The Pictorial History of the
Royal Canadian Mounted Police

1873-1973

The Pictorial History of the
Royal Canadian Mounted Police

S. W. Horrall, R.C.M.P. Historian
Foreword by W. L. Higgitt, Commissioner, R.C.M.P.

McGRAW-HILL RYERSON LIMITED
Toronto   Montreal   New York   London   Sydney   Johannesburg   Mexico
Panama   Düsseldorf   Singapore   São Paulo   Kuala Lumpur   New Delhi

ISBN 0-07-077366-1

1 2 3 4 5 6 7 8 9 10   BP-73   10 9 8 7 6 5 4 3

PRINTED AND BOUND IN CANADA

30882

ACKNOWLEDGEMENTS

Excerpts from "The Law of the Yukon" and "The Cremation of Sam Magee" by
Robert Service are quoted by permission of Ernest Benn Limited, Tonbridge, U.K.;
Dodd, Mead and Company, New York; and McGraw-Hill Ryerson Limited, Toronto.
  All pictures used in this book are from the collection of the R.C.M.P., except for those
listed below. The Publisher is grateful to the following for the loan of pictures and/or
permission to reproduce them:
Canada Wide Feature Service, Montreal, 247. Canadian Film Archives, Stills Library,
122. Robert Chambers/Miller Services, 126 bottom. Glenbow-Alberta Institute, Calgary,
Canada, 111 bottom, 114 top, 159, 167. Metro-Goldwyn-Mayer Inc., 123. L. Norris/
Vancouver Sun, 126 top. Provincial Museum and Archives of Alberta, 170, 193. Public
Archives of Canada, 12, 13, 20, 40 both, 112, 113, 115, 172, 173, 177, 191, 200.
Rolph-Clark-Stone Ltd. Paintings by Tom McNeely, 36 both, 37 left. Sergeant Preston of
the Yukon, Inc., 121 both. Toronto Sun, 120. Universal Films (Canada), 125.
  Every reasonable care has been taken to trace and give credit to all owners of copy-
righted material used in this book. The Publisher will welcome information enabling him to
rectify any errors or omissions.

Foreword

As we mark our hundredth anniversary it is most appropriate that a pictorial history of the Force be published so that all Canadians may have the opportunity to reflect upon the contribution made by the Royal Canadian Mounted Police to the history and development of our nation.

I hope the publication of this book will lead to a greater understanding and appreciation of the accomplishments of the Force and of the vast reservoir of experience it now has available to enrich its future.

As we move into our second century, we rededicate ourselves to the service of Canada and all Canadians.

W. L. Higgitt
Commissioner
Royal Canadian Mounted Police

Contents

"D" Division under Superintendent S. B. Steele leaving Fort Steele, British Columbia, August 1888.

The Great Lone Land

It seems to me that the best Force would be, Mounted Riflemen, trained to act as cavalry, but also instructed in the Rifle exercise. They should also be instructed, as certain of the Line are, in the use of artillery. This body should not be expressly Military but should be styled Police, and have the military bearing of the Irish Constabulary.

Sir John A. Macdonald, December 1869

From the wooded Precambrian Shield of northwestern Ontario and the Hudson Bay hinterland, the Canadian prairies stretch westward for over a thousand miles to the foothills of the Rocky Mountains. After travelling across the prairies in 1871, a British army officer, Lieutenant W. F. Butler, dubbed this remote and vast territory "The Great Lone Land," a wilderness subcontinent, where "one may wander five hundred miles in a direct line without seeing a human being, or an animal larger than a wolf." On early nineteenth-century maps it was often shown as part of the "Great American Desert," a largely treeless tract of undulating grassland inhabited by nomadic Indian tribes who followed their traditional way of life based upon hunting the enormous herds of buffalo which grazed on the prairie grasses. In 1670 King Charles II of England had granted most of the land and a monopoly of the trade in the territory to "The Governor and Company of Adventurers of England Trading into Hudson's Bay," or the Hudson's Bay Company as it was soon after called. The Company's servants came by sea across the Atlantic into Hudson Bay, seeking furs for the markets of Europe.

Gradually a string of trading posts was established from which the Company's agents exchanged trade goods with Indians for the valuable pelts with which the region was richly endowed. To protect the fur trade, settlers were discouraged. Within a few years, however, the Company's monopoly was challenged by the French Canadian *coureurs de bois* who had found a path to the western plains overland from the French colony of Quebec. A rivalry began between the Company and the Montreal fur traders which was to last until the two joined forces early in the nineteenth century.

By the 1860s the population of this vast wilderness, excluding Indians, amounted to some ten thousand souls, mostly of Métis, or mixed, racial origin. The only settlement of any significance was on the banks of the Red River and its tributaries adjacent to the Company's administrative centre at Fort Garry, in present-day Manitoba. Westward on the plains were the ancient tribal domains of the Blackfoot, Assiniboine, Cree and other tribes. Here the rule of law, the institutions of Western culture and the ways of the white man were found only in the isolated posts of the fur traders. The Company called its trading empire "Rupert's Land," after Prince Rupert, King Charles's cousin. To Canadians at the time of Confederation it was familiarly known as "the North-West."

Canada Purchases the Northwest

Like their neighbours to the south, Canadians had always felt that it was their destiny and their right to expand westward across the continent. The Fathers of Confederation had provided for the admission of the Northwest to Canada in the British North America Act. To the men who created the Dominion of Canada on July 1, 1867, the federation of Quebec, Ontario, New Brunswick and Nova Scotia was just the beginning of a movement which they hoped would end with the unification of all the British colonies in North America. The Northwest was the highway to the Pacific, the vital link which would bring British Columbia into Confederation. With it the dream of a "dominion from sea to sea" could become a reality. But before a railway could span the plains, or settlement begin, some means would have to be found to bring the institutions of law and order to this frontier society.

The Canadian Government would have preferred to wait a few more years, until the new Dominion was firmly established and the country's resources had increased, before taking on the responsibility for the Northwest. The question of the territory's future, however, was thrust upon the young nation by the same forces which had helped to bring about Confederation. Both the Hudson's Bay Company and the British Government were anxious to relinquish their responsibility for governing the territory. Canada could not leave the Northwest unprotected, possibly to go by default to her powerful neighbour as Oregon had done two decades before. The Canadians suspected that the Americans secretly desired to annex the Northwest. The republic had expanded rapidly during the Civil War. Large numbers of settlers had found their way into the territories immediately below the 49th parallel; the tide of settlement would soon spill over the border into British territory. The United States was in an aggressive mood following the Civil War, and its purchase of Alaska in 1867 was a dramatic warning to Canadians of its capacity to gobble up what was left of the North American continent. Speaking of the Northwest, Sir John A. Macdonald once wrote: "I would be quite willing personally to leave that whole country a wilderness for the next half-century, but I fear if Englishmen do not go there Yankees will." The necessity of acquiring the western plains was one of the first challenges to the vitality of the young Dominion, a test of its determination to expand and survive.

The only obstacle to Canadian sovereignty over Rupert's Land was the claim of the Hudson's Bay Company for compensation for relinquishing its rights and privileges. In 1869, after a long series of negotiations with the Company and the British Colonial Secretary in London, the Company's representatives agreed to surrender its title to the territory in return for £300,000 and certain land grants. In anticipation of the transfer, the Canadian Government, in June 1869, passed the "Temporary Government of Rupert's Land Act," which provided for the territory's administration by a Lieutenant-Governor and Council. In October a party of Canadian officials left Ottawa for the West to prepare for the closing of one of the largest real estate deals in history. The date scheduled for the formal transfer to Canada was December 1, 1869.

Sir John A. Macdonald Plans a Mounted Police Force

"The institutions of Law and Order, as understood in civilized communities, are wholly unknown," wrote Lieutenant Butler in the account of his journey across the Northwest published in 1872. With the transfer, the monumental task of establishing authority in the territory became the responsibility of the Canadian government. The man on whom that duty fell directly was Canada's first prime minister, Sir John A. Macdonald, the shrewd Scottish-born lawyer whose career would dominate Canadian political life until his death in 1891. In addition to being Prime Minister, Macdonald from 1867 to 1873 was also Minister of Justice, the

Sir John A. Macdonald, c. 1872. The creation of the North-West Mounted Police was primarily the work of Sir John A. Macdonald, the Scottish-born lawyer who became the first Prime Minister of the Dominion of Canada in 1867. In a semi-military mounted police force, modelled on the Royal Irish Constabulary, Macdonald saw a practical and economic means of establishing law and order on Canada's western frontier. Except for the five years he was in opposition, from 1873 to 1878, the Force remained under Macdonald's control until his death in 1891.

department responsible for the administration of justice in the Northwest.

What was uppermost in Macdonald's mind as he considered the problem of establishing law and order on Canada's frontier was the violence which had accompanied American expansion onto the western plains in the previous decade. The rush of settlers and miners into the American West had been followed by a series of Indian wars with the Sioux, Cheyenne and other plains tribes, which had cost the United States millions of dollars and the lives of hundreds of troops and settlers. Macdonald was aware that Canada did not have the resources to repeat the American experience. As soon as "emigrants" start moving into the Northwest, he warned Sir George-Etienne Cartier, "We are in constant danger of an Indian war, and once that commenced God knows where it may end." Macdonald was determined that law and order be established in advance of settlement, and a way found to prevent conflict between the native peoples and the settlers when they arrived. Fortunately for Macdonald, the rush for the Canadian West had not yet begun. With few settlers in the territory, there was still time to plan the westward extension of Canada's sovereignty.

Macdonald's answer was a paramilitary force of mounted police, trained and equipped for plains warfare but with primarily civil responsibilities; it would be the advance guard of settlement, establishing friendly relations with the Indian tribes and maintaining peace as settlers arrived. The Prime Minister obtained the idea for this type of force from two sources – the United States and Ireland. During the American Civil War, the Northern Army had successfully used units of mounted rifles to carry out extended incursions into enemy territory, attacking the flanks of the Confederate Army and harassing its lines of communication. Similar formations were later used against the Indians by the United States Army in the West, where they were found to be far more suitable to plains warfare than the traditional cavalry troop armed only with sabres or lances. Canadian military experts had watched the progress of the American Civil War, and the changes in the use of cavalry, with considerable interest. Following its conclusion, many of them urged the Canadian government to organize mounted rifle corps for use on the Canadian prairies.

To the mobility of a mounted rifle corps, Macdonald added the organizational structure and civil responsibilities of the Royal Irish Constabulary. This Irish force was well-known throughout the British Empire and had been used as a pattern for organizing numer-

ous police forces. The British Columbia Provincial Police was modelled on it in 1858, and in 1871 the Newfoundland Constabulary was reorganized along the same lines. The Irish Constabulary had developed against the background of rural unrest and civil disorders which were common features of early nineteenth-century Ireland. Unlike the English police forces, it was not under local control at the county or borough level, but under the central administration of the Irish authorities in Dublin. The Royal Irish Constabulary (it was granted the prefix "Royal" for its part in putting down the Fenian Rising of 1867) had wide territorial jurisdiction; its members were armed and subject to a military type of discipline and organization.

Louis Riel Delays the Organization of the Force

It is likely that Sir John A. Macdonald, as he sat in his office in the East Block of the Parliament Buildings in Ottawa in the winter of 1869/70 studying the organization of the Royal Irish Constabulary, did not realize that he had conceived of a police force which would one day be considered uniquely Canadian. The Prime Minister had originally planned to organize the mounted police in 1869, at the time of the scheduled transfer of the Northwest. Its first task would have been to police the settlements at Red River before moving westward on to the plains as settlers arrived. The

Métis at Red River, however, had never been consulted about the change in sovereignty. They had no guarantee that their rights would be safeguarded in the new Dominion, and they were alarmed by the activities of the Canadians already in the territory. Under the leadership of Louis Riel they decided to protect their rights by force. As a result, control over the Northwest was seized by Riel and his followers, and its transfer to Canada, as well as Macdonald's plan for a mounted police, had to be postponed.

The fate of the mounted police force now became tied to the settlement of the political crisis over the future of the Northwest. Macdonald continued with his plans for the force, but in the spring of 1870 the Government decided to accede to the demands of Riel's provisional government for the admittance of Red River

Louis Riel and members of the provincial government of Rupert's Land and the Northwest. A mounted police force was first planned by Sir John A. Macdonald in 1869 as part of Canada's preparations for assuming sovereignty over the lands granted to the Hudson's Bay Company. When the Métis settlers under Louis Riel obstructed the transfer of the territory to Canada, established their own government and demanded provincial status, the organization of the mounted police was postponed.

into Confederation as the Province of Manitoba. The decision removed at once the need for a federal police force in the only settled part of the territory. The administration of justice and the maintenance of law and order would now become the responsibility of the new provincial government under the terms of the British North America Act.

The Northwest was officially handed over to Canada on July 15, 1870. The part of it which was not included in the tiny new Province of Manitoba was designated "The Northwest Territories." It would be administered by a Lieutenant-Governor and council upon orders from Ottawa. The Prime Minister had earlier told Parliament that the Government intended to establish law and order in the Northwest Territories with a small force of mounted riflemen which would act as a constabulary. Following its formal transfer in July, however, the plan for a mounted police force was put aside. The territory was still sparsely populated and until large-scale settlement began Macdonald did not feel that Canada could afford to shoulder the responsibility for establishing order. British Columbia had yet to enter Confederation and the plans for a transcontinental railway were still a long way off. Furthermore, the Government found it necessary to maintain a large militia force at Fort Garry to protect Manitoba from possible unrest. This it was felt was already a big enough strain on the country's financial resources. Fortunately the old fear of American annexation was passing. Canada's existence was diplomatically recognized by the United States in the Treaty of Washington in 1871. The following year a joint commission began the task of surveying the western boundary between the two nations.

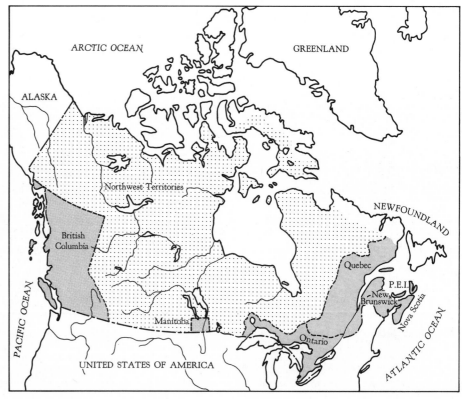

Canada's Frontier, 1870 to 1873

What the Canadian Government failed to realize fully was that conditions on the plains began to change rapidly following the American Civil War. Before the transfer law and order had been administered by a number of officials of the Hudson's Bay Company, who were appointed justices of the peace for that purpose. As a rule, however, the justices had confined their policing to the immediate neighbourhood of the Company's trading posts. Elsewhere, no attempt had been made to make the Indians, or white men who were not employees of the company, subject to British or Canadian criminal laws. In the interests of the fur trade, the

Canada in 1873. On July 1, 1867, Quebec, Ontario, Nova Scotia and New Brunswick had joined together to become the Dominion of Canada. By 1873 the Dominion had acquired Rupert's Land and the Northwestern Territory (1870) (naming the lands the Northwest Territories, and creating the small province of Manitoba from part of the area), British Columbia (1871) and Prince Edward Island (1873). The legislation of 1873 gave the North-West Mounted Police jurisdiction throughout the Northwest Territories, an area extending westward from Labrador to Alaska and northward from the American border to the Arctic Ocean. In practice much of this huge territory was still uninhabited and unexplored, and the duties of the Force were for many years confined to the prairie country which rolled westward from Manitoba to British Columbia.

Mapping the 49th parallel. Ox carts of the Boundary Commission leaving the Long River depot about eighty miles west of Fort Dufferin in 1873.

Personnel of the British North American Boundary Commission, 1873/1874. During 1873 and 1874 an Anglo-American commission surveyed and marked the boundary between Canada and the United States from Lake of the Woods to the Rocky Mountains. The trails and the supply depots established by the Boundary Commission were used by the N.W.M.P. on the first part of their trek westward in the summer of 1874. Among the personnel shown here are: Captain D. R. Cameron (seated third from the left), the British Commissioner; L. W. Herchmer (standing fourth from the left), the commission's commissary who was later Commissioner of the N.W.M.P., 1886 to 1900; and G. M. Dawson (standing sixth from the left), who in spite of a physical deformity was to become one of Canada's outstanding geologists and explorers.

Fort Whoop-up. In 1869 two traders from Fort Benton, Joe Healy and Al Hamilton, built a trading post at the junction of the Belly and St. Mary's Rivers, southwest of the present city of Lethbridge, Alberta. The following year it was partially burned by fire and a new building was constructed about three hundred feet north of the original site. First called Fort Hamilton, it was soon known as Fort Whoop-up, the most notorious of the whisky forts. Here a group of Blood Indians are shown outside the fort, while overhead flies the flag of one of the trading companies.

Fort Benton, Montana, in the 1870s. After the American Civil War Fort Benton, on the Missouri River about ninety miles south of the border, became the main centre of trade for the Blackfoot Country of western Canada. Until the arrival of the Mounted Police, the Fort Benton traders conducted an illicit and unscrupulous business with the Canadian Indians, exchanging rifles, ammunition and whisky for buffalo robes and furs.

Indians had been left to follow their tribal ways uninhibited by the judicial institutions of white society.

Following the war a new wave of traders from the northern outposts of the American West crossed the border into the foothill country of present-day Alberta, the tribal home of the Blackfoot, to compete with the Hudson's Bay Company. Tough, adventurous men, representing many nationalities, often veterans of the Civil War, they had little concern for the welfare of the Indians. They soon established themselves in fortified posts whose colourful names reveal something of their storied character – Slideout, Kipp, Standoff and the most notorious of all, Whoop-up. By 1870 these "free traders," as they were called, had captured most of the Blackfoot trade.

Liquor of one kind or another had always had an important part in the trade relations between the white man and the native population of North America. The early British colonists had brought rum; the French, brandy. The Hudson's Bay Company and its agents in the Northwest used liquor, usually rum; but the Company's monopoly had enabled it to exercise a control over its distribution which tended to prevent excessive misuse. The free traders brought cheap whisky with them from the distilleries of Chicago and St. Louis; it was often adulterated to improve its effect and increase the profits. One recipe called for a quart of whisky, a pound of chewing tobacco, a handful of red pepper, one bottle of Jamaica ginger, a quart of molasses and a dash of red ink. The effect of this concoction was said to be stunning.

Profits were high in this nefarious exchange of goods. The Indians had no use for the white man's money. In exchange for his furs the traders gave him rifles, ammunition and whisky. Whisky realized the greatest profits, and the Indians who craved the vile concoction sought out the traders who offered the most, often bartering their last possessions for a few cups of "Whoop-up bug juice." What followed was a trade war between the Montana-based free traders financed by American capital and the Anglo-Canadian Hudson's Bay Company and its agents. The result was that many of the Indians were stripped of their pride and their possessions; they became debauched and demoralized, and the old tribal institutions began to break down. Life became cheap; murder and robbery went unpunished. The Reverend John McDougall, a methodist missionary, has left a vivid firsthand account of the effects of the whisky trade:

Scores of thousands of buffalo robes and hundreds of thousands of wolf and fox skins and most of the best horses the Indians had were taken south into Montana,

and the chief article of barter for these was alcohol. In this traffic very many Indians were killed, and also quite a number of white men. Within a few miles of us, that winter of 1873/4, forty-two able-bodied men were the victims among themselves, all slain in the drunken rows. These were Blackfeet. . . . There was no law but might. Some terrible scenes occurred when whole camps went on the spree, as was frequently the case, shooting, stabbing, killing, freezing, dying.

Thus these atrocious debauches were continuing all that winter not far from us. Mothers lost their children. These were either frozen to death or devoured by the myriad dogs of the camp. The birth-rate decreased and the poor red man was in a fair way towards extinction, just because some men, coming out of Christian countries, and themselves the evolution of Christian civilization were now ruled by lust and greed.

Buffalo. Until the middle of the nineteenth century the central plains were one gigantic buffalo pasture from the North Saskatchewan Valley to the Texas border. The American bison, to use their proper name, had originally roamed over about one-third of the North American continent. To the Plains Indians, the buffalo were a source of food, shelter and clothing as well as a means of trading with the white man. Like the Indians, the N.W.M.P. frequently had to depend upon the buffalo during its first years in the West. Eventually, the buffalo head was adopted as the main emblem on the Regimental Badge of the Force.

To add to the difficulties a fresh outbreak of smallpox occurred in the winter of 1869/70. It took a heavy toll among the Blackfoot, who like many Indians believed that the disease was deliberately spread by the white man. But what was worse, the great herds of buffalo upon which the way of life of the Plains Indians depended began to disappear through indiscriminate slaughter. By 1873 conditions in the North-west Territories had deteriorated

to the point where the territorial officials believed that a major Indian rising was a distinct possibility.

The Canadian Government was well informed of the conditions in the Northwest Territories between 1870 and 1873, but it continued to delay the organization of the mounted police. Lieutenant Butler's published account of his 1871 visit to the Northwest vividly described the lawlessness and the disruptive effects of the whisky trade. In 1872 Lieutenant-Governor William Archibald informed Macdonald of the activities of the whisky traders,

Sioux Camp on Frenchman's Creek, 1874.
These Indians were of the Sisseton band of
Sioux that had sought refuge in British
territory in 1862, following the Indian mas-
sacres in Minnesota. The N.W.M.P.
encountered a friendly camp of these people
on the March West.

Buffalo bones at Swift Current, ready for
shipment to fertilizer factories in the East.
In 1870 the buffalo could be numbered in
the millions. The Indians believed that the
supply was inexhaustible. But the demand
for hides and the introduction of the repeating rifle resulted in a wanton slaughter
which had reduced them almost to extinction by 1885. With their passing, the
Indians were forced to give up their nomadic
way of life and settle on the reservations
offered to them by the government.

The Honourable Alexander Morris, 1869. Born at Perth, Upper Canada, in 1826, Alexander Morris entered politics as a conservative for Lanark in the Legislative Assembly in 1861. A strong supporter of Confederation, he was Minister of Inland Revenue in the federal Government from 1869 to 1872. In 1872 he was sent westward as Lieutenant-Governor of Manitoba and the Northwest Territories. Morris's persistent nagging about the necessity of establishing order on the prairies finally persuaded Sir John A. Macdonald to organize the N.W.M.P. in 1873.

and the Territorial Council of the N.W.T. urged Ottawa to take action. In the same year Colonel Robertson-Ross, the senior officer of the Canada militia, was sent from Ottawa to investigate conditions in the Northwest. Early in 1873 the Hudson's Bay Company endeavoured to get the federal Government to act, but Macdonald pointedly refused to establish law and order to protect the Company's trading interests. Like many eastern Canadians, the Prime Minister felt that much of the information coming out of the Northwest was exaggerated. But, more important, Macdonald still believed that the country could not afford to organize the mounted police until the militia force in Manitoba was disbanded. The Territorial Council passed an ordinance in 1870 prohibiting the importation, sale or barter of intoxicating spirits in the Northwest Territories. As with the criminal laws, however, there was no means of enforcing it in the area where it was most needed.

Alexander Morris and the Cypress Hills Massacre

The man who was largely responsible for finally getting the Government to proceed with the organization of the mounted police was Alexander Morris. Morris was a lawyer from Perth, Ontario. He represented Lanark in the House of Commons and was one of the earliest advocates of Cana-

dian expansion into the Northwest. In 1869 he had been appointed Minister of Inland Revenue, a post he resigned three years later to become Lieutenant-Governor of Manitoba and the Northwest Territories. Shortly after taking up his new duties at Fort Garry, Morris warned the Prime Minister that "the most important matter of the future is the preservation of order in the Northwest and little as Canada may like it she has to stable her elephant."

Although unwilling to proceed with the force's organization, Macdonald cautiously took steps to obtain the necessary legislative authority. In the fall of 1872 his deputy minister in the Department of Justice, his close friend and confidant Hewitt Bernard, began drawing up new plans for the establishment of the force. Bernard was the brother of Macdonald's second wife, Susan Agnes Bernard, whom the Prime Minister had married in London, England, in 1867. The legislation to organize the mounted police was included in a bill which also provided for the establishment of courts, the appointment of magistrates and the erection of jails in the Northwest Territories. Macdonald introduced the bill into the House of Commons on May 3, 1873. The Government's plans for administering justice in the Northwest attracted little attention in eastern Canada. Macdonald was careful to allay criticism of the expense of organizing the force by pointing out that its members would be customs officers and would therefore contribute to the public purse. The bill passed unopposed through Parliament and received Royal Assent on May 23, 1873. It did not, however, immediately establish the North-West Mounted Police. The Act was merely an enabling measure, giving the Government authority to implement its provisions by Order-in-Council. On August 30, 1873, an Order-in-Council was signed by the Governor General, Lord Dufferin, bringing the Force formally and legally into existence. It existed only on paper however. The Prime Minister's latest plan was to start recruiting in the spring of 1874 when, it was hoped, the militia in Manitoba could safely be reduced.

Morris found the Government's tardy action incredible. Early that spring he had warned Macdonald of unrest among the tribes. In July 1873 he sent Ottawa a long confidential report on the activities of the whisky traders at Fort Whoop-up, and the demoralizing effect they were having on the Blackfoot. The only response was a reply from Ottawa informing him that the Government didn't consider the situation at Fort Whoop-up serious enough to warrant the presence of a force there.

Unknown to Macdonald, an event had already occurred in Canadian territory which would soon force him hastily to change his plans. Early in May 1873 a dispute arose between a party of white wolf hunters from Fort Benton, Montana, and a band of Assiniboine Indians over the theft of some horses. The scene of this altercation was the Cypress Hills, a favourite hunting ground of the Plains tribes located in the southwest corner of the present Province of Saskatchewan. In the ensuing fight a number of Indians were killed, including women and children. It was months before full reports of the event reached the outside. To Canadians the death of the Indians became a cause célèbre, the "Cypress Hills Massacre," the murder of innocent and defenceless Canadian Indians by lawless American desperadoes. South of the border it was celebrated in Fort Benton as another victory over the murderous and treacherous redskins. The circumstances surrounding the fight will never be precisely known. The evidence collected later was contradictory, and in some instances highly prejudiced. The whites involved were by no means all Americans; there were British and Canadians among them too. But while they were not all American outlaws as the Canadians later insisted, they were representatives of the rival commercial system based in Montana.

The reports of the fight which reached Lieutenant-Governor Morris in August convinced him that a rising of the tribes against all the whites in the Northwest was a distinct possibility. His position was now justified. He had been warning Ottawa for months that something like this would happen unless steps were taken to establish order. He immediately renewed his pressure upon the Government to organize the mounted police, warning Macdonald of the serious consequences of failing to act. The Prime Minister still refused to believe that there was cause for alarm, but he took steps to extradite the white men involved, from the United States, to stand trial. Morris persisted, however. Dissatisfied with the Government's reply, he telegraphed a final urgent appeal on September 20, "What have you done as to Police Force. Their absence may lead to grave disaster." Morris's persistence finally did the trick. Macdonald prudently decided to proceed with the Force's organization. The "massacre," he told Lord Dufferin, "has so greatly excited the red men that we have decided to send the Force out before the close of navigation." Five days later, on September 25, 1873, the Force's first officers were appointed by Order-in-Council, and recruiting commenced in Ontario, Quebec and the Maritimes for three Divisions of fifty men each to be sent to Lower Fort Garry in Manitoba before the winter freeze-up.

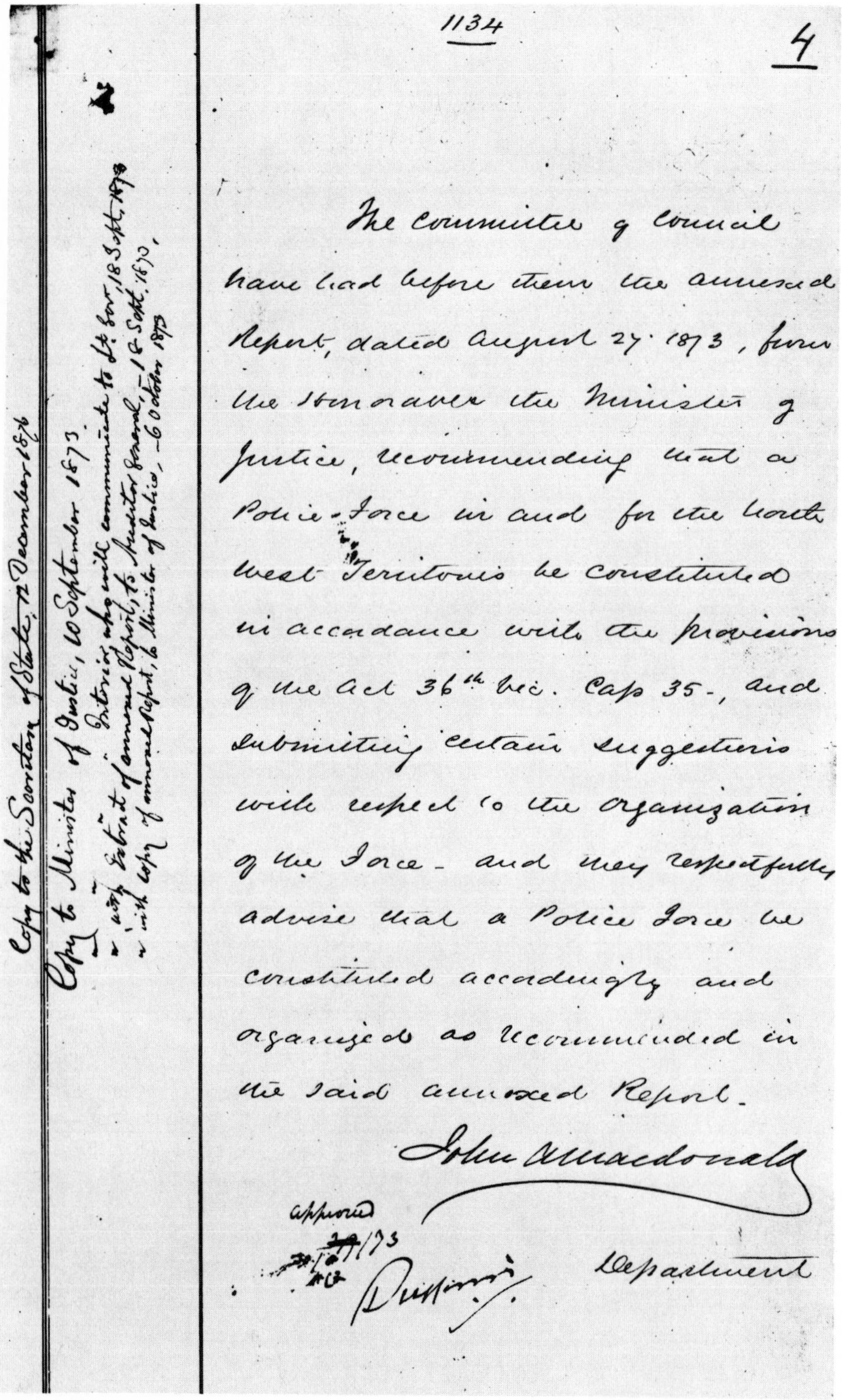

1134

4

The Committee of Council have had before them the annexed Report, dated August 27. 1873, from the Honorable the Minister of Justice, recommending that a Police-Force in and for the North West Territories be constituted in accordance with the provisions of the Act 36th Vic. Cap 35, and submitting certain suggestions with respect to the organization of the Force — and they respectfully advise that a Police Force be constituted accordingly and organized as recommended in the said annexed Report.

John A Macdonald

Approved

Department

[marginal notations:]
Copy to the Secretary of State, 17 December 1876
Copy to Minister of Justice, 10 September 1873.
Entering copy with communication to Lt. Gov. 18 Sept. 1873.
copy Extract of annual Report, to Auditor General, 15 Sept. 1873.
with copy of annual Report, to Minister of Justice, 6 October 1873.

The Establishment of the North-West Mounted Police

The Act of May 23, 1873, 36 Vic. Chap. 35, included precise provisions regarding the responsibilities and organization of the Force. Its duties were to preserve peace, prevent crime and apprehend criminals. In addition the members were required to act as court orderlies, jailers, customs officers and escorts for prisoners and lunatics. The Force was placed under the command of a "Commissioner" who would be responsible to the federal Minister of Justice, not the Lieutenant-Governor or the Territorial Council. Its authorized strength was not to exceed three hundred mounted men. No person was to be appointed to the Force unless "of a sound constitution, able to ride, active and able bodied, of good character, and between the ages of eighteen and forty years." Furthermore, the men were required to "be able to read and write either the English or French language." Interestingly enough, there were bilingual members among the first recruits, as well as some from the Province of Quebec who spoke only French.

Privy Council Order 1134, August 30, 1873. The North-West Mounted Police actually came into existence on August 30, 1873, when Lord Dufferin, the Governor General, approved an Order-in-Council recommending its formation. The original document shown here is now in the Public Archives of Canada, Ottawa.

The men were required to engage for a period of three years, at the end of which, if their service was satisfactory, they could obtain a free land grant of 160 acres in the Northwest Territories. During the few years that this last regulation was in effect, many men joined the Force, completed their three-year term of service and took up homesteads on the prairies.

One unusual provision was the appointment of all commissioned officers of the Force as ex-officio justices of the peace. By this regulation two officers sitting together in court had all the powers of a magistrate. This was contrary to the principle of an independent and impartial judiciary which had long been a practice of the British legal system. In effect the Mounted Police would bring an offender to court, prosecute him and also sit in judgment on the case. This provision was to some extent necessary. The Northwest was sparsely populated, the distances were great and there were few other persons qualified to act as magistrates. It certainly made the Force's task much easier. There was less chance of political interference or local sentiments obstructing the course of justice. In the early years of the Northwest Territories, justice was comparatively swift and sure. It was all a part of Macdonald's authoritarian and imperialistic approach to the problem of bringing law and order to the Canadian frontier – his concern for avoiding the American experience where

the English tradition of local policing bodies under local control was the usual practice. As a result the North-West Mounted Police was to play an important role in transforming the frontier society of the prairies into a settled agricultural community without the lawless traditions of the American West. To its credit the Force never seriously abused the extraordinary powers with which it was invested.

In choosing officers, Macdonald favoured men who had had previous military experience. This was a practice which was continued for many years and tended to emphasize the military nature of the Force, giving it a character and appearance little different from those of a regular army unit. The nine officers appointed on September 25 were: W. O. Smith, W. D. Jarvis, C. F. Young, J. F. Macleod, W. Winder, J. Carvell, J. M. Walsh, E. Brisebois and E. D. Clark. Macdonald had adopted rank designations similar to those in the Royal Irish Constabulary for the use of the officers – Superintendents, Inspectors and Sub-Inspectors. The officers, however, preferred the more prestigious and familiar military ranks to which they were also entitled.

Probably the best qualified of them for the task ahead was James Farquharson Macleod (later Commissioner of the Force and a Judge of the Supreme Court of the N.W.T.), who was a lawyer as well as a soldier. Macleod was born on the Isle of Skye, but he had been brought to Canada as a child by his father, a retired British army officer who settled north of Toronto. The young Macleod was educated at Upper Canada College, Queen's College at Kingston, and Osgoode Hall, admitted to the Ontario Bar in 1860. He was already familiar with the Northwest, having served as a brigade major in the Red River expedition of 1870. Another experienced soldier was William Dummer Jarvis, who came from a prominent Toronto family of the same name. His father, Sheriff W. B. Jarvis, had led the loyalist attack against the rebels on Yonge Street in Toronto in 1837. The son had started his military career in England as an officer in the East Suffolk Regiment. He later served in South Africa at the time of the Kaffir War. After returning to Canada, Jarvis served with the Canadian militia during the Fenian threat of 1866. Charles Young was another officer who had formerly served with a British regiment. Two others with active service to their credit were a French Canadian, Ephrem Brisebois, who had fought with the Papal Zouaves in Italy, and Jacob Carvell, a veteran of the Confederate Army. Edward Dalrymple

Attestation list, 1873. This is one of the
original engagement lists signed by the first
recruits at Lower Fort Garry on November
3, 1873. The first name on the list is that of
Sergeant Major Arthur Henry Griesbach,
who then witnessed the signatures of the
other recruits. Several of the men on this
list were to become well-known figures in
the early history of the Force and rise to
senior ranks – Samuel B. Steele, John Henry
McIllree, Robert Belcher, Laurence
Fortescue.

The first officers of the Force. On this document acknowledging receipt of their commissions are the signatures of the Force's first officers. The names from top to bottom are: W. D. Jarvis, C. F. Young, James F. Macleod, Jacob Carvell, E. A. Brisebois, J. M. Walsh, E. Dalrymple Clark, W. Winder, John Breden and G. A. French.

Clark, who was appointed paymaster, was the son of a British major general and a nephew of Sir John A. Macdonald by his first marriage. James Morrow Walsh became probably the most well-known of the early officers of the Force. He was a native of Prescott, Ontario, where he had been an officer in the local militia.

Macdonald had yet to find a suitable officer to command the Force. In order to proceed with its organization Lieutenant Colonel W. O. Smith, the commander of the militia in Manitoba, was temporarily appointed Commissioner. Smith had served as a British officer in the Crimean War

Lieutenant Colonel W. Osborne Smith. The first Commissioner of the Force was Lieutenant Colonel Smith, the Deputy Adjutant General of Militia District No. 10 (Manitoba). Smith was appointed temporary Commissioner on September 25, 1873, as a result of the Government's sudden decision to proceed with the organization of the Force. It was Smith who swore in the men of the first three divisions at Lower Fort Garry on November 3, 1873. His command lasted only a few weeks. In December he was relieved by his permanent successor, Commissioner G. A. French.

before coming to Canada in 1856. Upon orders from Ottawa, he began preparing accommodation for the new force at Lower Fort Garry, the old Hudson's Bay post about twenty miles down the Red River from Winnipeg. Here the recruits would spend the winter in training for the following spring when they would take up their duties on the plains.

The officers who were responsible for recruiting had no difficulty obtaining applicants, although there was little time to advertise and the pay was only seventy-five cents a day for sub-constables and one dollar a day for constables. Most of the recruits were native Canadians, largely from Ontario and Quebec, with a dozen or so from the Maritime Provinces. More than half of them had had military experience of one kind or another, usually in the militia. Only two of the recruits had formerly been policemen. Forty-six of them gave their previous occupation as clerk, while another thirty-nine stated they were tradesmen. There were a number of emigrants from the British Isles who had served in various British regiments. One of these was A. H. Griesbach, the Chief Constable or Regimental Sergeant Major (the N.C.O.'s like the officers preferred military titles). Griesbach had served with the Cape Mounted Rifles in South Africa before coming to Canada. Like Macleod and a number of the other recruits, he had already been to the Northwest with the Red River expedition in 1870.

Probably the most influential group of recruits came from the two batteries of Canadian artillery at Kingston and Quebec City. These two schools of gunnery were the only permanent Canadian military units. They provided an opportunity for Canadian militiamen to obtain full-time military training and service. A small

Commissioner George Arthur French, 1873–1876. The main bone of contention between Commissioner French and the officials in Ottawa was the location of the headquarters of the Force at Swan River. French insisted that the quarters provided there were unfit to live in. Above all, though, he protested the isolation of the site which made it almost impossible for him to carry out the command of the Force under

him. He had no regular means of communication with the divisions in the Blackfoot Country. Ottawa ignored him, communicating directly with Fort Macleod via Fort Benton. French merely received copies of the orders and instructions sent to Assistant Commissioner Macleod, often weeks later. His outspoken objection to the arrangement finally left him with no choice but to resign or be dismissed.

Original Warrant of Appointment. These warrants were issued only to the first three divisions recruited in 1873. The title "North-West Mounted Police" had not yet come into official use. Before receiving his warrant each member was required to take the Oath of Office, promising to perform his duties "without fear, favour or affection of or towards any person or party whomsoever." This oath has changed very little in the last hundred years.

number of N.C.O.'s from these batteries joined the mounted police. One of these was Samuel B. Steele (later Major General Sir S. B. Steele). As N.C.O.'s they brought with them the training and experience which were invaluable assets to the nascent force of mounted policemen. In spite of the customary political patronage, Macdonald was able to obtain a nucleus of experienced officers and N.C.O.'s which became the backbone of the Force.

Within a month the recruiting was completed and the men were hurriedly assembled at Collingwood, Ontario, for the journey westward. Early in October the first party left by steamship for Prince Arthur's Landing (Thunder Bay) at the head of Lake Superior. From here they proceeded by boat, wagon, or on foot over the Dawson Route to St. Boniface and Lower Fort Garry. "Judging from the first detachment, the Mounted Police are a fine body of men," reported the Winnipeg *Manitoban*. As the recruits made their way over the old fur-trading route, the weather turned cold and heavy snow

MOUNTED POLICE FORCE

OF CANADA.

I hereby appoint *George Berkley Hall*

to be a *Sub* Constable in the Police Force

of, in and for the North West Territories, under

Statute of Canada, 36 Victoria, Chapter 35.

Given under my hand at *Lower Fort Garry*

Province of Manitoba

this *Third* day of *May* A.D., 18*73*

[signature]

Commissioner of Police.

The first uniform of the Force. Taken in 1874, the earliest known photograph of members of the Force shows the first official uniform: scarlet Norfolk jacket, steel-grey or flesh coloured breeches, blue trousers with a double white stripe, black or brown boots, pill box hat or white helmet. By 1876 this uniform had been replaced by a more ornate and military style of dress.

Seated at the table is Sub-Inspector John French, brother of the Commissioner, who was killed in action at Batoche in 1885. The bearded officer behind French is Sub-Inspector F. J. Dickens, son of the novelist Charles Dickens.

heralded the coming of winter. The last party marched safely through the gates of the fort on November 1, but the Force's supplies and equipment were less fortunate. They were caught by the early freeze-up along the Dawson Route and did not reach their destination until after the New Year. Service in the Force officially began November 3, 1873. On that historic wintry day the entire force of mounted policemen, officers and men, was paraded inside the fort and sworn in by the Commissioner, Lieutenant Colonel W. O. Smith.

Macdonald, meanwhile, had found a permanent commanding officer for the Force. He was Lieutenant Colonel George Arthur French, the commandant of "A" Battery at Kingston, and Inspector of Artillery and Warlike Stores for the Canadian Militia. French had already made his mark as one of the "founding fathers" of the Canadian Permanent Armed Forces. The new commissioner was born in County Roscommon, Ireland, in 1841. He had been educated at the military colleges at Sandhurst and Woolwich, and had entered the Royal Artillery as a lieutenant in 1860. Shortly after, he came to Canada as adjutant of the Royal Artillery detachment at Kingston, Ontario. When the British Army was withdrawn in 1871, French was seconded to the Canadian Militia and given the task of organizing "A" Battery School of Gunnery. Although a strict disciplinarian, he was known

at Kingston as an efficient and energetic officer, with a genuine concern for the physical well-being and morale of those under his command.

French had barely accepted command of the hastily organized force before there were serious doubts regarding its future. Early in November Sir John A. Macdonald's Government was defeated in the House of Commons and resigned from office. A new Government was formed by the Liberals under the leadership of Alexander Mackenzie. The new Prime Minister had doubts about the fitness of Macdonald's novel force of mounted police as a means of establishing order in the Northwest. While the Government considered its future policy, Commissioner French proceeded to Lower Fort Garry to assume command of the partially completed force. He was appalled to find upon arrival that most of the men were still without uniforms or proper equipment, and that the horses purchased for their use were largely unbroken. With a firm hand he set about turning the "unleavened mass" of recruits, as he called them, into an efficient and thoroughly disciplined force.

In subzero weather the men began a rigorous training schedule. To alleviate the hard work, they organized dances and skating parties as well as a rifle match with the military which the Mounted Police lost, 302 to 370 points. The men were aware, however, of the uncertainty which for a time hung over their heads. Captain Clark, the paymaster, described the "great state of anxiety as to our future" in a letter to his uncle, Sir John A. Macdonald. In February 1874 French returned to Ottawa to ascertain the Government's future plans. Would the North-West Mounted Police, as its members were beginning to call it (neither the Act nor the Order-in-Council had provided a designation for the Force), be completed, to its full strength and despatched westward, or did the Government propose to take other steps to bring law and order to Canada's western frontier?

Recruiting

Recruiting notice, 1874. Commissioner French had no difficulty obtaining recruits. Throughout most of the Force's history, the number of applicants has far exceeded the positions available. One of the few exceptions to this was just before World War I, when poor pay in the Force and high employment generally compelled the Force to open a recruiting office in London, England.

NORTH WEST MOUNTED POLICE.

150 additional Constables and Sub-Constables being required for the above Force, the following information is published for the guidance of those desirous of joining the Force :—

(1).—Candidates must be active, able-bodied men of thoroughly sound constitution and exemplary character. They should be able to ride well, and to read and write either the English or French language.

(2).—The term of engagement is three years.

(3).—The rates of payments are as follow :—

Constables.............$1 per diem.
Sub-Constables......... 75 c. "

with free rations; a free kit on joining; clothing; boots; quarters; fuel; and light; and the Government is empowered to give a free grant of 160 acres of land to all well-conducted men on completion of three years' service.

(4.)—All transport expenses of those who are approved and accepted for service will be borne by the Government.

(5).—The undersigned will attend at

on the
for the purpose of of engaging suitable men.

G. A. FRENCH, Lt.-Colonel,
Commissioner N. W. M. P.

NORTH WEST MOUNTED POLICE.

Memorandum for the information of persons desiring engagement
in the above Force.

1. Lieutenant Colonel MacLeod, the Commissioner of the N. W. Mounted Police Force, will be at   Montreal, on the 25th and 26th, and at   Toronto, on the 29th and 30th instant, for the purpose of engaging recruits for that Force.

2. Applicants accepted for Service will be instructed to report to the Commissioner at Toronto on the 5th June, from which date free rations will be issued to them.

3. Recruits engaged in Montreal will be furnished with a Railway Ticket to Toronto, but no other expense incurred by them, prior to reporting for duty to the Commissioner at Toronto, will be defrayed from public funds.

4. Pay will commence on the date of arrival at Fort MacLeod or Cypress Hills, in the North West Territories.

5. Any expense incurred by applicants going to Montreal or Toronto to meet the Commissioner, or returning to their places of residence, must be borne by themselves, whether they are engaged or not.

6. A free Kit will be issued to each recruit at Toronto, but it is desirable that each man should take with him one suit of clothing to be worn while passing through the United States.

7. No trunks or boxes will be allowed. A waterproof bag and a valise will be supplied to each recruit at Toronto, which will contain one hundred pounds weight of clothing and sundries. Beyond these no baggage will be permitted.

8. Many applications are for employment in the "Manitoba" Mounted Police, the writers expressing a desire to go to that Province with a view to settlement after the expiration of their term of Police Service. The duties of the Mounted Police are entirely in the North West Territories, and the recruits about to be engaged will be stationed at Mounted Police Posts varying from 500 to 900 miles from the Province of Manitoba.

9. Applicants must be between the ages of Eighteen and Forty, active, able-bodied men of thoroughly sound constitution and must produce certificates of exemplary character.

10. They must be able to read and write either the English or French language: must understand the care and management of horses, and be able to ride well.

11. The term of engagement is three years.

12. The rates of pay are as follows:—

Constables.................................90c. to $1.20 per day.
Sub-Constables—1st year's service..... 50c. per day.
                     2nd and 3rd year's do. 75c.   do.   subject to good behaviour.

Extra pay at the rate of 15c. per day is allowed to a limited number of Artizans.

(OVER.)

13. Members of the Force are supplied with free rations, a free kit on joining, and an annual issue of clothing.

14. Married men will not be engaged.

15. The Governor in Council may, from and out of any of the lands of the Dominion in the Province of Manitoba or in the North-West Territories, make a free grant not exceeding one hundred and sixty acres, to any constable or sub-constable of the said Force, who, at the expiration of three years of continuous service in the said Force shall be certified by the Commissioner of Police to have conducted himself satisfactorily, and to have efficiently and ably performed the duties of his office during the said term of three years.

16. The form of engagement is as follows:

I do hereby contract, engage, promise and agree to and with the Commissioner of the Police Force constituted, by law in and for the North-West Territories of Canada, to serve in such Police Force for three years from   , and do hereby declare myself subject to all the provisions of the Act of the Parliament of Canada, 36 Vic., ch. 35, intituled: "An Act respecting the Administration of Justice and for the establishment of a Police Force in the North-West Territories," and the several Acts amending the same now in force or hereafter during my term of service to be passed, and to all rules, regulations or orders made by virtue of the said Acts or any of them, and that I will during the said term of service take care of and protect all articles of public property which shall from time to time be entrusted to me, and make good all deficiencies and damages occurring to such property while in my care or possession, except through fair wear and tear or unavoidable accident. And I do hereby declare and admit that by reason of such engagement no right accrues to me for any transport expenses returning from the North-West Territories of Canada on being discharged.

DEPARTMENT OF THE SECRETARY OF STATE,   }
        Ottawa, May 15th, 1877. }

Information for applicants, 1877. In the early years the vacant positions were filled by a recruiting drive which was carried out annually in eastern Canada. Until the railway reached the prairies, those accepted had a long journey ahead of them across the United States by rail, up the Missouri River by steam boat and overland to Fort Walsh or Fort Macleod, where they would be sworn in and issued uniforms.

The frontier conditions prompted the adoption of two basic qualifications for recruits which have remained unchanged. To begin with, the Government was unwilling to go to the expense of transporting a recruit to western Canada, training and equipping him, unless he would engage for a stated period of service. Also, the early Force had to maintain a degree of mobility. There were few settlements, living conditions were primitive and the Government was reluctant to accept responsibility for providing for the families of married men. Except in unusual circumstances the Force has only accepted single men, who have been required to engage for an initial period of service, usually three or five years.

Since the 1880s the main training centre for recruits has been "Depot" Division in Regina, Saskatchewan. As a result it is frequently referred to as "The Cradle of the Force."

ORDER FOR
LAYING OUT KIT FOR INSPECTION
— DRESS. —

Summer :—Serges, Breeches, Boots & Spurs, Side Arms, Carbines, Felt Hat.

Winter:—Serges, Breeches, Fur Caps, Moccasins & Stockings no spurs, Side Arms, Carbines.

FUR COATS AND PEA JACKETS TO BE HUNG ON PEGS

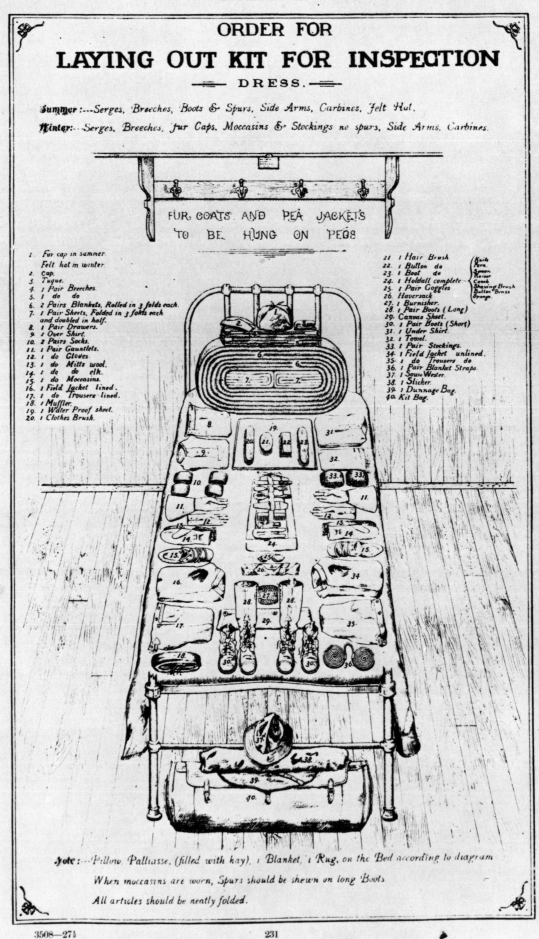

1. Fur cap in summer. Felt hat in winter.
2. Cap.
3. Tuque.
4. 1 Pair Breeches.
5. 1 do do
6. 2 Pairs Blankets, Rolled in 3 folds each.
7. 1 Pair Sheets, Folded in 3 folds each and doubled in half.
8. 1 Pair Drawers.
9. 1 Over Shirt.
10. 2 Pairs Socks.
11. 1 Pair Gauntlets.
12. 1 do Gloves.
13. 1 do Mitts wool.
14. 1 do do elk.
15. 1 do Moccasins.
16. 1 Field Jacket lined.
17. 1 do Trousers lined.
18. 1 Muffler.
19. 1 Water Proof sheet.
20. 1 Clothes Brush.

21. 1 Hair Brush.
22. 1 Button do.
23. 1 Boot do.
24. 1 Holdall complete.
25. 1 Pair Goggles.
26. 1 Haversack.
27. 1 Burnisher.
28. 1 Pair Boots (Long).
29. Canvas Sheet.
30. 1 Pair Boots (Short).
31. 1 Under Shirt.
32. 1 Towel.
33. 1 Pair Stockings.
34. 1 Field Jacket unlined.
35. 1 do Trousers do.
36. 1 Pair Blanket Straps.
37. 1 Sou' Wester.
38. 1 Slicker.
39. 1 Dunnage Bag.
40. Kit Bag.

Knife, Fork, Spoon, Razor, Comb, Shaving Brush, Button Brass, Sponge.

Note :— Pillow, Palliasse, (filled with hay), 1 Blanket, 1 Rug, on the Bed according to diagram.

When moccasins are worn, Spurs should be shewn on long Boots.

All articles should be neatly folded.

Form No. 84a.

North West Mounted Police Force, Canada.

DISCHARGE.

This is to Certify that *J. G. Donkin*

served as *Constable and Corporal*

in the above Force from *30 September 1884* to *12ᵗʰ March 1888*

and is now discharged in consequence of *his having been permitted*

to purchase his discharge

Dated at *Regina, N.W.*

13ᵗʰ March   1888.

L. W. Herchmer
Commissioner N. W. M. P.

Conduct during Service   *Good*

L. W. Herchmer
Commissioner N. W. M. P.

(printed vertically in center: This Discharge does not entitle the recruit named therein to any grant of Land.)

(Above) N.W.M.P. Discharge Certificate of Corporal John George Donkin, a young Englishman who tried his hand at homesteading in Manitoba before joining the Force. A former medical student, he served as a hospital steward during the North West Rebellion. Following his discharge, he returned to England, where he published a lively and colourful account of his experiences entitled Trooper and Redskin.

(Left) Rules and Regulations, R.N.W.M.P., 1909.

Northwest Mounted Police
RECRUITS WANTED.

APPLICANTS must be between the ages of twenty-two and forty, active, able-bodied men of thoroughly sound constitution, and must produce certificates of exemplary character and sobriety.

They must understand the care and management of horses, and be able to ride well.

The term of engagement is five years.

Members of the force are supplied free with rations, a free kit on joining, and periodical issues during the term of service.

Applications to be made to

RECRUITING OFFICER, N. W. M. Police.

At 677 Main Street, Winnipeg, between the hours of 9 a.m. and 6 p.m.   830F

(Left) Recruiting notice, 1893. The recruiting standards have always stressed physical fitness and good character. In addition, recruits have always been required to be British subjects ("Canadian citizens or British subjects resident in Canada" is the present qualification), but prior to World War I this was not strictly enforced, and men of many nationalities were recruited, particularly Americans.

OATH OF OFFICE

I, ...
(NAME IN FULL)

solemnly swear that I will faithfully, diligently and impartially execute and perform the duties required of me as a member of the Royal Canadian Mounted Police, and will well and truly obey and perform all lawful orders and instructions that I receive as such, without fear, favour or affection of or towards any person. So help me God.

Sworn before me at ....   Signature ....

in the Province of ....   Witness ....
(TO BE TAKEN BEFORE A COMMISSIONED OFFICER OF THE R.C.M.P., A JUSTICE OF THE PEACE, OR A COMMISSIONER FOR OATHS).

this .... day of ....

.... 19 ....

YOU ARE INVITED TO HELP "MAINTAIN THE RIGHT"

Join the
RCMP
Royal Canadian Mounted Police

(Above) *Oath of Office. For one hundred years every recruit entering the Force has been required to take the Oath of Office. The wording has changed very little. The form used today is almost identical to that of 1873.*

(Left) *Recruiting poster, 1953. For many years recruits received little better than a labouring wage – men joined the Force for adventure, for the military life or for an opportunity to reach western Canada and later to homestead. Few saw it as a career. The pay for a recruit in 1873 was 75 cents per day. This was reduced to 40 cents in 1880, raised to 60 cents in 1905, to 75 cents in 1912 and to $1.25 in 1935.*

Recent trends have raised the income level and improved the working conditions of policemen. This has attracted a different type of recruit, better educated, often a university graduate, highly motivated, and seeking a worthwhile, challenging career.

SERMENT D'OFFICE

Je, ... jure solennellement

(NOM AU LONG)

que j'accomplirai et remplirai fidèlement, diligemment et impartialement les devoirs exigés de moi comme membre de la Gendarmerie royale du Canada, et que j'observerai fidèlement et exécuterai ponctuellement toutes les instructions et ordres légitimes qui me seront donnés à ce titre, sans crainte de personne et sans faveur ni partialité envers qui que ce soit. Ainsi Dieu me soit en aide.

Assermenté devant moi ....   Signature ....

dans la province de ....   Témoin ....

(DOIT ÊTRE ASSERMENTÉ PAR UN OFFICIER BREVETÉ DE LA GENDARMERIE ROYALE DU CANADA, UN JUGE DE PAIX, OU TOUTE PERSONNE CHARGÉE DE RECEVOIR LES DÉCLARATIONS ASSERMENTÉES).

ce .... jour de

.... 19.........

30882

Recent recruiting literature reflects Canada's bilingual character. One requirement for recruits that has never changed is that they speak and write either French or English. As a result there have always been French Canadians as well as English Canadians in the Force. Some of the first officers appointed were French Canadians and the recruits of 1873 included a group from Quebec who spoke only French. Mindful of the aspirations of French-speaking Canadians, Commissioner Mac-Brien in 1933 initiated a policy of posting, as far as possible, bilingual members to "C" Division, Quebec, and the French-speaking areas of "J" Division, New Brunswick.

Uniforms and Badges

*Sergeant of the North-West Mounted
Police in the first official uniform; 1874.*

*Sergeant of the North-West Mounted
Police in Dress Uniform, 1898.*

Paintings by Tom McNeely, reproduced courtesy of Rolph-Clark-Stone Ltd.

Sergeant of the Royal Canadian Mounted
Police in Review Order of Dress, 1973.

The first Guidon of the R.C.M.P.

The Regimental Badge of the R.C.M.P.

Badges and buttons of the N.W.M.P. and R.N.W.M.P.

The R.C.M.P. Long Service Medal. Approved by Royal Warrant and first issued in 1935, the medal is awarded to regular members of the Force who have completed twenty years of good conduct and satisfactory service.

OFFICERS

Commissioner	Deputy Commissioner	Assistant Commissioner	Chief Superintendent	Superintendent	Inspector	Sub-Inspector

NCO's

Corps Sgt. Major	Sgt. Major	S/Sgt. Major	Staff Sergeant	Sergeant	Corporal

APPOINTMENT

Instructor	First Aid Instructor	Rough Rider	Musical Ride	Dog Master

Air Pilot	Air Division	Drum Major	Bandsman

MARKSMEN

Distinguished Marksman	Marksman	Distinguished Marksman	Marksman

LONG SERVICE

Five Years	Ten Years	Fifteen Years

Insignia of the R.C.M.P., 1973.

*I*nto the Unknown

A Canadian force, hastily raised, armed, and equipped, and not under martial law, in a few months marched 2,000 miles, through a country for the most part as unknown as it proved bare of pasture and scanty in the supply of water. Of such a march, under such circumstances, all true Canadians may well feel proud.

From "Report of G. A. French, Commissioner, N.W.M.P., December 1874."

The change of government which took place in Ottawa in November 1873 had a profound effect upon the future history of the North-West Mounted Police. A political storm had been building up all that summer over charges that members of the Conservative Government had accepted bribes during the federal election of the previous year. On November 6, three days after the first members of the Force were sworn in at Lower Fort Garry, Sir John A. Macdonald resigned from office. His successor was Alexander Mackenzie, a dour stonemason from Sarnia, Ontario, who like Macdonald was a native Scot. Mackenzie was hard-working, earnest, abstemious in his habits and a strong supporter of the temperance movement – quite a contrast to his coarse, joking and frequently inebriated predecessor. The new minister responsible for the Mounted Police was A. A. Dorion, the leader of the Quebec wing of the Liberals.

Mackenzie, the Whisky Trade and the Mounted Police

Under the Liberal Government, a new sense of urgency and concern replaced Macdonald's parsimonious and procrastinating policy regarding law and order in the Northwest. To a large extent this new approach was a result of Mackenzie's willingness to accept Lieutenant-Governor Morris's assessment of conditions in the Territories. Morris had always maintained that the suppression of the whisky trade and the establishment of friendly relations with the Indian tribes were the keys to establishing order in the West. The Cypress Hills Massacre convinced him that the situation was rapidly deteriorating and that the country could find itself embroiled in a full-scale Indian war. He lost no time in notifying the new Government of the latest threat. There are now at least "six forts of United States traders, fully armed and equipped," ready to defy Canadian authority, he informed Ottawa. The Mounted Police, he warned, are "insufficient," the Government must get London to maintain a British regiment in the Northwest.

Mackenzie decided that the whisky trade must be stopped as quickly as possible; but for a while he was uncertain how this task was to be accomplished. Like Morris, he did not feel that a mounted police force was suitable.

Hewitt Bernard. As Deputy Minister of Justice from 1867 to 1876, Hewitt Bernard was closely associated with Macdonald's plan for a mounted police force. The Force's early organization and the march to the foothills were carried out under his direction. Born in Jamaica, Bernard emigrated to Canada in the 1850s. He became a close friend of Macdonald and from 1858 to 1866 acted as his private secretary. The two became brothers-in-law in 1867 when Macdonald married Bernard's sister, Susan Agnes Bernard.

Antoine-Aimé Dorion, December 1873. When the Liberals came to power in November, 1873, Dorion, the leader of the Quebec Rouges, succeeded Sir John A. Macdonald as Minister of Justice. With Bernard, Dorion persuaded Prime Minister Mackenzie to continue with the plan for a semimilitary police force to establish order in the Northwest Territories.

In May, 1874, Dorion resigned to become Chief Justice of the Province of Quebec.

He at first decided to seek the assistance of American troops. To Lord Dufferin he proposed a joint Canadian-American military expedition, with the American soldiers empowered to enter Canadian territory and carry out police duties. The United States Government had repeatedly urged Ottawa to bring order to the foothill country north of Montana. Early in December 1873 Washington complained through official channels that its efforts to suppress the trade in Montana were being hampered by the easy way in which American Indians could obtain liquor north of the border.

Lord Dufferin described the Prime Minister's proposal as "a very objectionable plan, and quite incompatible with the dignity of the Dominion." In an effort to dissuade Mackenzie from taking a course of action which might endanger Canadian sovereignty, Dufferin wisely pointed out the advantages of acting independently:

. . . even though the expense might be considerable, an expedition organized by Canada itself would have its advantages. In the first place the mere fact of putting forth her strength for the purpose of asserting her jurisdiction and repressing outrage in those wild districts, would flatter in a very legitimate manner the national pride of the Dominion . . . in the next place we should appear upon the scene, not as the Americans have done, for the purpose of restraining and controlling the Indian tribes, but with the view of avenging injuries inflicted on the red man by the white.

In the end the Governor General's sounder advice had its effect. The Prime Minister decided upon a purely Canadian expedition. He was still opposed, however, to the idea of using soldier-policemen. It was only under strong pressure from Dorion and Hewitt Bernard, who had been retained as Deputy Minister of Justice by the Liberals, that he finally agreed to give the assignment to the North-West Mounted Police.

Early in March 1874 French received instructions to carry on with the organization of the force. Recruiting started for a further three divisions, comprising 150 men, and preparations began for the procurement of supplies and equipment for an expedition into the Northwest. The Governor General described the Government's final plan, and the task which lay ahead for the Mounted Police to the British authorities:

It is the intention of my Government about the month of June to send off an expedition consisting of three hundred mounted riflemen fully equipped accompanied by a mountain gun or two, into the Northwest for the purpose of capturing a band of desperadoes who have established themselves in some fortified posts in our territory in the neighbourhood of the Belly River.

The expedition will be commanded by Col. French, an artillery officer, and though nominally policemen the men will be dressed in scarlet uniform, and possess all the characteristics of a military force.

The Liberals had decided to act boldly on the question of establishing order in the West. Macdonald had intended to distribute the Mounted Police in detachments at the Hudson's Bay posts along the North Saskatchewan trade route from Fort Ellice to Edmonton. He proposed to use the trading posts as bases from which the Force would move onto the southern plains, should trouble arise. Mackenzie planned to march the Force right into the robbers' roost, suppress the whisky trade and establish a post in the heart of Whoop-up country.

It was a daring plan and one for which there were few precedents. Commissioner French had a difficult task ahead of him. He had just three months in which to recruit, train and prepare his command for duty. There was little accurate information about the territory it would be entering, and no reliable maps. Once it was out on the prairies, the Force would have no direct means of communications with the East, and the logistics of the expedition would require it to take sufficient supplies and equipment to sustain itself for several months.

The tribes of the Blackfoot Confederacy were reputedly warlike and unfriendly. There was no way of knowing how they would react to the presence of a strange military force camping on their tribal hunting grounds. They had already attacked American troops south of the border, and in 1870 had inflicted over two hundred casualties on a combined army of Cree and Assiniboine raiders.

Dufferin was right in realizing the attention such an expedition would attract. During the summer of 1874 the eyes not only of eastern Canada but of the United States and Britain, too, would be focussed on the progress of the small column of red-coated policemen.

The Organization of the Force Continues

Commissioner French was heartened by the Government's decision. He had already informed Dorion that the 150 men under his command would be quite insufficient for confronting the more than two thousand warriors reported to be at the disposal of the Blackfoot. Throughout April and May, the Commissioner hurried back and forth between Ottawa, Kingston and Toronto, frantically ordering supplies, buying horses and selecting recruits. There was no shortage of the latter. There were so many applicants, in fact, that French was able to accept only the "exceptionally desirable men." The Toronto *Mail* reported more than fifteen hundred men offered themselves for the 150 positions available. The Commissioner was fortunate in obtaining another thirty men from the two schools of gunnery at Quebec City and Kingston. Like the first contingent, most of those recruited in the spring of 1874 had had some military experience of one kind or another.

The new recruits came from a variety of backgrounds. It was the desire for romance and adventure, or the opportunity to satisfy their curiosity, that attracted them to the Force, rather than the seventy-five cents a day most of them would earn as sub-constables. One of them was Jean D'Artigue, a school teacher from France who gave up his career because he had read Fenimore Cooper and wanted to find out what life on the frontier was really like. Another was Cecil Denny, a young Anglo-Irish aristo-crat (later Sir C. E. Denny); then there was William Parker, the educated son of an English country parson who had grown tired of labouring on a farm in Ontario and wanted excitement. Michael Kirk from Donegal, Ireland, was one of several ex-members of the Royal Irish Constabulary. One interest-ing recruit was Joseph Francis, a veteran of the Crimean War whose account of the "charge of the Light Brigade" would no doubt capti-vate many a campfire audience in the months ahead. The youngest of them was fifteen-year-old Fred Bagley, the son of a former sergeant in the Royal Artillery who en-listed as a trumpeter. One English-man was reported to have inheri-ted £30,000 shortly after joining the Force. He was so anxious to see the Northwest however that he refused to resign and collect his inheritance.

The assembly point for the new recruits was the New Fort in Toronto. Here they were organ-ized into three Divisions ("E",

"Interior of the Officers' Car at 11 P.M." On June 6, 1874, the second contingent of the N.W.M.P. consisting of 217 officers and men, and 244 horses left Toronto for Fort Dufferin Manitoba. To reach their destination they travelled by rail as far as Fargo, North Dakota, stopping at Sarnia, Detroit, Chicago and St. Paul en route. While in the United States they were re-quired to dress in civilian clothes. This scene of the officers' sleeping quarters on one of the trains was sketched by a journal-ist who accompanied them, Henri Julien.

"D" and "F"). For the next few weeks they were fully occupied with mounted drill, servicing their equipment and practising with the two nine-pounder field guns which had recently arrived from England. For small arms, the Force was issued with Snider-Enfield carbines, hardly a match for the latest repeating rifles reported to be in the hands of the whisky traders and Indians.

Public excitement and specu-lation grew as the time approached for the departure from Toronto. One newspaper reported five hundred outlaws in fortified posts ready and able to defend them-selves with repeating rifles. French anticipated "hot work" for the Force once it confronted the whisky traders. Jean D'Artigue's friends in Montreal tried to dis-suade him from joining the expedi-tion, warning him that he risked losing his scalp. The Toronto *Mail* wished the men "God Speed." It felt they had enough pluck, discipline and ability to crown their efforts with success. If a few of them should lose their scalps, it could offer only the comforting thought: "Sharp be the blade, and sure the blow and short the pang to undergo."

French frequently warned the men of the dangers and hardships ahead in the hope that the feeble-hearted would drop out before the expedition began. By the time the march was under way, French was glad to report that more than thirty had decided not to "rough it" and had taken their leave.

In deciding upon a uniform for the Force, the government followed the recommendations of numerous observers who had spoken of the long-established respect among the Indians for the traditionally red-coated British soldier. Morris had advised Macdonald that fifty men in red coats would be better than one hundred in any other colour. The first official uniform was fairly simple compared with the military styles of the day. It consisted of a plain scarlet Norfolk jacket, steel grey or flesh-coloured breeches, blue trousers with a double white stripe, long boots with spurs, a white helmet and a forage cap, or pill box, and a dark blue cloak. Later a more elaborate type of military uniform came into use. It was several years before the Force acquired buttons and badges with its own insignia. To the Indians the marching column would appear unmistakably as soldiers of the Queen.

The jumping-off point for the expedition was the small settlement of Dufferin, Manitoba, just inside Canadian territory about sixty miles south of Winnipeg.

Fort Dufferin, Manitoba 1873. In 1872 the British North American Boundary Commission established its headquarters and main supply depot on the west bank of the Red River, just north of the international border. It was designated Fort Dufferin in honour of Canada's Governor General, the Earl of Dufferin. Here on July 8, 1874, the N.W.M.P. began its epic march to the foothills of the Rocky Mountains.

Here the Government had acquired some of the buildings occupied by the Boundary Commission for the use of the Force while it made its final preparations for the trek westward. In order for the Toronto contingent to reach Dufferin with all possible speed, arrangements were made for it to travel by train through the United States to the nearest rail point at Fargo, North Dakota. From here the men and horses would have a march of 150 miles before joining the three divisions from Lower Fort Garry.

The Departure from Toronto

The day of the departure from Toronto was June 6, 1874. The scene at Union Station resembled that of a military force leaving for war. Two trains were needed to transport the 16 officers, 201 men, 244 horses and their equipment. Thousands turned up at the station to see the men off, and a military band added to the excitement which ran through the crowd. Relatives and friends were busy exchanging last farewells. "Be a good boy," Fred Bagley's mother cautioned him, "say your prayers regularly and come back soon." One father was heard to warn his son: "I would rather hear of your death than your dishonour."

To the strains of "Auld Lang Syne," the train carrying the horses pulled away from the platform. The second train followed shortly after, with the crowd cheering, rockets firing and the band playing "The Girl I Left Behind Me." With the men went

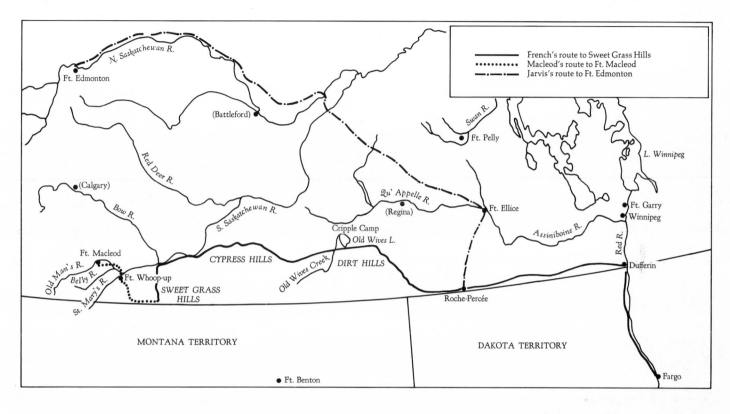

The route of the March West. In 1874 the
Mounted Police moved westward across
open, uninhabited prairie. Today farms,
highways and cities stand upon the route
over which they struggled. The distance
from Fort Dufferin to the Belly River was
781 miles. By the time Commissioner
French with "D" and "E" Divisions had
reached the Force's headquarters at Swan
River on the return trip, they had ridden
almost two thousand miles in three and a
half months.

Henri Julien, a Montreal journal-
ist whose accounts and drawings
of the Force's progress would do
much to publicize the epic march
before it.

The Force Assembles at Dufferin

After brief stops at Chicago and
St. Paul, the three divisions arrived
at Dufferin on June 19. They
found their comrades from Lower
Fort Garry, under the command of
Assistant Commissioner J. F.
Macleod, already there to greet
them. On the night of their arrival
a severe hail-and-thunder storm
flattened their tents and stampeded
the horses. D'Artigue, in his book
*Six Years in the Canadian North-
West*, described it as a "dazzling
and continuous glare of lightning,
which seemed like one sheet of fire
above our heads; crashes of thunder which appeared to shake the
earth to its very centre, and a
hurricane which in spite of our
efforts, blew down our tents."

With the exception of a small detachment which had been sent to
Fort Ellice, the site designated as
headquarters, the entire Force was
gathered together for the first and
only time in its history.

While preparations for the
departure got under way at Dufferin, French rode to Fort Garry to
see Lieutenant-Governor Morris
and discuss the route he would
take. Morris had secured a party
of Métis guides for the Force
under the leadership of Pierre
Léveillé. The Commissioner's latest instructions called for him to
march westward to the Belly
River, leave a small force there and
proceed on north to Fort Edmonton. French wanted as far as possible to use the trail taken by the
Boundary Commission. This way
the Force would have a ready-

"Camp of the N.W.M.P. at Rivière Courte," by Henri Julien. On July 24, 1874, the Force passed Roche-Percée and camped on the banks of the Souris River at Rivière Courte, or Short Creek, close to the present town of Estevan, Saskatchewan. Here the Commissioner found good water, grass and wood.

made trail to follow and accurate information on the location of feed and water. The Government, however, was anxious that the Force should not remain too close to the border. His final orders, therefore, required him to follow the boundary for only about two hundred miles, march northwest for a short distance and continue westward to the Belly River, well away from the 49th parallel. Captain Cameron, one of the boundary commissioners, warned him that on the parched prairie north of the border he would probably lose 40 per cent of his horses.

The March West

French returned to Dufferin on July 1 to find Macleod, a "capital fellow," had the wagons loaded and the supplies issued ready for the departure. On July 8, 1874, the great trek began. French decided to march for just a short distance the first day to see that all was in order. About five o'clock on a hot afternoon, the temperature over 90 degrees Fahreinheit, the command was given to proceed. To the accompaniment of bugle calls, shouts and the rattle of the Red River carts, the astonishing cavalcade got under way.

The expedition consisted of 275 officers and men, 142 draught oxen, 93 head of cattle, 310 horses, 114 Red River carts, 73 wagons, two 9-pounder field guns, two mortars, mowing machines, portable forges and field kitchens.

"A Lancer of the N.W.M.P.," by Henri Julien. There are no extant photographs of the March West. Fortunately a pictorial record was made by the Montreal journalist and artist, Henri Julien, who accompanied the expedition. Many of Julien's lively sketches were later published in the Canadian Illustrated News.

Several men were left behind suffering from malaria and typhoid. Two of them succumbed shortly after, the first members of the Force to die in its service. The column moved to a small lake about two miles from Dufferin where camp was made for the night. On the following day the struggle to reach the foothills before the winter snows arrived began in earnest.

Once under way, the red-coated column made an impressive sight. First came "A" Division riding on dark bay horses. It was followed by "B" on dark browns and "C" on chestnuts drawing the field guns and ammunition. Behind these came "D" on greys, "E" on blacks, and finally "F" Division mounted on light bays. To the rear was a string of ox carts, wagons, cattle and mowing machines. When closed up to proper intervals, the formation was about a mile and a half in length. However, owing to the uneven pace of horses and oxen and the breaking of axles and wheels, it usually stretched across the prairie for four or five miles.

After a few days on the march the men settled down to a steady routine. "The cooks," French reported, "got into the way of cooking and baking in the open air, and loaves of bread no longer have the appearance of lumps of dough." By following the Boundary Commission's trail, the daily marches could be arranged with some certainty of finding wood, grass and water when camp was made for the night. The weather was hot throughout July, the temperatures climbing daily to over 90 degrees. Usually each day's march was started in the early hours of the morning and a halt called before the afternoon sun became too hot. In spite of this the warm weather began to have a bad effect on the horses and oxen.

"Scene in the N.W.M.P. Camp," by Henri Julien. During the March West, and for many years after, the only entertainment to be found in the isolated police posts was that provided by the members themselves. Anyone who could sing, dance or play a musical instrument soon found a demand for his talents. One of Commissioner French's earliest suggestions was the formation of a band to relieve the monotony and loneliness. Eventually, a band was organized at Swan River in 1876.

"Evening Guard Parade," by Henri Julien.

"A Halt to Cut Hay," by Henri Julien. Included among the equipment taken by the expedition were several mowing machines. Wherever good grass was found, a stop was made to cut hay for later use.

With the "air full of locusts and everyone tormented by mosquitoes," the Boundary Commission depot at Pembina was reached on July 12. Here the men camped in a thunderstorm which rained hailstones as large as "walnuts" on their tents. As it was Sunday, a brief halt was called in the daily routine to allow for the holding of religious services. French, who kept a daily diary, noted the Sunday practice of religious worship:

> *Had regular church parade under the senior officer of each persuasion; I took the Church of England party myself, the number being in excess of all other persuasions. Much pleased to hear many of the men singing hymns in the afternoon and evening; unfortunately, the language of a great many is by no means Scriptural.*

"Storm on the Third of August," by Henri Julien. On the night of August 3/4 the expedition was hit by a tremendous thunderstorm. Nearly all the tents were blown down, but fortunately the horses were prevented from stampeding.

"Crossing the Dirt Hills," by Henri Julien. On August 6 the Force left the Boundary Commission Road and began the difficult ascent of the Dirt Hills. Even though the men dismounted to assist in hauling the wagons and guns, the steep slopes were so hard on the horses that French had to rest them all the next day.

Jean D'Artigue recalled, what "a grand sight to see three hundred men standing in the wilderness, several hundred miles from civilization, giving thanks and offering prayers to their Creator."

On July 24 the Commissioner's diary recorded the arrival at "Roches Percées," the unusual outcropping of limestone 270 miles west of Dufferin:

Left at 4 a.m. Great rivalry between the troops as to who should be off first. "A" Troop got off at 3.30, marched 16 miles to St. Peter's Springs, found a dirty mud hole, set to work and made several wells, placed a barrel in one and banked it round with stones for the benefit of Macleod, and any others who might come on. Watered nearly 300 horses from this well. Soil generally poor, no wood or water of consequence. In afternoon marched for Roches Percées and passed it, camping on the banks of the Souris at Short Creek. Very good camping ground, wood, water, and grass . . . 26½ [miles].

By the time he had reached Roche-Percée French knew he would have to revise his plans. With the easiest stretch of the march behind them, many of the horses and oxen were already showing signs of exhaustion. Only the fittest would be able to survive the uncertain journey ahead. At Roche-Percée he had hoped to find fresh horses waiting for him from Fort Ellice. These it turned out were not available. French

Superintendent Edward Dummer Jarvis. On August 1, 1874, "A" Division under Superintendent Jarvis with six sick constables and nearly sixty of the weakest horses left the main column at Roche-Perceé and proceeded northwest via the Saskatchewan trade route to the Hudson's Bay post at Fort Edmonton. On the journey ahead many of the horses and oxen died as a result of starvation and exposure. In almost desperate condition the Division finally straggled in to Fort Edmonton in bitterly cold weather on October 27. Early in 1875 Jarvis began the construction of Fort Saskatchewan a few miles downstream from the Hudson's Bay post.

decided, therefore, to send "A" Division under Inspector Jarvis with the weaker horses and oxen directly to Fort Edmonton via the North Saskatchewan trail. Jarvis's party would have a long march of over eight hundred miles ahead of it, but was assured of finding food and shelter at the Hudson's Bay posts, and winter quarters would be waiting once it reached Edmonton.

On July 29 the remaining five divisions moved on to the Boundary Commission post at Wood End. Here they remained a day gathering firewood before continuing on westward along the Boundary trail. Gradually, on their right there appeared a line of low hills, the Coteaux of the Missouri, or the Dirt Hills as the Métis drivers called them. On August 4 the column left the border trail for good and swung northwest up the parched bare slopes of the Coteaux.

With each day's march now the expedition became a test of endurance and determination for both men and horses. The terrain and the heat were especially hard on the animals. French's diary tells the story: August 7 – "Horses so played out by the severe descent of the Dirt Hills that I resolved to give them a day's rest"; August 10 – "The saline water and bad feed is telling severely on the horses." By the middle of August most of the mounts were "half-starved" and in very poor condition.

The ordeal began to have an effect on the men too. Day after day they had been on the move, from early dawn until well after dark, frequently stopping to help the animals haul the wagons over hills and gullies. They were often obliged "to drink liquid, which when passed through a filter was still the color of ink." Many were suffering from dysentery, and typhoid made its appearance once again. On August 13 the column reached Old Wives Creek, a few miles south of the present city of

Moose Jaw, Saskatchewan. Here they found good feed and water, and French decided to rest a few days while Macleod went south to Wood Mountain depot to buy a supply of oats. At Old Wives Creek they were visited by a curious band of Sioux who dubbed French "Wachasta Sota," "Man with Power."

On August 19, the Force moved about two miles northwest of Old Wives Creek to a small lake where there were also grass and water. Here French decided to establish Cripple Camp for the weakest of the animals and the men who were too sick to continue. On August 20, the main Force moved on leaving behind 28 horses, 7 men (5 of them ill), and a quantity of stores.

With each passing day, now, the Force was getting closer to its target. But the condition of the horses was growing steadily worse. On August 31, Macleod rejoined the march with a much-needed supply of oats. Two days later, to everyone's excitement, they sighted their first herd of buffalo. Five of the beasts were killed, and the men enjoyed a welcome meal of fresh meat.

The appearance of the buffalo alleviated the shortage of food for the men, but the horses began to die of starvation and exhaustion. For miles around, the prairie had been stripped bare of grass by the migrating herds of buffalo. On September 6, the column reached the South Saskatchewan River, and camped close to the site of the

Louis Léveillé N.W.M.P. guide and interpreter. For many years the Force depended upon the Métis for guides and interpreters. Among the most well-known of these were two brothers, Louis and Pierre Léveillé. Before coming to the Northwest, their father was reputed to have fought under Napoleon at Waterloo. Pierre, who weighed over three hundred pounds, acted as chief guide on the March West. Louis assisted with the erection of Fort Walsh and acted as interpreter there at many of the crucial meetings between the Force's officers and the Indian chiefs. He died at Maple Creek on May 29, 1888.

present city of Medicine Hat, over seven hundred miles from Dufferin. On the following day they found neither grass nor good water and the men drank "liquid mud for tea."

The Arrival at the Belly River

On September 8, a cold wind from the north brought heavy rain. By morning five horses were dead. Two days later the Belly River was sighted. Finally, on September 12, the Force reached its objective and camp was made on the banks of the Belly close to its junction with the Bow.

French could hardly believe what he saw. Slowly he began to realize how grossly exaggerated and erroneous was the information he had been given in Fort Garry and Ottawa about conditions at the Belly River. Here the Force was supposed to find Fort Whoop-up and hundreds of outlaws ready to do battle. All they discovered, he angrily reported, were "three deserted log huts without roofs."

Even worse was the lack of feed and water for the livestock. For two months the Force had been on the march, believing that at the end of its journey it would find "a perfect garden of Eden," with a climate "milder than Toronto." Instead, French noted, the vicinity "for at least sixty or seventy miles in every direction is little better than a desert, not a tree to be seen anywhere, ground parched and poor, and wherever there was a little swamp it was destroyed by the buffalo."

"The Sweet Grass Hills in Sight," by
*Henri Julien. Failing to find Fort Whoop-up
at the junction of the Bow and Belly Rivers,
the N.W.M.P. turned south to seek shelter
for their starving and exhausted animals.
On September 15 they sighted the snow-
capped buttes of the Sweet Grass Hills,
where they found excellent feed and water.*

The expedition was now in a desperate situation. Every day horses and oxen were dying from starvation and cold. The men were tiring. Their uniforms were tattered and most of them were now marching on foot so as not to weaken the remaining horses. Unless the animals found food and a place to rest, without delay, the expedition might collapse completely. Léveillé advised French that he would lose most of the horses if he tried to get through to Fort Edmonton. The only alternative was to turn south to the Sweet Grass Hills. Here the guides assured him he would find good grazing and water. There at least they would be close to Fort Benton, Montana, where they could replenish food stocks and obtain essential supplies.

On to the Sweet Grass Hills and Fort Benton

As the weary column resumed its march on September 14, it ran into vast herds of buffalo "in every direction." Cecil Denny recalled a sight which would soon be gone from the Western plains: "As far as the eye could reach, thousands and tens of thousands were in sight, the country being fairly black with them." On the seventeenth, the cold wind and the rain returned, and began to take its toll of the horses once more. The next day, with the Rocky Mountains in sight to the west, the Force entered a coulee close to the West Butte of the Sweet Grass Hills, about six miles north of the boundary. To everyone's relief they found good pasture and French decided to call a halt.

After resting for a few days French took Macleod and a small party of men and empty carts to Fort Benton, almost one hundred miles to the south, to report his position to Ottawa and obtain fresh supplies. Upon his arrival, the Commissioner found two telegrams already awaiting his attention. From the first he learned that the Government approved his suggestion that he leave a large force in the vicinity of the Belly River. The second informed him that his headquarters had been moved from Fort Ellice further west to a new site near Fort Pelly, the proposed seat of government for the Northwest Territories.

To the authorities, French tersely summed up his position: "Force on way back – state of affairs on the Bow and Belly Rivers has been greatly exaggerated – I leave a large force in that vicinity under Major Macleod." After leaving instructions with Macleod (whom he would never meet again), and procuring fresh horses, the Commissioner returned to the border. On September 29 with "D" and "E" Divisions he began the return march of more than eight hundred miles to Fort Pelly.

Fort Mc Leod N.W.T.

Fort Whoop-up

To the tall, dignified Macleod now fell the task of building a post and establishing law and order in the foothills. While at Benton arranging for supplies, he hired an experienced guide and interpreter, Jerry Potts, the son of a Blood Indian woman and a Scottish trader. Potts, a short strongly built man, with his knowledge of the plains and his uncanny sense of direction was to become an invaluable asset to the Mounted Police. From Potts, Macleod learned that Fort Whoop-up was at the junction of the Belly and St. Mary's Rivers, farther west than originally reported. With Potts to guide him, he rejoined the three remaining divisions, "B", "C" and "F", and marched north to search for the notorious stronghold of the whisky traders.

On October 9, the small column drew rein on some high ground overlooking the confluence of the two rivers. Below it, about three hundred feet from the banks of the Belly, the monosyllabic Potts pointed out the wooden stockades and bastions of Fort Whoop-up. After cautiously positioning his men, Macleod strode boldly through the main gate. All he found were a few Indians and a friendly trader, Dave Akers, who hospitably invited the men to a meal of buffalo meat and vegetables. The fort was searched from top to bottom but not a dram of whisky was to be found. Slowly Macleod began to realize that with the approach of the Force most of the whisky traders in the foothills had either fled south across the border, or had turned to more legitimate business.

"Fort Macleod, N.W.T., 1874," by R. B. Nevitt. The first post built by the Mounted Police in the West was Fort Macleod on an island in the Old Man's River. As a result of frequent flooding this site was abandoned in 1883 and a new post constructed on higher ground. This sketch was drawn by Richard Barrington Nevitt, who accompanied the Force on the March West as Assistant Surgeon. Although born in Savannah, Georgia, Nevitt received his education and medical training in Toronto. After leaving the Force in 1878, he returned to Toronto to become one of the city's leading gynecologists and obstetricians.

Fort Macleod Established

What was uppermost in the assistant commissioner's mind now was the need for winter quarters. With Potts guiding them, the three divisions left Fort Whoop-up and moved northwest. Three days later they came to the banks of the Old Man's River. Here their guide led them to a site beside the river where they found good pasture and groves of tall cottonwoods with which to build. Work began immediately upon the construction of stables for the exhausted animals. The task was saddened by the death of a constable who had contracted typhoid during the march westward. His body became the first of many to rest in the little cemetery marked out between the post and the river.

Within a few weeks the log walls of a police post began to rise around the perimeter of a barrack square. Around the square were soon clustered the rough shanties of the traders who had arrived from Fort Benton to provide the Force with supplies. By the end of the year a new settlement had appeared in the vast wilderness of the Canadian West. Upon French's instructions it was named Fort Macleod after its commanding officer. Above its barrack square flew the Union Jack. The symbol that authority had finally arrived in Whoop-up country.

Commissioner James Farquharson Macleod, C.M.G. One of the cornerstones of the Force's peaceful understanding with the tribes of the Blackfoot Confederacy was the personal relationship between Macleod and the Indian chiefs. The handsome Commissioner treated the tribal leaders with courtesy and respect. His honest and understanding enforcement of the law gained their respect. They called him Stamixotokan ("Bull's Head"). Macleod was appointed

Commissioner on July 22, 1876, following French's resignation. On October 31, 1880, he gave up the command of the Force to become a stipendiary magistrate for the N.W.T. His death occurred at Calgary on September 5, 1894.

Assistant Commissioner Macleod's quarters at Fort Macleod, 1875.

To anyone who had thoughts of defying that authority, Macleod left no doubt that justice would be swiftly but fairly enforced, and the offenders heavily penalized. As the Commanding Officer of the Mounted Police and a magistrate, his authority in the remote frontier community was almost absolute. To the Force's credit, however, it never seriously abused the extraordinary powers with which it was endowed.

Shortly after their arrival, an Indian named Three Bulls complained that a party of traders at Pine Coulee, about fifty miles to the north, had given him two gallons of whisky for two horses. Macleod moved quickly. A detachment hurried north under Inspector L. N. F. Crozier to investigate. Crozier returned with five men under arrest, four whites and a "coloured man" named Bond. The accused were tried before Macleod and the other officers for having liquor in their possession. The two ringleaders were each fined $200 and the others $50; their equipment was confiscated and the whisky spilled. The first blow had been struck against the whisky trade.

Macleod Meets the Indian Chiefs

The arrest of the whisky traders had an immediate effect upon the Force's relations with the native population. Since the arrival of the Mounted Police, the Indians had been watching the strange visitors to their lands very closely. Macleod sent invitations to the chiefs to meet with him and several of those of the Blood and Peigan tribes came to the fort. Finally, on December 1, 1874, he was visited by a "very fine old Indian," Crowfoot, the head Chief of the Blackfoot.

Macleod greeted the chiefs ceremoniously and treated them with respect and dignity. After distributing presents of tobacco, he explained the reasons for the Force's presence. The Mounted Police, he informed them, had not come to take away their lands, but to teach them the laws of the white man. All who broke those laws, white or Indian, he promised, would be equally punished. As to their lands, the government would send "its great men to speak with them later."

The March West, 1874.

Jerry Potts, N.W.M.P. guide and interpreter. Jerry Potts was born about 1840. His father was Andrew Potts, a Scot employed by the American Fur Company at Fort Mackenzie on the Missouri River. His mother was Crooked Back, a member of the Black Elk band of Bloods. Following the death of his father, the young Potts spent much of his early life with his mother's people. He was no stranger to the violence of frontier life. He killed his first man at the age of twenty-three and made a name for himself as a warrior in many battles with the Blackfoot against their enemies. In 1874 Assistant Commissioner Macleod engaged him at Fort Benton as a guide and interpreter. Potts's experience of the frontier was to be invaluable to the Force in its first years in the West. It was he who led the Force to Fort Whoop-up and the Old Man's River where Fort Macleod was built. In 1877 he acted as interpreter at the signing of Treaty No. 7. Jerry Potts continued to serve the Force until his death at Fort Macleod in 1896.

With his diplomacy Macleod gained the confidence of the chiefs. The trust which the Indian leaders placed in him was to be vital to future relations between the Government and the tribes. They welcomed the new order that was promised by the arrival of the Mounted Police. The whisky trade was destroying their people and they had begun to realize that the buffalo would not last forever. Now there was hope of finding a new way of life. One old Indian summed up the change wrought by the arrival of the police in a few words: "Before you came the Indian crept along, now he is not afraid to walk erect."

"Writing-on-Stone," by J. de C. Fletcher.

Fort Calgary about 1878. In order to police the Blackfoot and Sarcee Indians who frequented the area, an Order-in-Council of April 10, 1875, authorized the establishment of a post on the Bow River. By the end of August, fifty men of "F" Division under Inspector Brisebois had started the construction of a fort at the junction of the Bow and Elbow Rivers. At first it was referred to as the Bow Fort. Later it was called Fort Brisebois. Finally Assistant Commissioner Macleod suggested the name Calgary, meaning "clear, running water" in Gaelic.

The site shown here is now in the heart of downtown Calgary.

By the close of 1874 law and order had been firmly established on Canada's frontier. The violence and lawlessness of the whisky trade era were things of the past. The task ahead for the police now was to maintain peace with the tribes, as settlers came and the railway began to snake its way across the land.

Upon his return to Manitoba, French found, to his surprise, little appreciation for the task which the ill-equipped and badly misinformed Force had accomplished. The march, he discovered, had become a political issue.

The attack upon it was led by the Toronto *Mail*, a leading conservative paper, which described the expedition as a "signal failure" and accused the government of seeking a "little glory for itself."

Red Crow, Chief of the Bloods. As a warrior, Red Crow led many war parties against the Cree, Assiniboine and other enemies of his tribe. With arrival of the Mounted Police and the disappearance of the buffalo, he was among the first to realize that the Indian would have to adjust to a new way of life. As an example, he became the first of his people to build a house and start ranching.

Crowfoot, Chief of the Blackfoot. Formerly a proud warrior, Crowfoot like Red Crow became a proponent of peace, preaching friendship with the white man and leading his people during the difficult period of transition which followed the arrival of the N.W.M.P. He refused to join Sitting Bull in a war against the whites, and in 1877 signed Treaty No. 7, committing his tribe to a sedentary life on a reserve. On his grave near Cluny, Alberta are inscribed the words: "Father of His People."

To this criticism were added the tales of mismanagement spread by deserters and political appointees that French had removed from the Force as unsuitable. The Commissioner soon found that in fighting bureaucratic incompetence to create an efficient and disciplined organization, he had trodden on many toes. In his outspoken and often tactless manner he pursued what he believed were the best interests of the Force. Among officials in Ottawa there was little understanding of the conditions faced by the police in the Northwest Territories. Eventually his relations with the Government over the administration of the Force reached an impasse. In 1876, much to the regret of most of those under his command, he resigned and returned to a successful career in the British Army, attaining the rank of major general and a knighthood before his death in 1921.

Although it may not have immediately received the recognition it deserved, the westward trek had been the making of the Force – which may have lost some of its glitter and glamour by the time it reached the foothills, but had survived the ordeal and successfully accomplished the tasks for which it had been sent. As a test of determination and endurance, the march left an indelible sense of achievement upon those who had participated. For those who succeeded them, the March West became a source of pride, an example of duty and service upon which the Force's future traditions and esprit de corps would be founded.

A Century of Weapons

During the past one hundred years the Force has been issued with a wide variety of small arms. The following represent the most important of these along with the approximate dates during which they were in service.

Snider-Enfield Carbine MK III.
Calibre: .577, Single Shot, 1874 to 1885
As far as fire-power was concerned these weapons were already obsolete when first used in 1874. The Indians and plainsmen were already using the newer, more effective repeating rifles. Like most of the other carbines issued to the Force it was carried in a rifle-bucket attached to the saddle behind the rider's right leg.

Winchester Model 1876.
Calibre: .45 – 75 W.C.F., 8 Rounds, 1878 to 1914
The Winchester proved to be very popular and was in service longer than any other shoulder-arm issued to the Force. It was carried, as shown here, in a sling attached to the pommel of the California stock saddle.

Lee-Metford Magazine Carbine MK I.
Calibre: .303, British, 6 Rounds, 1895 to 1914
The first bolt-action weapon issued to the
Force.

Ross Carbine MK I.
Calibre: .303, British, 5 Rounds, 1905 to
1907. The MK I proved unsatisfactory
and was replaced by an improved model,
the MK II, which was issued from 1909
to 1912.

Lee-Enfield.
Calibre: .303, British, 10 Rounds
Several models of the Lee-Enfield were
issued from 1902 to 1969. The one shown
here is the short Magazine Lee-Enfield
No. 1, MK III, in service from 1920 to
the 1940s.

Winchester Model 70.
Calibre: .308, 5 Rounds, 1960 to the present.

F.N. C1 (A1).
Calibre: 7.62 mm. Nato (or .308), 20
Rounds, 1960 to 1969
Used largely for competitive shooting.

Adams Side-rod Ejector Model.
*Calibre: .450 Adams, 6 Shots, 1874 to 1875
From 1875 to 1886 a second model, with an
improved ejection mechanism, was issued.*

Enfield.
Calibre: .476, 6 Shots, 1883 to 1905

Colt "New Service."
*Calibre: .455 and .45 Long, 6 Shots, 1904
to 1954
The Adams and the Enfield had both been
carried on the left side. The Colt was worn
on the right, attached to the new Sam
Browne Belt.*

Smith and Wesson.
*Calibre: .38 Special, 6 Shots, 1954 to the
present
A snub-nosed model was also issued for
plainclothesmen.*

Maxim Nordenfelt Air-cooled Machine Gun. Calibre: .303.
Acquired in 1898 for service on the summit of the White Pass during the Yukon Gold Rush. This weapon is now on display in the R.C.M.P. Museum, Regina.

It is often believed that the N.W.M.P. operated a Gatling Gun during the second Riel Rebellion. This is quite untrue. The Force acquired its first machine guns in the Yukon during the Gold Rush. These were in service for only a short time. Since then a very small number of machine guns have been in use from time to time, notably during the two World Wars. None of them were ever fired in anger.

Seven-pounder bronze Mark II guns at "Depot" Division, Regina. These are three of the four guns of this type which the Force obtained from the Department of Militia in 1876 to reinforce the defences of Fort Walsh, in preparation for the arrival of the American Sioux. All three of these guns saw action in 1885, two at Cut Knife Hill and one at Duck Lake. The four guns are now in the R.C.M.P. Museum, Regina.

The Force received two more of these seven-pounder guns from the Yukon Field Force in 1900. One of these later blew up. The other is still at Dawson in the Yukon.

The Force's first artillery pieces were the two nine-pounder guns and the two mortars taken on the March West in 1874. Two more nine-pounder guns were transferred from the Department of Militia in 1885. These four guns and the two mortars are also now at Regina.

In addition to the field guns from the early days, some of the larger ships of the Marine Division were equipped with artillery. One of these guns, from the former R.C.M.P. S. Wood, is also now on display in the Regina Museum.

Trooper and Indian

Three years ago when the Mounted Police came to my country, I met and shook hands with Stamixotokan (Commissioner Macleod) at the Belly River. Since that time he has made me many promises and has kept them all – not one of them has he broken. Everything that the Mounted Police have done has been for our good.

Red Crow, Chief of the Bloods,
at the signing of the Blackfoot Treaty, September, 1877

The Force's main task between 1874 and 1885 was the establishment and maintenance of amicable relations with the Indians of the N.W.T. Avoiding the American experience of frontier wars was one of the Canadian Government's main concerns during this period. The Canadian experience, fortunately, was to be somewhat different from that below the border. Miners and settlers had still not arrived in the Canadian West in sufficient numbers to challenge the warlike tribes for their hunting lands. By the time settlement did get under way on the prairies, the Indian had safely adopted a sedentary life on a reserve, and put away his war paint. In this peaceful change the buffalo were a key factor. Their rapid disappearance forced the Indians onto reserves before settlement began.

There was, too, the cooperation of the Indian leaders who had seen the futility of resistance on the American frontier and wished for a peaceful transition. Their cooperation was vital, for the Indians, particularly the Blackfoot, were for a time militarily far superior to the N.W.M.P. There was also the legacy of largely good relations which had existed between the Hudson's Bay Company, the British forces and the Indians. The red tunic was in many ways the symbol of that inheritance. The lack of settlement also enabled the Force to tackle the problem of establishing law and order with a power and authority which would not have been otherwise possible.

The task, nevertheless, was a difficult one, and the tact, confidence and understanding with which the N.W.M.P. handled it did much to pave the way for the construction of the C.P.R. and the peaceful settlement of the West.

The Indian Treaties

The Canadian Government began making treaties with the Indians of the Northwest shortly after the transfer of the Territories in 1870. The Indian claim to the land had to be extinguished if the country was to be opened up for peaceful settlement. The treaty system had been used since British colonial days as a means of extinguishing the aboriginal rights to the land. Under this system, the Indians gave up their territorial claims in return for a number of agreed benefits. In the case of the treaties reached with the Indians of western Canada, these usually included: (1) an allotted reserve set aside for homes and agricultural use, (2) hunting and fishing rights while the territory remained the property of the crown, (3) an annuity of $5 a head to each man, woman and child ($25 for chiefs, $15 for councillors), (4) the establishment of schools and the provision of agricultural implements and livestock.

By 1875 the Government had acquired title to all the territory west of Manitoba except that claimed by the Saskatchewan Indians and the tribes of the Blackfoot Confederacy. With the outbreak of hostilities between the American Sioux and the United States Army in the spring of 1876, the Canadian authorities were anxious to reach agreements with the remaining tribes.

"The Last Great Council of the West," by Sydney Hall. In 1881 the Marquis of Lorne, the Governor General of Canada, made a tour of the Northwest Territories. His visit was of special significance to the Indians, for his wife, Princess Louise, was a daughter of the Great White Mother herself, Queen Victoria.

The Governor General was accompanied by Sydney Hall, an artist for the London Graphic, correspondents from the London Times and the Toronto Globe, a French chef and six servants. The viceregal party was escorted throughout its tour by a troop of the N.W.M.P.

The Governor General in this sketch by Hall is shown holding council with the Blackfoot at Blackfoot Crossing on September 10, 1881.

N.W.M.P. officers at Fort Walsh, 1878.
Back row, l. to r.: Sub-Inspectors Neale,
Dickens, Antrobus, McIllree, Frechette,
Denny.
Seated: Assistant Commissioner Irvine,
Commissioner Macleod, Surgeon Kittson.
Front: Sub-Inspector Clark.

Treaty No. 6

Early in 1876 Superintendent
Walker was instructed to take a
troop and proceed to Battle Ford
at the junction of the North
Saskatchewan and Battle Rivers,
the site soon to be designated as
the seat of government for the
Northwest Territories. His orders
were to establish a Mounted
Police post and prepare to provide
an escort for the commissioners
who had been appointed to con-
clude a treaty with the Cree and
Assiniboine Indians of the Saskatchewan country at Fort Carlton.

In July 1876, Walker left the
Force's headquarters at Swan
River with a command made up
largely of members of "E" Division. At Battle Ford a site was
chosen on the high ground between
the two rivers, and a small party
under Inspector Frechette commenced the construction of the
post while Walker moved on to
Fort Carlton with the bulk of his
command to await the treaty
commissioners.

Troop of the N.W.M.P. on parade at Fort
Macleod, 1878.

Noncommissioned officers, Fort Walsh, 1878. Standing, l. to r.: Sergeant W. Piercy, Staff Sergeant T. Dunne, Staff Sergeant G. Harpur, Sergeant Douglass, Sergeant P. Macdonald, Staff Sergeant Ferland, Sergeant Gille, Sergeant R. Giveen.
Seated: Sergeant Major S. Horner, Staff Sergeant T. Lake, Sergeant Major J. Francis (Francis was reputed to have ridden in the Charge of the Light Brigade), Staff Sergeant F. Norman.
Front: Sergeant J. Calvin, Sergeant Bradley, Sergeant Major J. Barwis.

The commissioners appointed for Treaty No. 6 were the Lieutenant-Governor of Manitoba, the Honourable A. Morris; W. J. Christie, the Chief Factor of the Hudson's Bay Company; and the Honourable James Mackay, a Scottish Métis and a member of the Manitoba Government. Pierre Léveillé, the North-West Mounted Police guide, acted as interpreter.

The negotiations began at Fort Carlton on August 18, 1876, where more than two thousand excited Indians had gathered to meet with the commissioners. To the accompaniment of drums and tribal dancing, the chiefs assembled to hear the words of the Great White Mother's representatives. Dressed in a cocked hat and wearing a uniform trimmed with gold braid, the Lieutenant-Governor addressed the assembly, outlining the terms of the treaty. After several days of feasting and discussion, the chiefs signed their adherence to the treaty on August 23. As a result, the Cree and Assiniboine Indians surrendered their title to more than 120,000 square miles of central Saskatchewan and Alberta. Throughout the proceedings the presence of the Mounted Police in their scarlet tunics had had a salutary effect, discouraging any attempts by those dissatisfied with the terms of the treaty from disrupting the negotiations.

Treaty No. 7

The two commissioners appointed to treaty with the tribes of the Blackfoot Confederacy were the Honourable David Laird, Lieutenant-Governor of the Northwest Territories, and Commissioner J. F. Macleod of the North-West Mounted Police. The date set for the commencement of the negotiations for Treaty No. 7, or "the Blackfoot Treaty" as it was commonly called, was September 17, 1877. The site chosen was Blackfoot Crossing on the Bow River. The place was a favourite camping and burial ground of the Indians and its choice had been insisted upon by Crowfoot, the Chief of the Blackfoot.

Towards the end of August, Inspector Crozier arrived at the location with a party of men from "F" Division at Fort Calgary. A few days later he was joined by Commissioner Macleod with a detachment from Fort Macleod. In all, 108 officers and men participated in the treaty ceremonies. By the middle of September, a vast camp of several thousand persons – missionaries, traders, Indians and police – had assembled.

The Indian camp was a brilliant sight with the Indians in their ceremonial dress and their lodges freshly painted in bright colours. At the appointed time the chiefs approached the official tent of the commissioners accompanied by a thousand mounted braves, shouting and discharging their firearms. As the chiefs took their

Fort Walsh 1878. A group of Cree and Assiniboine Indians with members of the N.W.M.P. inside the stockade of the fort.

places on the buffalo robes before the tent, one of the Force's nine-pounder guns fired a salute, and the band, under Sergeant Major T. H. Lake, struck up the "Maple Leaf Forever." After Crowfoot had lit a stone pipe, taken one puff and passed it to Lieutenant-Governor Laird, the conference opened.

The key to the successful signing of the treaty was the bond of trust which had developed between Commissioner Macleod and the two Indian chiefs, Crowfoot and Red Crow. Macleod's honesty and sincerity had won their respect. Unlike many white men before him, he had treated the Indians as equals. He had been scrupulous in keeping the promises he had made to them and fair in his enforcement of the law. They accepted his advice, and Macleod made it clear to them that the terms of the treaty gave them and their tribes the best chance of adapting to a new way of life. "The advice given to me and my people has proven to be good," said Crowfoot, at the signing.

If the police had not come to this country, where would we all be now? Bad men and whisky were killing us so fast that very few of us would have been alive today. The Mounted Police have protected us as the feathers of the bird protect it from the frosts of winter. I wish all my people good, and trust that all our hearts will increase in goodness from this time forward. I am satisfied. I will sign the treaty.

On September 22, 1877, the treaty was signed and the Blackfoot, Blood, Peigan, Sarcee and Stoney Indians surrendered their title to what is today the southern part of Alberta.

N.W.M.P. *patrol with lances at Fort Walsh, 1878. The red and white pennons used by the Force in the early days are still carried in the R.C.M.P. Musical Ride.*

Policing the Indians

The Force was frequently called upon to keep the peace among the Indian tribes themselves. Contact between the tribes often brought out traditional rivalries and hostilities. To prevent intertribal violence the Mounted Police had to act firmly and boldly. Although numerically and militarily in an inferior position, they handled difficult situations with confidence and courage. To have allowed the Indians to flout and disregard the law could have been disastrous while they were still in an independent, warlike state.

A typical incident occurred in May 1877 when a Saulteaux chief named Little Child rode into Fort Walsh to complain that his small band had been terrorized, assaulted and intimidated by a party of South Assiniboines.

It appears that Little Child's fifteen lodges had made camp in the Cypress Hills with a large band of Assiniboines, over 250 lodges, that had recently arrived from Montana. One of the Assiniboines, Crow's Dance, had formed a war lodge of about two hundred young men, and informed the Saulteaux that henceforth he would control the hunting in the area and the Saulteaux would be subject to his authority. If they did not comply with the Assiniboines' wishes, their camp would be destroyed. Little Child had protested the strong-arm methods. If any harm came to his people, he would report the matter to the "White Mother's Chief." The Assiniboines had replied by tearing down the lodges of the Saulteaux, killing nineteen dogs, assaulting the men and frightening the women and children. As to Little Child's threat to report the matter to the Mounted Police, Crow's Dance had promised to give them the same treatment.

Here was a challenge to authority which had to be met head-on unless the Force was to be discredited and authority undermined. The story of the incident would travel quickly across the plains and the action of the Mounted Police would be closely observed. Within an hour, of receiving the complaint, Walsh and another officer, and fourteen men, with Louis Léveillé as guide, left Fort Walsh for the Assiniboine camp, thirty miles to the northeast.

Superintendent Walsh and his party rode throughout the night to locate their objective. Just as dawn was breaking they sighted the Assiniboine camp. Walsh and Léveillé moved closer to reconnoitre. The camp was sleeping, unaware of their presence. The Superintendent decided to take the troublemakers by surprise. At a small butte nearby, Surgeon Kittson and three constables were detailed to prepare a breastwork of stones to which the police could, if necessary, retreat and make a stand. With the remaining men, Walsh set out towards the Indian camp.

East End Detachment. With the influx of the American Sioux in 1877 a number of new detachments were established to maintain a close watch on the unwelcome visitors. East End was located between Fort Walsh and Wood Mountain at the east end of the Cypress Hills. It remained an important post while the Sioux remained camped nearby on Frenchman's Creek.

At a sharp trot the party passed the lodges with the slumbering occupants and quickly surrounded the war lodge. In the lodge, Walsh found Crow's Dance and nineteen other warriors. The sleeping Indians were dragged from their beds, arrested and hurriedly hustled out of the camp. By the time the rest of the camp realized what had happened, Walsh and his prisoners had rejoined Kittson. While the men sat down to a well-earned breakfast, Léveillé returned to the Indian camp to inform the Assiniboine chiefs that Walsh wished to speak with them.

At the appointed time the chiefs assembled to meet the daring officer. Walsh lectured the chiefs for permitting Crow's Dance and his warriors to terrorize the other Indians. The law of the White Mother protected all. The captives, he informed them, would be taken to Fort Walsh for trial. Back at the Fort, Crow's Dance was sentenced to six months at hard labour. The incident had a salutary effect upon the Indians. Walsh had made it clear that the Force was determined to uphold authority.

The American Sioux

Probably the most serious threat to peace in the Canadian West at this time was the arrival of the American Sioux. For years the Sioux had been fighting a losing battle to protect their traditional hunting lands from the encroachment of white civilization. The discovery of gold in the Black Hills of Dakota brought a new wave of miners and settlers. The events which followed were a familiar story of broken treaties and violence and atrocities on both sides. The tragedy of the Sioux might well have been repeated in the Canadian West had white settlement advanced while the Canadian Indians continued their nomadic warlike existence.

In 1875 the American authorities informed the Sioux that unless they settled on the reserves allocated to them they would be considered enemies of the United States. The Indians refused and in the spring of 1876 the United States army began a campaign to force them onto the reserves. The climax of the Sioux resistance was annihilation of five troops of the 7th United States Cavalry under the command of Lieutenant Colonel George A. Custer in the Valley of the Little Big Horn in June 1876. The defeat of Custer, however, was the beginning of the end. They could not hope to defeat the large military forces now closing in to harry them from all sides. Tired and hungry, they gradually retreated northward to seek refuge in Canadian territory.

The arrival of the Sioux threatened to endanger the peaceful relations which Canada was in the process of establishing with its own tribes. The Sioux were traditional enemies of many of the Canadian Indians. Their presence would also strain the already dwindling herds of buffalo.

The task for the North-West Mounted Police was a difficult one. The Sioux would have to be watched closely. There must be no revival of intertribal warfare. The Sioux must obey Canadian laws and above all they must not be allowed to use Canadian territory as a base from which to attack Americans south of the border. Fort Walsh in the Cypress Hills now became the Force's main centre of operations. The post that had been established there in 1875 was reinforced and enclosed by a fortified stockade. Its new importance was recognized when in 1878 the headquarters was moved there from Fort Macleod.

The first news of the migrating Indians was brought to Fort Walsh by scouts in November 1876. A large party of Sioux, they reported, were moving north towards the trading post at Wood Mountain. Within a few days, Walsh and a party of twelve men were on their way east to meet with the fugitives. Upon his arrival at Wood Mountain, Walsh found about two thousand Sioux under Black Moon, the tribe's hereditary chief, camped close to the trading post. A council was called and the Indians informed

Superintendent James Morrow Walsh was probably the only white man that Sitting Bull ever completely trusted. "Sitting Bull's Boss," the American press called him. A flamboyant individual who frequently did not do things "by the book," Walsh enjoyed the attention that was focussed upon him. He had a deep admiration for the Indians, but his humane concern for them did encourage them to remain in Canada. An angry Prime Minister finally removed him from Fort Walsh with strict instructions that he was to have no more dealings with Sitting Bull.

Walsh retired from the Force in 1883. For a while he engaged in the coal business in Winnipeg. With the discovery of gold in the Klondike, however, Walsh found himself once more back on the frontier. In 1897 the government made him Administrator of the Yukon. At the same time he was reappointed a superintendent of the N.W.M.P. and given command of the Force in the Yukon. He died at Brockville, Ontario, in 1905.

Walsh that they were tired of being hunted and had come to the land of the Great White Mother to find refuge. Walsh warned them firmly that they must obey the law and above all they must not raid the United States from north of the border.

Black Moon's band was followed early in 1877 by two more groups of Sioux, the first under Chief Four Horns, and finally a large band under Sitting Bull, who by now was recognized as the leader of the Sioux resistance. Again Walsh visited the newcomers and firmly emphasized the conditions they must observe, if they were to remain. At their meeting, Sitting Bull informed Walsh that he had "buried his weapons on the American side," that he would do no wrong in the country of the White Mother, and that his heart was good save when he came into contact with the Long Knives (United States Cavalry).

While in Sitting Bull's camp at Pinto Horse Buttes, the Superintendent had an opportunity to impress the visitors with his determination to enforce the law. His scouts noticed that White Dog, a South Assiniboine who was in Sitting Bull's camp, was riding a stolen horse. Although accompanied only by four Mounted Police and two scouts, Walsh boldly arrested the horse thief and confiscated the stolen animal. To White Dog's surprise, his Sioux companions refused to come to his assistance.

Fort Walsh, 1878. With large numbers of Indians frequenting the Cypress Hills in order to hunt, the location of a post there was soon recognized as a necessity. A site was chosen on the headwaters of Battle Creek, close to where the massacre had taken place just two years before. Here, in the summer of 1875, "B" Division under Walsh began the construction of the fort which would eventually be named after him.

With the Sioux influx in 1877 the fort became an important base of operations. The Force's headquarters was located here from 1878 to 1882. Once the Sioux departed, however, and the Canadian Indians settled on their reserves, its prominence declined. It was finally abandoned by the Force in 1883.

Sixty years later Commissioner Wood acquired, for a horse breeding station, the property on which the Fort had been situated. From 1943 to 1968 horses were bred and raised here for the R.C.M.P. Musical Ride. Today it is a National Historic Site.

In June 1877 Assistant Commissioner Irvine arrived from Fort Macleod to meet with Sitting Bull who had now become the key figure in the Sioux affair. With Walsh at his side, the assistant commissioner held a formal council with the Sioux leader and his followers. As the peace pipe was passed around, Irvine saw ample evidence of the recent struggle between the Sioux and their enemies. Many of the Indians were proudly sporting the scalps of American soldiers and the weapons and articles of uniform they had seized. Like Walsh, he firmly reminded the Indians that they must obey Canadian laws. Above all, he warned, they must not attack United States troops south of the border. We are British Indians, the chiefs told Irvine. We have suffered greatly at the hands of the Long Knives and have come to the land of the Great White Mother to find peace.

The arrival of the Sioux created an international crisis for Canada. Ottawa was anxious for the refugees to return to the United States. During the summer of 1877, the government began diplomatic negotiations with Washington in an effort to persuade the American authorities to induce the Sioux to return. As a result, the United States Government appointed a commission to negotiate with Sitting Bull and his followers. The site set for the meeting of the two sides was Fort Walsh, where it would be the task of the Mounted Police to act as mediators.

Early in October, Commissioner Macleod left Fort Walsh with a lance troop to meet the United States Commission at the border. The two commissioners appointed by the United States government were Brigadier General A. H. Terry and the Honourable A. G. Lawrence. Terry was an unfortunate choice. He had been one of the commanders in the recent campaign against the Sioux, and Sitting Bull and his followers regarded him as one of their arch-enemies.

Macleod met the Commissioners near Kennedy's Crossing on the Milk River on October 15. The American delegates had come north with an escort of three companies of United States 2nd Cavalry. Also, with the commissioners were two journalists, J. B. Stillson of the New York *Herald* and Charles Dehill of the Chicago *Times*, evidence of the attention now focused upon this remote corner of the Canadian frontier. "Colonel Macleod," Stillson wrote, "whose fame as a gentleman and officer had reached the commission far below this latitude of 49 degrees north, approached General Terry on horseback and clad in his scarlet uniform at the head of a small but brilliant retinue, passed the stone monument [boundary marker] on the left of the road and paused on United States soil to receive the American guests. General Terry saluted him and both dismounted and shook hands."

While the cavalry escort made camp, the United States commissioners, their aides and the two journalists began the journey north to Fort Walsh. Behind them rode the troop of mounted policemen, "their red uniforms and the red and white pennons affixed to their lances contrasting beautifully with the monotonous dun colour of the plains," wrote Stillson.

The historical meeting between Sitting Bull and the United States commissioners took place in the officers' mess of Fort Walsh, the largest room available, on October 18, 1877. Here under the mediation of Commissioner Macleod, the two sides came face to face. The American commissioners and the representatives of the press sat at small tables. Opposite on buffalo robes sat Sitting Bull. Beside him sat Spotted Eagle, the Sans Arc war chief, naked to the waist, a cartridge belt over

Sitting Bull was born about 1834, the son of Jumping Bull, a Hunkpapa Sioux. An injury early in life left him slightly lame. Hence the name "Lame Bull," or Sitting Bull.

By the 1860s he had gained a considerable reputation as a medicine man and had become prominent in Sioux councils. Although he did not actually take part in the fighting at the Little Big Horn, to millions of Americans he was the leader of the Sioux resistance. Of Sitting Bull, Walsh said, "In my opinion he is the shrewdest and most intelligent living Indian."

his painted chest, a long three-bladed war hatchet in his hand, glaring defiantly at the Americans. Between the antagonists stood Constant Provost, the interpreter.

The formalities were opened by the tall, bearded General Terry, who explained to the Sioux leaders that the Commission had been sent by the President of the United States to make a "lasting peace" with them and their people. They would be given a full pardon, the

Rain-in-the-Face. One of the Sioux chiefs at the Battle of the Little Big Horn who fled to Canada, Rain-in-the-Face was famous among his own people as a warrior. For a time it was erroneously believed that he had actually killed Custer.

general promised, none would be punished, if they would hand over their arms and horses and go to the agencies assigned to them.

To the Indian leaders these terms were quite unacceptable. They were being asked to "surrender unconditionally" to an enemy they both hated and mistrusted. In his reply, Sitting Bull bitterly reviewed the broken treaties and promises to which his tribe had been subjected for many years. To show his trust in the Mounted Police, he turned and shook hands with Macleod and Walsh, informing Terry that in Canadian territory he had found peace and here his people would stay.

Once the other Indian leaders had indicated their rejection, the meeting came to an end; the negotiations had reached an impasse. If the Indians hoped for better terms, they were to be disappointed. For the Americans had no intention of bargaining, and later attempts by the Canadian and British governments to effect a change in the United States attitude came to nothing. This was partly because the American authorities were not anxious for the troublemakers to return. If they wished to remain in Canada, so much the better, as far as Washington was concerned.

By the summer of 1878 it began to look as if the Sioux would remain in Canada for good. But what diplomacy could not do, the dwindling herds of the buffalo would soon accomplish. As their traditional source of food diminished, the Indians began to realize that they must accept a sedentary way of life. There was no point in defending a land that was now empty of buffalo. The Canadian government continued to insist that they were refugees, and had no intention of granting them reserves north of the border. They must return south.

By 1879 Sitting Bull's influence was on the decline, and in small bands the Sioux began to return. The Sioux leader and a small group of intransigents still refused, however, to trust the Americans. In 1880 the Macdonald Government decided to take a firmer stand. Walsh, Ottawa felt, had been a bad influence upon Sitting Bull, showing too much deference to him and encouraging him to remain in Canada hoping for better terms. In July Walsh was replaced in the Cypress Hills by Superintendent L. N. F. Crozier.

Without the same admiration and sympathy for the Indian as his predecessor, Crozier lost no time explaining the Government's new policy. Visiting the remaining Sioux camps, he urged them to accept the American terms. The Government, he warned them, would no longer supply them with food. Unless they returned to the United States, they would starve.

A few weeks later, Spotted Eagle and 65 lodges gave themselves up to the military authorities at Fort Keough. Sitting Bull continued to procrastinate. Only after a winter of starvation did he finally surrender with 187 men, women and children at Fort Buford in July, 1881. Perhaps the most famous of all Indian leaders, within eleven years he was dead, killed in a fight with Indian police on the Standing Rock Agency, South Dakota.

Handling the Sioux had required patience and diplomacy. Fortunately there were no serious incidents during their sojourn in Canada. With their return to the United States, the Government could now get on with the task of settling its own Indians on reserves. As to the Force, the departure of the Sioux from the Cypress Hills enabled it to reduce its strength at the isolated border posts and turn northward to face new problems brought by the growth of settlement and the coming of the railway.

Settlement

In 1874, the white population of the Northwest Territories numbered only a few hundred, mostly traders, missionaries, Hudson's Bay personnel, and a few settlers. There were no railways, telegraph lines, regular mail services or newspapers. The new police posts at Fort Macleod, Fort Walsh and Fort Saskatchewan attracted settlers. By 1878 there was a substantial village of several hundred persons adjacent to Fort Walsh. The settlers congregated around the posts to provide the many services required by the police, or to trade with the Indians who camped in the area. Battleford grew rapidly after it was designated as the territorial capital in 1876. In the same year it was linked by telegraph to Fort Pelly and Winnipeg. In 1877 the line was extended west to Edmonton which

Settlement at Fort Walsh, 1878. The presence of Indians and Mounted Police in the Cypress Hills soon attracted settlers. By 1878 a village had sprung up adjacent to the fort. Its regular population was about five hundred, but in summer this could expand to from three thousand to four thousand persons. The settlement boasted two hotels, restaurants, pool rooms, a

tailor shop, a photographer, as well as trading posts for the companies of I. G. Baker and T. C. Power.

The village provided the members of the Fort with an opportunity to escape the routine of barrack life. There they could spend their pay on girls, liquor, Perry Davis's Painkiller at the barber shop, or poker at the rear of Cloustre's Pool Room.

still had less than a thousand inhabitants. The Territories' first newspaper, the *Saskatchewan Herald*, began publishing in Battleford in 1878.

The number of settlers did not begin to increase steadily until the railway had been constructed across the Prairies in 1881 to 1883. The first train was unloaded at Winnipeg in 1877, but construction across the plains did not really get under way until four years later when W. C. Van Horne became General Manager. By October 1881 the track had arrived at Brandon. A year later it reached Regina, which had just become the new capital. By August 1883 the line was through to Calgary. In its wake there came a steady stream of settlers. Many were construction workers. Towns soon sprang up along the route – Medicine Hat, Moose Jaw, Maple Creek, Swift Current – and the older frontier posts like Calgary grew rapidly. In 1881 the white population was about 7,000, in addition to 5,000 Métis and 2,000 to 3,000 Indians. By the census of 1884/85, the white population had climbed to over 23,000.

The positioning of the early police posts had been determined by the location of the Indians' hunting grounds and the need to control the whisky trade. Once the Indians had been placed on their reserves, the Force was gradually redeployed to police the growing settlements along the railway. To meet its new responsibilities the

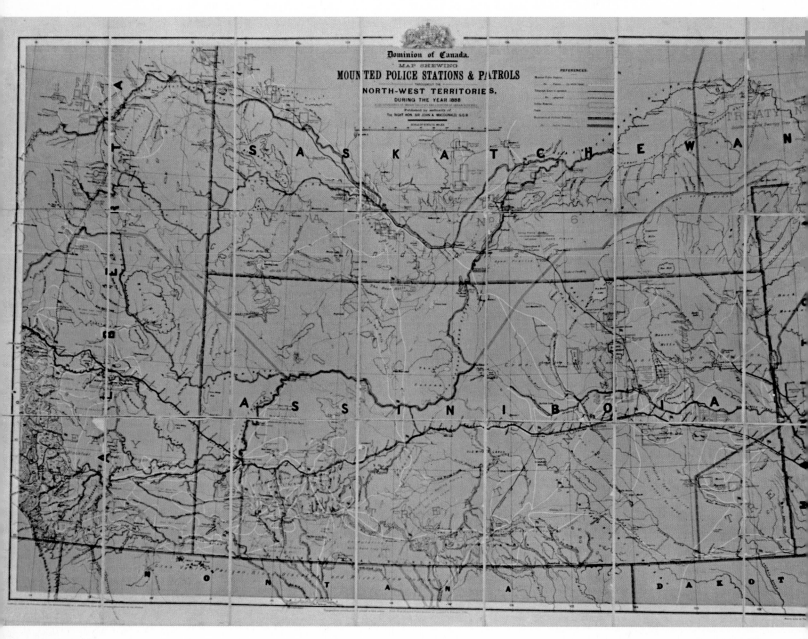

N.W.M.P. posts and patrol routes, 1888.

Government in 1883 increased its statutory strength from three hundred to five hundred men. Detachments and divisions were soon established at the new urban centres. In 1882, Headquarters was moved to a more central location on the flat open prairie beside the Wascana Creek on the outskirts of the new capital of Regina (Pile of Bones). By the time of the Northwest Rebellion the transformation was complete. In 1884 the strength and distribution of the Force was as follows:

"A" Division, Maple Creek – with detachments at Medicine Hat, Swift Current   48

"B" Division, Regina – with detachments at Moose Jaw, Moosomin, Qu'Appelle, Wood End, Shoal Lake   129

"C" Division, Fort Macleod – with detachments at Standoff, Kootenai, Pincher Creek, Crow's Nest, Whoop-up, St. Mary's   68

"D" Division, Battleford – with detachments at Carlton, Fort Pitt, Prince Albert   200

"E" Division, Calgary – with detachments at Fort Saskatchewan, Kicking Horse Pass, Moberley, Laggan, First Crossing   112

    ——

Total Strength   557

Crime

In spite of the lack of established institutions the young communities of western Canada were generally as law-abiding as any of the older settled parts of the country. The population was small but so was the incidence of serious crime. During 1883, for example, the principal cases tried by the officers were: 1 murder, 13 cattle killing, 18 theft, 29 gambling, 29 horse stealing, 97 non-payment of wages and 101 infractions of the liquor ordinances.

The Force was invested with exceptional powers with which to control crime. The original legislation made all officers justices of the peace. By later amendments, the commissioner and assistant commissioner became ex-officio magistrates. The police prosecuted and sat in judgment. Court proceedings were often quite irregular, but the officers endeavoured to interpret the law to suit frontier conditions under which normal procedures could not be followed, seeking to uphold the spirit rather than the letter. At first there was little criticism from the white population while the Mounted Police's main duty was policing whisky traders and controlling Indians. There were no lawyers to question the exercise of their authority or the methods which they used. On one occasion an accused man appearing before Macleod began to argue a point of law. He was quickly silenced by the magistrate with the comment, "We want justice in this country, not law."

Apart from the liquor ordinances, horse stealing was the most common criminal offence. The apprehension of the offenders was aggravated by the close proximity of the border, or "medicine line," as the Indians called it. White and Indian on both sides of the line went north or south as the case might be to steal horses and return with the stolen property. While the Force had much power in Canadian territory, the authorities below the border did not. It was found difficult therefore to recover horses stolen in Canada once they had been taken across the border.

It was the Force's role in enforcement of the prohibitive liquor laws however that was most difficult, bringing public criticism and a challenge to their former authoritarian status. At a time when the average consumption of liquor by Canadians was four gallons for every man, woman and child, it was hardly surprising that the new settlers resented the existing regulations against importation of liquor into the Northwest. Most of them were single men, and drinking became a common means of seeking relief and relaxation from the hard conditions under which they lived and worked.

A liquor permit. An 1875 ordinance prohibited the importation of liquor into the N.W.T. except for sacramental or medical use, and then only by special permission in writing from the Lieutenant-Governor. The measure became very unpopular with a growing number of thirsty settlers. In 1882 Lieutenant-Governor Dewdney used his discretionary authority to begin issuing printed permits like this one. While the permit system made liquor more easily available to settlers, it made the Force's task of enforcing the law far more difficult.

The original legislation against the importation, sale or barter of liquor in the Northwest Territories had been aimed at preventing the Indians from drinking. The unrest and violence among the Indians was widely attributed to the availability of liquor. As long as the small white population felt threatened by the Indian presence, it loudly praised and supported the strenuous efforts of the Mounted Police to suppress the whisky trade. Gradually, however, as the Indian threat diminished and the railway arrived with new settlers, the public praise turned to general condemnation of the liquor laws and the efforts of the police to maintain them.

In 1875 the Territorial Council tightened up the stringent liquor ordinance. The importation and manufacture of intoxicants in the Northwest was forbidden "except for medicinal and sacramental purposes" and even then only "by special permission in writing of the Lieutenant-Governor." Although the Northwest was not entirely "dry," this law was strictly and on the whole successfully enforced until about 1882. Its enforcement was not too difficult at first. The population was small, the few trails into the Northwest could easily be watched and travellers effectively searched under the broad powers with which the police were endowed.

With the appointment of Edgar Dewdney as Lieutenant-Governor in 1882, this situation began to change. His predecessor, Charles Mackintosh, had tightly restricted the importation of liquor, but Dewdney took advantage of the loophole in the 1875 Act which allowed for the importation of liquor by special permission of the Lieutenant-Governor to begin a policy of freely issuing liquor permits. The requirement that the liquor be used only for medicinal or sacramental purposes was widely overlooked. Within a short time the citizens of the Northwest were plagued by an epidemic of hypochondria. With tongue in cheek, the Calgary *Herald* commented on this deterioration in the health of the local population:

> *The prohibitory laws of the Northwest enact that certain quantities of liquor may be brought into the Territory for medical purposes. Calgary must be a very unhealthy place and Governor Dewdney's sympathetic soul is stirred to its profoundest depths, that the health of the denizens of this valley may recover.*

The Macleod *Gazette* calculated that "for every gallon of liquor used as medicine, one hundred are used as the average man uses it, for ordinary drinking."

In addition to the irregularities of the permit system, the police were also faced by a vast increase in smuggling brought about by the extension of the railway across the prairies. The railway almost overnight multiplied the possibilities for smugglers and equally increased the difficulties of enforcing the law. It was impossible for the police to be at every railway stop to search every

Review Order Parade, "E" Division, Calgary, 1883.

train, its freight or the belongings of the hundreds and thousands of settlers who began to arrive.

Smugglers showed considerable ingenuity and imagination to avoid detection. Liquor began to arrive disguised as sardines, coal oil and books. A shipment of canned apples consigned to a justice of the peace at Qu'Appelle was found to contain rum. In two barrels of oatmeal addressed to a clergyman the Mounted Police discovered ten gallons of whisky.

One of the more imaginative smuggling ventures took place in Lethbridge. As the police, "heads lowered," watched silently, a coffin was lifted from an incoming train and placed in a waiting hearse. The driver of the hearse, a renowned smuggler, was disguised in a "black suit of woe."

As the police stood quietly by, the cortege drove away with its coffin of liquor to celebrate the "funeral."

By 1885 most of the Force's efforts were directed toward enforcing the liquor ordinance. The regulations were being widely and openly flouted and the police received little cooperation from the public, the government or the courts. It was difficult to obtain informants. Local magistrates dismissed liquor cases on the flimsiest of excuses. Western lawyers prided themselves on their ability to find loopholes in regulations. The use of undercover agents by the police brought cries of tyranny and oppression. Their critics attacked the wide powers of search-without-warrant enjoyed by the police and the authoritarian position of the officers as justices of the peace

and magistrates. The Force was damned when it succeeded in obtaining a conviction, reported the Commissioner, and assailed by the temperance forces when it failed. The enforcement of the unpopular liquor laws was a sobering experience for the Force. It was not until after the Rebellion that the laws were finally changed to conform to the general consensus of opinion and this "most disagreeable duty," as Irvine once called it, came to an end.

Inspector S. B. Steele, seated centre, with members of his detachment policing the construction of the Canadian Pacific Railway in 1885.

An escort of the N.W.M.P. welcomes the first through train from eastern Canada to the West Coast as it arrives in Calgary, July 1886.

Policing the Railway

One of the special tasks imposed upon the Force in the period before the Rebellion was the maintenance of order along the line of railway construction. The C.P.R. reached Maple Creek in 1882, Calgary and Laggan, near the summit of the Kicking Horse Pass, by 1883. To police the railway, the Force organized a detachment under Inspector S. B. Steele to follow the construction. Thousands of labourers were used to lay the track, and it was essential to maintain order among them, if the railway was to be completed on schedule. The workers lived under rough conditions in construction camps. To maintain order in these camps the police enforced the *Act for the Preservation of Peace in the Vicinity of Public Works*, which prohibited gambling and drinking for an area of ten miles on each side of the railway line. In gratitude for the service it performed Van Horne wrote Commissioner Irvine:

Our work of construction for the year 1882 has just closed, and I cannot permit the occasion to pass without acknowledging the obligations of the Company to the . . . Police whose zeal and industry in preventing traffic in liquor and preserving order along the line under construction have contributed so much to the successful prosecution of the work.

In policing the railway the Force also encountered its first experience with labour unrest. The first serious strike occurred in 1883 when the C.P.R. reduced the wages of its engineers and firemen. Reinforcements were rushed to Moose Jaw and Broadview to guard railway property from unruly strikers, and guards were provided to protect those who refused to leave their jobs. Another serious strike occurred in 1885 at

Regina, N.W.T., in 1884. In 1882 Regina replaced Battleford as the seat of government for the Northwest Territories. Its name was chosen by Her Royal Highness the Princess Louise, daughter of Queen Victoria and the wife of the Governor General. This photograph looking south down Broad Street was taken from the C.P.R. depot. Just to the left of centre is the N.W.M.P. Regina Detachment, a small single-storey building standing by itself.

N.W.M.P. Headquarters, Regina 1885. The Force has occupied this site just outside Regina since 1882. The first buildings were shipped in prefabricated sections from eastern Canada over the newly completed railway, and erected according to plans laid out by Inspector Steele. The headquarters of the Force was located here from 1882 to 1920, and for ninety years it has been the main training centre for recruits.

Diverse Duties and Talents

For many years members of the Force represented every facet of civil authority in the Northwest. They were only gradually relieved of these duties as government departments, federal and territorial, were established and officials appointed to replace them. In the meantime they performed a diverse number of duties in maintaining services essential for public order and welfare. The Force assumed responsibility for many of the mail services between settlements, either carrying the mails themselves or awarding contracts. As late as 1883 members were still acting as postmasters, and police barracks were still serving as post offices. Until 1879 members acted as agents for the

Beaver Crossing in the mountains after twelve hundred men walked off the job over a pay dispute. When a mob of strikers tried to prevent the arrest of one of their leaders who was inciting violence, Inspector Steele rose from his sickbed to confront them with a rifle in his hands. After the Riot Act had been read, he warned them that if necessary he would use force to preserve peace and order.

Under the watchful eye and firm hand of the Force the construction of the railway was completed without serious disruption from labour disputes. The members found strike duty distasteful, however, and the cost of their involvement was to sow the seeds of alienation between themselves and organized labour.

Indian Department in most matters relating to Indian affairs. At border points customs were collected. The Force's surgeons, often the only medical practitioners for miles around, attended Indians and settlers as well as the police. The Mounted Police took care of lunatics, escorting them to the nearest asylum at Brandon. Until the erection of jails, persons sentenced to prison terms served their sentences in Mounted Police guardrooms. Those given hard labour were put to work on the post's woodpile. For a time, meteorological readings were kept by detachments. Much of the information for the 1881 census was collected by members of the Force. They administered territorial ordinances which regulated the spread of contagious diseases, the control of glanders, prairie fires, stallions-at-large and vital statistics.

Social Life of the Pioneer West

For many years the posts of the Force were the centres of the social life of the small communities in which they were situated. The members organized dances, bands, sporting events, in which the local population customarily participated. Often the posts had small libraries, the only ones for hundreds of miles; the books were sent out by relatives or friends, and the members subscribed to the leading American, Canadian and British newspapers and magazines. A copy of the London *Times*, *Harpers*, *Punch* or the *Tatler*, although many weeks old, was read and reread with great interest by the lonely and isolated Westerners.

Christmas was always a time for special celebrations and the annual Christmas dinner given by the Police was often one of the main social events of the year in the rough pioneer settlements. At Fort Macleod in 1876 the men prepared a lavish Christmas dinner at their own expense, paying seventy-five cents a pound for butter and six dollars a dozen for eggs. Following a cricket match the entire community, police, civilians, even the six prisoners from the guardroom, sat down to a feast of buffalo roasts, beef, venison, geese, plum pudding and pies – but no liquor. After dinner the company was entertained with songs and recitations accompanied by a piper.

Another highlight of the pioneer social scene was the "Barracks Ball." "We gave a grand ball to the civilians last Friday night," wrote a constable from Calgary in 1882.

We subscribed $250 and had the best supper ever given in this part of the country. We had the barrack rooms decorated with bead work, mottoes made of cartridges, revolvers and rifles on the walls. The music was two violins, a flute and banjo. Our Captain opened the ball with a little halfbreed and then we danced till 12 o'clock and then had supper. There was only one white woman and she was Dutch with hair like my tunic.

White women, of course, were few and far between, young unmarried ones quite rare. One sergeant reported that during his three years of service he never saw a white woman. Two other members, lonely for feminine attachments, advertised in the Montreal *Star*: "Two lonely Mounted Policemen desire to correspond with a limited number of young ladies for mutual improvement."

Variety or dramatic groups were another common form of entertainment. In 1878 the members at "C" Division, Battleford, organized the "Mounted Police Star Minstrel and Variety Troupe." The Saskatchewan *Herald* carried the following report of its second performance which was given in the Assembly Hall.

The programme was extensive and embraced farce, sentimental and comic songs; and excellent selections of instrumental music —all of which were rendered and well received. McIntosh gave "Masa's in the Cold, Cold Ground"; Robert Wyld "Battleford Races"; Whitehouse "Nigger on the Fence"; Harry Walker "Lady Nell"; Wyld "Tapioca"; Wardern "Old Folks at Home," "Mother Says I Musn't," and "Come under my Plaidie."
The performance ended, the report continued, with two farces, "The Photographer" and the "Egyptian Mummy" which kept the well-filled hall in "roars of laughter."

Interior of the officers' quarters at Fort Macleod about 1880. The officers were socially and economically well above the ordinary rank and file. A recruit constable started at forty cents a day. The lowest pay for a commissioned officer was one thousand dollars a year.

How the other half lived. In contrast to the comfortable accommodation of the officers, this scene of a barrack room shows the rough and crowded conditions under which the enlisted men lived.

The early bands of the Force entertained at official ceremonies and on festive occasions. The first band was organized at Swan River in February 1876. The instruments were shipped all the way from Winnipeg by dog team, the members paying for them themselves. The band made its first public appearance on the Queen's birthday, May 24, 1876. Later it was transferred to Fort Macleod and Calgary. In 1877 it was at Blackfoot Crossing for Treaty No. 7, playing "God Save the Queen" in the official closing ceremonies.

The State of the Force

In May 1875 Major General Selby Smyth, the Adjutant General of the Canadian militia was sent westward to investigate the criticism of the Force's management. In his confidential report, Selby Smyth stated that for a hastily established force it was in "very fair order" and organized on "sound principles." As to the men, he reported that the constables and N.C.O.'s were an "able body" and composed of "excellent material," but some of the inspectors "fall short" of the required ability. By 1880, however, a noticeable decline had begun in the morale and efficiency of the rank and file. This was primarily due to the government's determination to reduce expenditure and its unwillingness to contemplate improvements for an organization which it was widely believed would be disbanded once the Indian problem was settled.

The most serious blow to the Force's efficiency was the reduction in pay in 1879. The constable's pay was cut from seventy-five cents to forty cents a day. Those who wished to re-engage upon the expiration of their term were paid fifty cents. Better salaries could easily be found labouring on the C.P.R. "The consequence of this remarkable regulation," wrote Sam Steele, "was that none of the old hands would re-engage." To make matters worse the government discontinued the free grants of 160 acres of land which had been a useful inducement in the past.

Commissioner Acheson Gosford Irvine was the first native Canadian to command the Force. He was born in Quebec City on December 7, 1837. Like many of the other early members of the Force he had served with the militia in the Red River expedition of 1870. From 1871 to 1875 he commanded the Provisional Battalion of Rifles posted in Manitoba. In 1875 he was appointed a superintendent in the N.W.M.P. He served as Commissioner from 1880 to 1886. When violence threatened in 1885, Irvine hastened north from Regina with every available man in an effort to head off the rebellion. After a forced march of more than 300 miles in winter weather, he arrived at Fort Carlton to find that the fighting had already begun. Following his retirement from the Force in 1886, Irvine was for many years warden of Stony Mountain Penitentiary. He died in Quebec City in 1916.

The commanding officer's residence, Battleford, 1885. L. to r.: Constable Fontaine, Superintendent Neale, Inspector Sanders, Commissioner Irvine, Assistant Surgeon Miller, Assistant Commissioner Crozier.

Working conditions for the rank and file were abysmal in many cases and resulted in several "bucks," or organized demands for improvements. At Fort Macleod in 1883 an accumulation of grievances finally spilled over. The men complained of the triviality of their duties and the senselessness of the disciplinary regulations. For months their rations had consisted of beef, bread and tea three times a day, the meat being frequently unfit for human consumption. They had not been paid regularly. Their worn out uniforms had not been replaced. To survive they were forced to borrow money on interest to buy food and clothing for themselves. A manifesto, signed by every constable, listing the complaints was drawn up and presented to the Commanding Officer, Superintendent Crozier. Eventually changes were made and the conditions improved.

There was no shortage of potential recruits, however, even at forty cents a day. The positions were usually filled, as was the custom of the day, through government patronage. The forty or fifty places which became vacant every year as men took their discharge were filled by the sons of party supporters. Generally speaking they came from a rural background with little education and little experience beyond manual labour at home or in lumber camps. In the Commissioner's opinion, young men from rural districts made the best type of recruit, as they were accustomed to hard work and understood the management of horses.

N.W.M.P. detachment under the command of Inspector F. J. Dickens at Fort Pitt, 1884. Dickens (right foreground with sword), was the third son of the English novelist Charles Dickens. Before his appointment in 1874 as an inspector, he had served in India as a superintendent of police. Dickens was invalided in 1886 because of acute deafness. He died a few months later, on the eve of commencing a lecture tour of the United States.

The Flames of Discontent

The Indian treaties had been signed by both sides in the hope that they would lead to a peaceful transition in the Canadian West. At first the Indians did not take up the reserves allotted to them. They continued to follow the buffalo. The Government's policy was based on the principle that the tribes would live in their traditional way until they could support themselves by farming. The buffalo, it was believed, would last for many years. Unfortunately, the vast herds disappeared almost overnight.

The winter of 1877/78 was a bad one. The grass was poor and the remaining herds moved south across the border. The Canadian Indians were forced to follow them and hunt in Montana. By the winter of 1878/79 the end was in sight. The chiefs had hoped that their people would have many years to adjust to a new way of life. But, once on their reserves, the proud hunters were reduced to begging for rations and assistance.

On November 1, 1880, Assistant Commissioner Acheson Gosford Irvine took over the command of the Force. Earlier in the year Irvine had visited Dublin to study the management and organization of the Royal Irish Constabulary. He was impressed by what he saw. At the Constabulary's training depot in Phoenix Park he found carefully selected, well-educated recruits undergoing a modern training program which included lectures and instruction on many subjects relating to police work. (Training in the Force consisted largely of foot drill, equitation and instruction in the use of small arms.) In the Irish countryside he saw a smart and efficient police force carrying out its duties.

Upon assuming command, Irvine recommended the establishment of a training depot, higher standards for selecting recruits and the development of a better training program. In 1883 the Force's headquarters at Regina became the main training centre for recruits but there was little change in their instruction. With the cutbacks in government expenditure the substance of Irvine's recommendations was largely ignored.

While Irvine had progressive ideas for improving the standards and efficiency of the Force, his own ineffective leadership added to the general decline. Nicknamed "Old Sorrel Top," the Commissioner was a "thorough gentleman," far too kindly and good-natured to wield authority. Not a forceful personality, he gained the affection of his subordinates, but not their respect. He failed to rule his officers who in many cases ran their posts to suit themselves, much to the detriment of the Force's morale and efficiency. Neglected by the government and beset with internal problems, the Force's condition, but for the outstanding example of a few individuals, was at a low ebb by 1885.

The abrupt change came at a time when the responsibility for administering the Indians passed from the Mounted Police to the newly reorganized Department of Indian Affairs. Disputes between the Indians and the officials of the Department over the administration of the reserves became frequent. Only the restraint of the chiefs and the resourcefulness of the Mounted Police prevented many incidents from developing into violent conflict.

The most serious incident among the Blackfoot took place at the Indian Agency at Blackfoot Crossing in 1882. A dispute arose between an employee of the Agency and Bull Elk, a minor chief, over the purchase of some meat. Angered by the treatment he had received, Bull Elk fired his rifle at the Agency buildings, frightening the employees. The Mounted Police were notified and Inspector Dickens with two men moved to arrest the offender. A crowd of excited Indians gathered around, jostling them and preventing Dickens from making the arrest. It was a tense moment and order was only restored when Crowfoot arrived to calm his younger followers. After the old chieftain promised to take Bull Elk into custody himself, Dickens withdrew. Later Superintendent Crozier arrived with a larger force and effected the arrest. It was an ugly incident, however, and did much to drive a breach in the hitherto good relations between the Force and the Blackfoot.

Big Bear, Chief of the Plains Crees. Big Bear refused to sign Treaty No. 6 on the grounds that it did not grant him immunity from hanging. Although he did sign in 1882, he continued to agitate for better terms, and his lodge became the rallying point for all the discontented Indians of the Saskatchewan.

The estrangement of the Cree was more serious than that of the Blackfoot. Some of the Cree bands refused to sign the treaty in 1876. Under the leadership of Poundmaker and Big Bear they continued to agitate for better terms, refusing to settle on their reserves. Big Bear signed in 1882, but the discontent continued.

In 1883, a band of Cree under Piapot pitched their camp on the C.P.R. right-of-way. Corporal Wilde and a constable from Maple Creek were sent to investigate. Wilde's demand that they move was greeted with defiance and ridicule. The Indians refused and tried to provoke the two policemen by jostling them and discharging their firearms. It was a

challenge to authority; to retreat would have resulted in a loss of face. Wilde decided to take the upper hand. Coolly producing his pocket watch, he announced that he would give the Indians fifteen minutes to comply with his order to move. When the time was up, he dismounted, strode over to Piapot's lodge and began dismantling it. Faced with Wilde's bold action the Indians backed down.

Another serious confrontation took place the following year. In June 1884 Big Bear and Poundmaker arranged to hold a Thirst Dance on the Little Pine Reserve west of Battleford. More than fifteen hundred Indians from the neighbouring reserves gathered for the event. A dispute arose over the issuing of rations, and the farm instructor on the reserve complained to the Mounted Police that he had been assaulted by one of the Indians. Eventually, Superintendent Crozier set out from Battleford with a force of twenty-five men to arrest the offender. When he arrived the dance was in full progress, and in the large crowd the farm instructor was unable to identify the Indian who had assaulted him. Getting an unfriendly reception, Crozier decided to withdraw to the agency buildings on Poundmaker's reserve and wait until the dance was over. On the following day he met with Poundmaker and the other chiefs. The large assembly of Indians was in a hostile mood and the younger braves ready to fight.

Assistant Commissioner Lief Newry Fitzroy Crozier. "Paddy" Crozier was born in Newry, Ireland, in 1846, the third son of St. George B. Crozier, a Doctor of Music. His father later emigrated to Belleville, Ontario. Before his appointment as an inspector in the N.W.M.P. in 1873, Crozier had served as an officer in the 15th Argyll Light Infantry. A capable and efficient officer, his service had been outstanding until the Duck Lake affair clouded his career. He retired from the Force in 1886 and died in Belleville 15 years later.

The chiefs refused to hand over the offender, but Crozier persisted. Positioning his men, he strode into the mob of threatening faces and with the aid of an interpreter was able to identify and arrest the culprit. Only the unruffled action of the police prevented a war.

But for the rising tide of unrest among the Métis of Saskatchewan, the discontent of the Indians might have been safely contained. As in 1870, however, the Métis once again felt threatened by the spread of white settlement. They wished to obtain title to their river-front lots on the North Saskatchewan, and petitioned Ottawa; but their grievances went unheeded. With the government seemingly indifferent, they decided to take the law into their own hands. Louis Riel was recalled from Montana, where he had been teaching school, to lead them. Early in 1885 a provisional government was set up with the support of Big Bear and some of the Cree bands. The Blackfoot remained aloof from the conspiracy. Crowfoot wisely believed that the cause would fail, and in any case he and his people were reluctant to side with their traditional enemies, the Cree. As early as July 1884 Riel's return and the agitation among the Métis and Indians were being reported by the officers commanding posts in the north. The detachments along the North Saskatchewan were reinforced, but Ottawa still seemed unconcerned. By the spring of 1885 only a shot was needed to fan the flames of rebellion.

"The Fight at Duck Lake" as depicted by the Canadian Illustrated War News, July 4, 1885. With Commissioner Irvine only hours away with over 100 reinforcements, Superintendent Crozier impetuously marched out of Fort Carlton with a force of N.W.M.P. and Prince Albert Volunteers to confront the Métis rebels. The battle which resulted took place about two miles from the small settlement of Duck Lake. "When I found that the enemy were more numerous by far than we were," wrote Crozier, "that they were in ambush almost all around me, and had every advantage of ground and cover on their side . . . I deemed it prudent to abandon my attempt to push on to Duck Lake, and to withdraw my force." With heavy snow falling, the force hastily retreated to Fort Carlton on their sleighs, leaving some of the dead and wounded behind. They were joined at the fort within a few minutes by a shocked Irvine, who was dismayed to find that Crozier had rashly engaged the rebels without waiting for him.

Easterners were stunned when news of the fight reached them by telegraph on the evening of March 27. Few of them had suspected that the Métis agitation would lead to rebellion.

"The Siege of Fort Pitt," from Canadian Illustrated War News. *A detachment was established at the Hudson's Bay trading post of Fort Pitt in 1883 when Inspector Dickens and twenty-five men were sent to the fort to keep watch on the Cree bands in the area. The detachment was isolated. It was surrounded by Indian reserves and the nearest post was more than one hundred miles away down the Saskatchewan River at Battleford.*

When Dickens heard of the outbreak of the rebellion he prepared the post for a siege. Its occupants were shocked on April 2, 1885, to receive the news that white civilians on the nearby Frog Lake Reserve had been massacred. A few days later more than two hundred hostile Crees under Big Bear took up positions in front of the post. The Cree leader offered to guarantee the safety of the civilians in the fort, if they would surrender. He urged the Mounted Police to escape, warning them that he would not be able to prevent his younger braves from killing them.

Once the civilians decided to give themselves up, Dickens realized he would have to try to leave. There was little chance of relief from the outside, and if he remained he would be risking the lives of the entire command. After destroying surplus stores and ammunition, the small party of police set out at dawn on April 16 in a hastily built scow to drift downstream to Battleford. They arrived there safely a few days later.

Rebellion

The final break came early in March 1885. The rebels seized the trading post and its stores at Duck Lake, and sent an ultimatum to Superintendent Crozier calling upon him to surrender Fort Carlton. Crozier responded to the threat of violence as he had done successfully so often in the past. On March 26 he marched out of Fort Carlton with a force of 56 Mounted Policemen and 43 members of the Prince Albert Volunteers. Fearless and confident, he hoped to overawe the dissidents with a show of force and nip the rebellion in the bud, but boldness was no longer enough to prevent what lay ahead.

Unknown to Crozier, the Métis were determined to resist. Ahead of him was a superior force under the leadership of Gabriel Dumont, an experienced tactician in the art of plains warfare. The two forces clashed about two miles from Duck Lake. Caught by the deadly fire of the carefully deployed Métis riflemen, the force of Mounted Police and volunteers was forced to retreat, suffering twelve killed and eleven wounded. The Second Riel Rebellion had begun.

Duck Lake was an important psychological victory for Louis Riel, but it was a short-lived one. Already hundreds of militia troops were on their way from eastern Canada over the newly completed railway. Within a few days an army had been assembled. Under the command of Major General

F. D. Middleton it soon moved forward to crush the rebels. In the military campaign which followed the North-West Mounted Police were to play an important part. After a series of indecisive engagements, the rebels were finally defeated at Batoche on May 9, 1885.

Big Bear with his captors at Prince Albert, July 1885. L. to r.: Sergeant Smart, Constables Colebrook, Nicholls and Sullivan.

Following the defeat at Batoche and the capture of Riel, Big Bear and the insurgent Crees fled north across the Saskatchewan River. Although followed closely by a combined force of militia and Mounted Police, the old warrior managed to elude his pursuers and, turning south, surrendered to a N.W.M.P. detail under Sergeant Smart near Fort Carlton on July 2, 1885. Later he was transferred to Regina where he was tried and convicted of treason-felony. He was sentenced to three years in prison. He was released in 1887 but died shortly after.

Riel's hopes for an independent Métis nation died in the rifle pits at Batoche, but the defeat of the rebellion marked the beginning of a new order for western Canada. The frontier era was gone forever. The Indian and the Métis were finally subjugated. Never again would they threaten the peaceful settlement of the Canadian provinces. Soon the Northwest Territory would be covered with the villages and farms of thousands of newly arrived settlers. The North-West Mounted Police had been established to bring law and order to a frontier society. With the growth of settlement, it would have to face new challenges and new responsibilities.

Gabriel Dumont. Among the Métis casualties at Duck Lake was their military commander, Gabriel Dumont, who was wounded in the head. Although an able and experienced fighter, the Métis general was frequently prevented by Riel from using his forces to their best advantage.

Riel surrendered after the defeat at Batoche, but Dumont managed to escape to Montana. In 1886 he joined Buffalo Bill Cody's "Wild West Show," and toured the United States and Europe. Later he was allowed to return home to Saskatchewan.

Louis Riel's death as noted in the records of a Winnipeg undertaker. The Métis leader was sentenced to death after being convicted of high treason in a trial which attracted the attention of the entire country. His death was to divide the nation. To many Canadians he was a martyr and patriot, to others a murderer and a rebel.

The execution took place in a specially constructed yard at the rear of the N.W.M.P. guardroom in Regina where he had been held during his trial. The hangman was Jack Henderson who, strangely enough, had been a prisoner of Riel at Fort Garry in 1870. After the execution the body was handed over to a friend of the Riel family for burial at St. Boniface.

The Military Record

For many years the Force was little different in manner and appearance from a regular military formation. Internally, it was organized and run on regimental lines. Its members, by and large, considered themselves soldiers who had, in addition, certain civil responsibilities. After the first unadorned uniform was abandoned in 1876, the men looked like members of another unit of the Canadian militia. Not until after the broad-brimmed felt hat was officially adopted in 1901, did the Force begin to have a distinctive style of dress of its own. As with the uniform, the early members soon dropped the police-style ranks in favour of the more socially prestigious military ones.

When Canada went to war the members of the Force felt that it was as much their responsibility to fight as to maintain law and order. They were often frustrated in time of war, however, in their attempts to retain their identity as a fighting unit of the Mounted Police. For the Force was not organized under Army regulations and its members who volunteered for active service had to be transferred to the Department of Militia or National Defence. Nevertheless, the military tradition remained very strong. The Force was proud of its war record. Recruiting usually favoured those who had previous military experience, particularly war veterans. It was not until after World War II that the military character of the Force began to decline and the civil side of its nature gradually came to the fore.

In the last hundred years members of the Force have died on active service in western Canada, South Africa, the Atlantic, Siberia and western Europe. In addition to many individual honours and awards, the Force's military record is preserved on its Guidon, or regimental colours. The first Guidon was presented to the Force in 1935 by the Governor General, Lord Bessborough. It carried the following campaign honours: North West Rebellion, 1885; South Africa, 1900–02; France and Flanders, 1918; Siberia, 1918-19. In addition it bore the badge of the Canadian Provost Corps in recognition of its service with that formation during World War II. A new Guidon was presented to the Force by H.M. Queen Elizabeth II in July 1973.

During the rebellion of 1885 members of the N.W.M.P. saw action at Duck Lake, Fort Pitt, Cut Knife Hill, and Batoche, and in the pursuit of Big Bear. With the outbreak of war in South Africa in 1899, over two hundred members were granted leave of absence to serve with the Canadian contingents. Unable to fight under their own colours, they provided a nucleus of officers and men for two battalions of mounted rifles: the 2nd C.M.R., commanded by Commissioner L. W. Herchmer and the Lord Strathcona Horse, commanded by Superintendent S. B. Steele. One of the mounted policemen who volunteered for service in South Africa was Reg. No. 3588 Constable James H. MacBrien, later Major General Sir James H. MacBrien, Chief of the Canadian General Staff and Commissioner of the R.C.M.P.

At the outbreak of war in 1914, the Government refused to allow members to volunteer for active service, believing that essential police services had to be maintained. Many Westerners felt that the Force should be sent overseas as a distinctive representative of the prairie provinces. Commissioner Perry urged the Government to permit the Force to recruit for war service, but his request was refused. Members felt very strongly that they should be given an opportunity to fight. Finally, in protest, Perry tendered his resignation.

Fortunately, the need for cavalry reinforcements in the spring of 1918 brought a change in the Government's attitude, Perry withdrew his resignation and the Force was given authority to commence recruiting. Within a short time 12 officers and 726 men had been given leave of absence and transferred to the armed forces. On arrival in Englang in June 1918, the older members were organized into a cavalry squadron known as "A" Squadron, R.N.W.M.P. Under the command of Superintendent G. L. Jennings, it saw action in France and Belgium.

A further opportunity for active service came in 1918 when the Canadian Government decided to support the allied intervention in the Russian Civil War. In July of that year, Perry received authority to recruit another cavalry squadron of 6 officers and 184 men. This became known as "B" Squadron, R.N.W.M.P., C.E.F.S. It left Vancouver for Vladivostok in the fall of 1918 under the command of Superintendent G. S. Worsley, a former R.M.C. cadet who had once served with the British Army in India. After several months spent kicking its heels outside Vladivostok, it returned to Canada in June 1919.

With the commencement of hostilities in 1939, the personnel of the Force's marine and air services were transferred to the Royal Canadian Navy and the Royal Canadian Air Force. In addition, the Force was given the opportunity on this occasion to send overseas a representative unit from the land force. As a result, 125 officers and men were organized as No. 1 Provost Company, R.C.M.P., 1st Canadian Division. The Company sailed for England in December 1939. Its members later saw action in the Dieppe Raid and the fighting in Sicily and Italy, and on the Western Front.

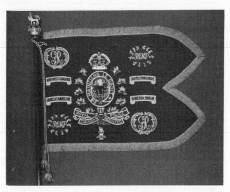

The Lord Strathcona Horse received an enthusiastic sendoff on Parliament Hill, March 8, 1900. The regiment was horsed, equipped, clothed and armed at the expense of Lord Strathcona. In its ranks were seven officers and twenty-six men of the N.W.M.P., including commanding officer Sam Steele, seated fourth from left. One of those to join was Sergeant A. H. Richardson, who was awarded the Victoria Cross for rescuing a companion under heavy fire at Wolve Spruit, July 5, 1900. He remains the only person to win this award while a member of the Force.

(Top left) Members of "D" Squadron, 2nd Canadian Mounted Rifles, pause in the offensive against the Boers near Majuba Hill. "C" and "D" Squadrons of the 2nd C.M.R. were composed almost exclusively of members of the N.W.M.P. Among them were veterans of police work in the Canadian North, like Inspector Moodie, Sergeant Murray Hayne, who had helped to build Fort Constantine in the Yukon, and Sergeant F. J. Fitzgerald, who was to lose his life in 1911 whilst on patrol from Fort McPherson to Dawson.

(Top right) Sergeant W. Grennan of "A" Squadron, R.N.W.M.P., on duty near Mons, Belgium, 1918. The members of "A" and "B" Squadrons during World War I as well as the men of No. 1 Provost Company in World War II donned army uniforms, but they continued to wear the badges and other insignia of the Mounted Police.

(Above) Recruits for overseas service, "Depot" Division, Regina, 1918. The training centre in Regina became a military camp once the Force was given authority to recruit for war service. Westerners jumped at the opportunity to serve overseas with the Mounted Police, and the Force's quota, as well as its accommodation, was soon filled.

(Top) "B" Squadron on parade near Vladivostok, Siberia, 1919.

(Above) Members of "B" Squadron outside their barracks in Siberia. The only members of "B" Squadron to see action in Siberia were a small party which was attacked by Red Army partisans whilst escorting a trainload of horses along the Trans-Siberian Railway. For their part in that engagement Farrier Sergeant J. E. Margetts was awarded the Meritorious Service Medal and Corporal P. Bossard the Military Medal.

(Above) Members of "B" Squadron, R.N.W.M.P., sightseeing in Yokohama, Japan, on their way home from Siberia in 1919.

No. 1 Provost Company, R.C.M.P., on the march in Sussex, England, July 1942.

The duties of No. 1 Provost Company included traffic control and communications. Here its members are undergoing motorcycle training in England, 1940.

The Passing of the Prairie Frontier

The year 1885 marks the dawn of a new era in the history of western Canada. With the defeat of Riel and the completion of the C.P.R. a curtain gradually fell upon the old frontier society which had threatened the peaceful and orderly settlement of the prairies. The nomadic ways of the Indian and the Métis were gone forever. Their resistance to the expansion of Western civilization died with them at Batoche.

Their defeat had been hastened by the ribbon of steel which now linked the territory with the east and ended its former isolation. Gone were the lawlessness and violence which Butler had found fifteen years earlier. The "Great Lone Land" was ready at last for one of the biggest migrations in human history.

At first the flow of settlers was only a trickle, but as the nineteenth century came to a close and the twentieth began, the century which Sir Wilfrid Laurier had prophesied would be Canada's, the trickle became a stream and the stream a flood as thousands upon thousands arrived to begin life anew on the vacant western prairie. Before them the frontier was pushed northward into the Yukon and the Arctic.

Only the outbreak of the Great War stemmed the tide of hungry land seekers. In 1891 the territory between the borders of Manitoba and British Columbia was home to about ninety thousand persons, including Indians and Métis. During the next

twenty-five years they were joined by more than a million immigrants. In 1905 the N.W.T. were divided to establish the new provinces of Alberta and Saskatchewan. In one generation the prairies were filled up. The vast open spaces over which the Force had marched in 1874 had been replaced by farms, towns and cities.

The Force was fortunate in the two men who would lead it through the period of growth and settlement which followed the rebellion. With the end of the frontier it had to find a new role on the prairies; as a military organization, it was no longer needed. There were many who said it had served its purpose and should be disbanded. Unless the Force adjusted to the new conditions which followed settlement, it would probably disappear.

Commissioner Lawrence William Herchmer, 1886–1900. While Herchmer was responsible for efficiently reorganizing the Force, his command in many other respects was a very stormy one. As a civilian, his appointment to Commissioner was greatly resented by a number of senior officers who felt the position rightly belonged to one of them. Their resentment increased when he promoted his brother, Superintendent W. M. Herchmer, to the vacant position of Assistant Commissioner. In addition, he unfortunately had an overbearing, brusque and ill-tempered personality which endeared him to few and made enemies of many. In short order the relations between the Commissioner and many of the officers and men became very strained.

To add to his problems, Herchmer made himself an implacable foe of Nicholas Flood Davin, member of Parliament and publisher of the Regina Leader. His tyrannical and irrational behaviour was soon widely discussed throughout the N.W.T. and there were demands for an investigation. Matters came to a head shortly after the death of his benefactor, Sir John A. Macdonald, in June 1891. The Government ordered the Honourable E. L. Wetmore, Judge of the Supreme Court of the N.W.T., to hear charges against the Commissioner and investigate his command. Wetmore's report absolved Herchmer of any serious charges but found he had acted in an overbearing manner and had misunderstood his authority. The Commissioner found little favour with the Liberals who came to power in 1896. When he went to South Africa his absence was used as an excuse to retire him.

Commissioner Lawrence William Herchmer

Although he owed his appointment as commissioner, in 1886, to the close friendship between his family and Sir John A. Macdonald, Herchmer was in many ways an ideal choice to succeed Irvine. He had had many years of experience living and working in the West and, perhaps more important, he had the necessary political support required to undertake a thorough reorganization of the Force. Added to this were his own boundless energy and determination.

The future commissioner was born in England in 1840, when his father, a Church of England clergyman from Kingston, Ontario, was chaplain to the Bishop of Bristol. The Herchmers were of German origin. Their forebears had come to the American colonies in the eighteenth century with the Hessian troops hired by the British, and had settled in New York State. After the American Revolution the family migrated to Upper Canada where it was granted land near Kingston. Here the Herchmers and the Macdonalds were neighbours. The Commissioner's father was a childhood friend of John A. Macdonald.

Herchmer was educated at Trinity College, Toronto, and the Royal Military College, Woolwich. In 1858 he obtained a commission in the H.M. 46th Regiment and served with it for four years in India and Ireland. After returning to Canada he became

commissary for the British North America Boundary Commission. In 1878 Macdonald appointed him an Indian agent in Manitoba. Eight years later he was promoted to Inspector of Indian Agencies.

The new commissioner's first task was to improve the internal organization and administration of the Force, implementing many of the reforms which Irvine had suggested earlier. After careful study, "Regulations and Orders" were published in 1889 to provide a systematic guide to the internal administration, duties and operation of the Force. At many posts new buildings replaced the crude log structures of the frontier days. A new riding school was built at Regina. Training was reorganized and placed on a systematic and permanent footing. More emphasis was placed on lectures, and attention was given to the duties and responsibilities of a police officer. Advanced training courses were started for N.C.O.s.

Herchmer was determined to improve the morale of the Force and the class of men admitted. Recruiting standards were more carefully enforced to prevent the engagement of medically unfit applicants. Recruits were required to undergo a probationary period of service to ensure their suitability. Discipline was tightened up and heavier punishment meted out to defaulters. Persistent offenders were not re-engaged.

R.C.M.P.RIDING SCHOOL.
ERECTED.1888.DESTROYED.1920

Riding School, Regina. Mounted training was greatly improved by the building of a commodious riding school at "Depot" Division in Regina in 1888. The building was destroyed by fire in 1920.

The Patrol System

Herchmer's most important accomplishment, however, was in transforming the Force into primarily a police service designed to meet the needs of the new communities. In appearance and organization it remained military, but its duties became largely civil in nature. The keynote of this change was the prevention of crime by the organization of an extensive system of patrols maintaining continuous surveillance, as far as possible, over every corner of the territory and every activity of its inhabitants.

Under the patrol system, the members of the Force were gradually distributed throughout the Territories in small detachments, usually consisting of an N.C.O and one or two constables. These became the operational centres of the new system. The task of the detachment members was to maintain a constant patrol over the district assigned to them, making their presence known to every settler, gaining their confidence, assisting them in any way possible, and reporting on every occurrence.

A Patrol Report Form was prepared on which the members were instructed to note "everything that has come under their observation, movements of doubtful characters, conditions of crops, prospects of hay, the ownership of any particular fine horses they may see, and to each report a rough map should be attached."

Drunkards were dismissed and unsuitable officers forced to resign. As a temperance measure, 4 per cent beer was introduced to the barracks at a cost of five cents a pint in an effort to keep the men from the hard liquor of the neighbouring saloons.

The Commissioner endeavoured to improve working conditions so that able men would be encouraged to stay and make a career of the Force. In this regard the most important reform was the introduction of a pension plan for N.C.O.s and constables in 1889. Efforts were made to improve the quality and variety of food in the messes, and more comfortable living accommodation gradually appeared. Recreation rooms were provided at the larger posts, with books and games for the off-duty hours. Nonprofit canteens were established to supply the men with necessary items at cheap rates. Teams were organized to participate in local sports. Variety and dramatic groups were encouraged. By 1895 a considerable change had taken place in living and working conditions, and the Force had reached the high degree of efficiency on which its later reputation was to rest.

First N.W.T.-Manitoba football championship, "Depot" Division, Regina, May 1891. On the occasion of Queen Victoria's birthday the Regina barracks was the scene of a two-day football tournament to decide the championship of the N.W.T. and Manitoba. The Regina population "turned out in force" for the games and were entertained by the Force's band. There were three teams, representing Moosomin, Winnipeg and the N.W.M.P. A fourth, Calgary, failed to appear. The winner was Winnipeg which defeated Moosomin by two points in the final game.

N.W.M.P. football team, 1891. Commissioner Herchmer, (in the back row, wearing a white summer tunic), actively encouraged organized sports in the Force. This team includes (fourth from left, middle row), Inspector A. C. Macdonell, later Major General Sir A. C. Macdonell, a prominent Canadian military leader during World War I.

Each settler was asked if he had any complaints, and requested to sign the report to verify that he had been visited. Copies of the patrol reports from the detachments were then forwarded to the Divisional Headquarters where they were assembled to give a comprehensive picture of the activities in the area under its jurisdiction. To provide effective communications many of the detachments, gradually, were equipped with telephone or telegraph facilities.

Men's barrack room at Battleford, 1898. Early detachments had been low log buildings chinked with mud. By the 1890s these were being replaced on the prairies by permanent frame structures which provided more spacious and comfortable accommodation. The men were still required, however, to sleep on wooden boards stretched between two wooden trestles.

The network of patrols soon proved an effective deterrent to rural crime. The system began in 1886 with a coordinated scheme of patrols along the border from Manitoba to British Columbia to prevent smuggling and the movement of stolen horses. In 1887 it was extended throughout the N.W.T. There was a resultant drop in the incidence of horse and cattle stealing. To prevent evasion, flying patrols were introduced in 1890 which did not follow regular trails.

The patrol system had other benefits too. It brought the police and the settlers into close contact, promoting good will and cooperation. The lonely settlers were usually glad to see a visitor, and the police could often count on a meal or a bed for the night, if it was needed. When the system was in full operation, the members of the Force covered about one and a half million miles a year on horseback.

At its height, from 1887 to 1895, the patrol system provided an effective means of policing. But its success was the seed of its own destruction. The preventive effect of any police service is difficult to measure. Why the need for such a large and expensive police force, argued its parliamentary critics, when there was so little crime and the old threat of Indian unrest had gone. Its strength had been increased in 1885 to 1,000. No other rural area of Canada had such a large police force. As a result there were repeated calls for its reduction. In 1893 it was reduced to 850, later to 750. By 1898, 250 of these had been sent to the Yukon to police the Gold Rush. The Force on the prairies was reduced to 500 men just at the time that settlement began to increase rapidly. It should have been increased to keep pace with the growing population. Instead, its former effectiveness was slowly undermined.

Indians—The Last War Cry

The 1885 rebellion broke the back of organized resistance by the Indians. In the decade which followed, the great majority of them adjusted to a peaceful and orderly way of life. Many tribal customs were dropped as the former nomads began living in houses, adopting Western dress and speaking English. An undercurrent of the old ways remained, however, which surfaced from time to time, sending a wave of anxiety through the white population. In the United States the Ghost Dance revival resulted in renewed bloodshed and there were fears the movement would spread northward. The Force, therefore, continued to keep a close watch on the reserves. In addition, efforts were made to discourage the Sun Dance and other rituals which harkened back to the warrior ways of the past.

One of the customs which proved difficult to wean them from was the old practice of horse stealing, especially among the Bloods. The arrest of Indian horse thieves was frequently hazardous because many of them continued

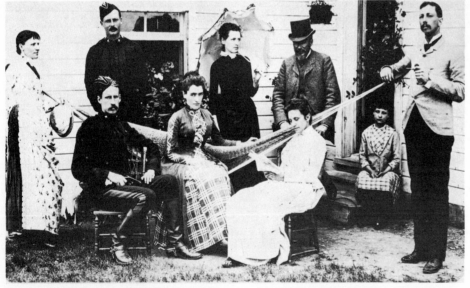

N.W.M.P. polo team, Fort Macleod, 1892.
L. to r.: George Ross, Inspector H. J. A.
Davidson, S. Heap, Inspector M. H.
White-Fraser and Inspector M. Baker.

Among other sports organized by the
members of the Force were cricket, rugby,
baseball and tennis. In September 1890 the
N.W.M.P. cricket team visited Winnipeg
for a week to play against the Winnipeg
Cricket Club and other local teams.

A social afternoon at Fort Macleod, 1899.
Standing, l. to r.: Mrs. C. E. D. Wood,
Inspector J. O. Wilson, unknown woman,
Mr. John Cowndry, one of the first bankers
in the N.W.T., Mr. C. E. D. Wood,
ex-constable of N.W.M.P. and owner and
publisher of the Macleod Gazette.
Sitting: Inspector Z. T. Wood, Mrs. Z. T.
Wood, Mrs. J. O. Wilson and Emily
Horan, the family maid.

At first the isolation, the cost of living
and the lack of the usual amenities in the
Northwest tended to discourage family life.
Commissioner French had brought his
family out to Swan River in 1874 and a few
of the other officers had followed his example. There were no restrictions in the
original regulations against the engagement
of married men, but the frontier was
generally considered a man's world and

most of the early recruits had been single.
A few married ones had left their families in
the East. The growth of settlement on the
prairies after the rebellion brought with it
the necessities for maintaining normal
family life and more and more men were
attracted to the Force as a career.

(Top) Writing-on-Stone Detachment, 1891. For centuries the Indians had used the sandstone cliffs of the Milk River Valley about 75 miles southeast of Lethbridge to carve pictographs recording their feats in battle. A detachment was built here in 1889 as a link in a regular system of patrols which extended south and east from "K" Division headquarters in Lethbridge to Kipps Coulee, Milk River, Writing-on-Stone, Pendant d'Oreille (noted for its many rattlesnakes), Manyberries and Willow Creek. At this last detachment, the "K" Division patrols connected with those coming west from "A" Division at Maple Creek.

(Above) Banff Detachment, 1888. In 1888 the Canadian Pacific Railway opened a hotel at Banff in the Rocky Mountains. The site soon became an internationally known holiday resort, with tourists coming from all over the world to visit the surrounding national park.

(Right) Members of the Pincher Creek Detachment, 1895. Broad brimmed felt hats were widely adopted for wear by the men long before they became part of the official uniform. The white regulation helmets and pill boxes gave little protection either from the sun or the rain. Dogs were very popular, especially large ones, both as pets and for hunting.

Almighty Voice. After shooting Sergeant Colebrook, Almighty Voice eluded capture for over a year before he was finally trapped on a bluff near Duck Lake. With two other armed Cree braves he decided defiantly to resist authority and seek a warrior's end. In the ensuing fight the three Indians as well as two mounted policemen and a civilian were killed.

Reward notice for the capture of Almighty Voice. The authorities soon realized that Almighty Voice could not continue to remain at large unless he was being harboured and aided by other Indians. A reward of five hundred dollars was posted for information leading to his capture, but even this unusually high sum failed to tempt informers.

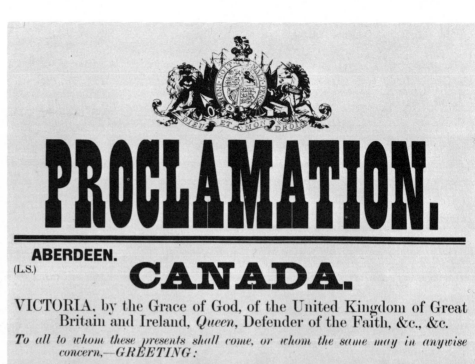

PROCLAMATION.

ABERDEEN.

(L.S.)

CANADA.

VICTORIA, by the Grace of God, of the United Kingdom of Great Britain and Ireland, *Queen*, Defender of the Faith, &c., &c.

To all to whom these presents shall come, or whom the same may in anywise concern,—GREETING:

A PROCLAMATION.

E. L. NEWCOMBE,
Deputy of the Minister of Justice, Canada.

WHEREAS, on the twenty-ninth day of October, one thousand eight hundred and ninety-five, **COLIN CAMPBELL COLEBROOK**, a Sergeant of the North-West Mounted Police, was murdered about eight miles east of Kinistino, or about forty miles south-east of Prince Albert, in the North-West Territories, by an Indian known as "Jean-Baptiste," or "Almighty Voice," who escaped from the police guard-room at Duck Lake;

And Whereas, it is highly important for the peace and safety of Our subjects that such a crime should not remain unpunished, but that the offenders should be apprehended and brought to justice;

Now Know Ye that a reward of **FIVE HUNDRED DOLLARS** will be paid to any person or persons who will give such information as will lead to the apprehension and conviction of the said party.

In Testimony Whereof, We have caused these Our Letters to be made Patent and the Great Seal of Canada to be hereunto affixed.

Witness, Our Right Trusty and Right Well-beloved Cousin and Councillor the Right Honourable Sir JOHN CAMPBELL HAMILTON-GORDON, Earl of Aberdeen; Viscount Formartine, Baron Haddo, Methlic, Tarves and Kellie, in the Peerage of Scotland; Viscount Gordon of Aberdeen, County of Aberdeen, in the Peerage of the United Kingdom; Baronet of Nova Scotia, Knight Grand Cross of Our Most Distinguished Order of Saint Michael and Saint George, &c., Governor General of Canada.

At Our Government House, in Our City of Ottawa, this Twentieth day of April, in the year of Our Lord one thousand eight hundred and ninety-six, and in the Fifty-ninth year of Our Reign.

By command,

CHARLES TUPPER,
Secretary of State.

DESCRIPTION OF THE AFORESAID INDIAN "JEAN-BAPTISTE" OR "ALMIGHTY VOICE":

About twenty-two years old, five feet ten inches in height, weight eleven stone, slightly built and erect, neat small feet and hands; complexion inclined to be fair, wavey dark hair to shoulders, large dark eyes, broad forehead, sharp features and parrot nose with flat tip, scar on left cheek running from mouth towards ear, feminine appearance.

Gun drill at Fort Macleod, 1894. The artillery of the Force in 1874 had consisted of two nine-pounder muzzle loading steel guns and two brass mortars, all of which were taken on the March West. In 1876 four seven-pounder guns were obtained from the Department of Militia in Winnipeg, and in 1886 two more nine-pounders were received from "A" Battery, Royal Canadian Artillery. The guns and mortars shown here are the original ones that were hauled across the prairies in 1874. One of the guns and the two mortars are now in the R.C.M.P. Museum, Regina.

Men and supplies leaving Regina for Wood Mountain, May 1895.

to carry firearms. Policemen pursuing the thieves were on several occasions fired upon by the fleeing Indians. Herchmer advised disarming the Indians. He saw no reason for them still to carry weapons when there was little left to hunt and no one to fight. The Commissioner, who had been an Indian agent for many years, believed the answer to policing Indians was the creation of an Indian Police under the direction of the Department of Indian Affairs.

The first serious threat to peace occurred not on the prairies but just over the border in British Columbia. In 1887 trouble erupted between the Kootenay Indians under Chief Isadore and the local settlers. Anxiety grew when the chief and his followers raided the provincial jail at Wild Horse and released an Indian charged with the murder of white miners. Fearing that the situation would get out of hand, the British Columbia government appealed to Ottawa to send a force of Mounted Police to the area to restore order.

The task was assigned to "D" Division at Fort Macleod under Superintendent S. B. Steele. In June 1887 a force of three officers and seventy-five men set out by rail for Golden, B.C. From Golden they followed the Columbia River trail south for 150 miles to the junction of the Kootenay River and Wild Horse Creek. Here they erected Fort Steele, the first and only N.W.M.P. post of its kind in British Columbia. After several months of very careful diplomacy, Steele was able to restore harmony between the Indians and settlers, and the division withdrew in

August 1888 via the Crow's Nest Pass to Fort Macleod, leaving behind four members who had died of mountain fever.

The most alarming incident on the prairies was the murder of Sergeant Colin Colebrook by a young Cree named Almighty Voice, from the One Arrow Reserve. The Indian had been arrested in October 1895 for cattle killing and brought to the Mounted Police guardroom at Duck Lake. During the night he managed to escape. On the following morning he became the subject of a widespread manhunt. He was discovered a few days later by Sergeant Colebrook and a Métis guide on a trail near the reserve. Although the Indian was armed, Colebrook slowly approached the fugitive, trusting that he would submit to authority. When the sergeant was just a few feet away, Almighty Voice raised his gun and shot him through the left breast, killing him almost instantly.

With the rebellion fresh in the minds of many, Colebrook's murder was cause for concern. Already that year two members of the St. Mary's detachment had been fired upon by a Blood Indian whom they were trying to arrest for horse stealing; and a Blackfoot named Scraping High had shot and killed the ration issuer on the Blackfoot Reserve. Unless Colebrook's murderer was quickly apprehended, other young Indians might be encouraged to follow his example and defy authority.

(Top) Officers at Regina, 1897. L. to r.: Inspector M. Baker, Superintendent A. Macdonell, Inspector J. Begin, Superintendent S. B. Steele, Inspector C. Starnes, Inspector Z. T. Wood.

(Above) Church parade in full dress uniform at "Depot" Division, Regina, in the 1890s. The members of the band are wearing sabretache badges on their helmets. Except for officers, helmet badges for the other ranks had not yet come into use. In the top left-hand corner is the new barracks completed in 1887 and known as "B" Block.

Anxiety increased when in 1896 Sergeant Brock Wilde of the Pincher Creek Detachment, formerly a member of the 2nd Life Guards, was shot and killed while attempting to arrest a Blood Indian named Charcoal. Like Colebrook, Wilde disregarded his own safety and endeavoured to take the wanted man alive. As he rode up to the fleeing Indian, Charcoal turned and fired at him hitting him in the right side. The Indian then rode on a few yards, turned, rode back to where the sergeant had fallen and shot him again in the stomach.

Charcoal was soon caught, tried and hanged at Fort Macleod, but Almighty Voice still managed to evade capture. His exploits began to attract the sympathy of some Indians and Métis. The Police realized that without assistance he could not remain hidden. The Government posted a reward of five hundred dollars for his capture, but with no result. Finally in May 1897 he was sighted with two companions by a search party under Inspector J. B. Allan and chased onto a bluff in the Minnichinas Hills near Duck Lake. Allan's party entered the bluff but withdrew after the Inspector and a sergeant were wounded.

N.W.M.P. contingent at Queen Victoria's Diamond Jubilee in London, England, 1897. As the nineteenth century closed, the quest for empire among the European powers was at its height. In 1897 representatives from every corner of the British Empire gathered in London in a brilliant display of imperial wealth and power to celebrate the sixtieth anniversary of Queen Victoria's ascension to the throne. For the N.W.M.P., the occasion marked its international debut. In the Service Order of Dress shown here – felt hat (worn officially for the first time), red cloth tunic, white gauntlets, blue breeches, black boots and Model 76 Winchester rifle – the men made a distinctive impression. Their appearance to the British crowds exemplified the dash, romance and courage which had extended the British red across the maps of the world. This style of dress was soon to become a symbol of the Force. It has been retained over the years with little basic change.

The three Indians dug in on the thickly wooded bluff and prepared to fight it out to the death, taunting their enemies and calling on them to fight. Corporal Hockin, upon whom command now devolved, decided to rush their position with the remaining members of the party. The decision was disastrous. Hockin, Constable Kerr and a civilian, Mr. Grundy, the postmaster from Duck Lake, were killed.

News of the engagement had by now reached the outside, and the authorities rushed reinforcements to the scene from Prince Albert and Regina with two field guns. With more than a hundred police and volunteers surrounding the area, the bluff was now heavily bombarded. When the police finally advanced the three Indians were found dead. Herchmer was criticized for the excessive force used, but the Commissioner felt it was justified. Unless such an open defiance of authority was quickly and effectively silenced, others would follow their example.

Two troops of the N.W.M.P. escorting H.R.H. the Duke of Cornwall and York, later King George V, during his visit to Calgary, September 28, 1901. His Royal Highness can be seen (in uniform, wearing a bearskin hat) to the left of centre, riding between the two troops.

This was one of the last occasions on which the old style full dress uniform was used by the Force. Regulations had already been passed on January 1, 1901, to replace it with the new style worn at Queen Victoria's Diamond Jubilee.

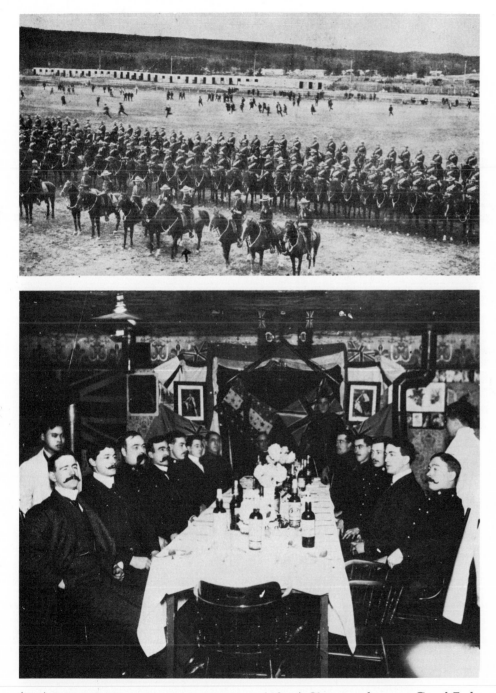

(Top) *R.N.W.M.P. contingent participating in the ceremonies inaugurating the Province of Alberta at Edmonton, September 1905. His Majesty King Edward VII had bestowed the title "Royal" on the Force in 1904 in recognition of its past service.*

(Above) *Christmas dinner at Grand Forks Detachment 1903.*

Settlement

Under the driving leadership of Clifford Sifton, the Minister of the Interior, the Canadian government in 1896 began a vigorous campaign to attract settlers to the prairies. Pamphlets were printed and distributed throughout the United States and Europe advertizing the quality of the soil and its suitability for agriculture. 160 acres were offered free to anyone who would come and settle on them. Assisted sea passages were provided. The C.P.R. ran reduced rail-fares on its colonist cars from the ports of embarkation. With the world emerging from a long depression, and the growing demand for wheat, the great land rush gradually gained momentum.

To ensure the success of the program every official from the Minister down to the mounted policeman was enlisted to advise and assist the new settlers. The police became land agents, agricultural experts, welfare officials and immigration officers. Often the immigrant's first contact with officialdom upon stepping off the train was the local detachment of the N.W.M.P. The police would give advice on the remaining land available in the area, sometimes driving the settlers out and helping them choose their homesteads. The police issued seed grain, quarantined livestock, and wrote copious reports on crop and soil conditions. If a settler lost a cow, he came to the police. If his crops failed and he had insufficient means

"The Talk Paper," by C. M. Russell.
The well-known Western artist Charles
Russell used the Force as a subject for many
of his paintings.

"*The Tampered Brand,*" *by the Canadian artist and novelist Arthur Heming. Heming's black-and-white wash drawing portrays the investigation of a common offence at this time, the stealing of cattle by changing their brands.*

The painting was purchased by the R.C.M.P. in 1958 and now hangs in the officers' mess at Regina.

to get his family through the winter, he applied to the local detachment for welfare. The time and effort needed to assist settlers placed an additional burden on the Force, but it also gave the Commissioner a new weapon with which to answer the demands for its reduction.

John Cashel under arrest at Calgary 1903. In 1902 a rancher near Lacombe mysteriously disappeared and foul play was suspected. The investigation was assigned to Constable Alick Pennycuick who was rapidly making a name for himself as the Force's foremost detective. After months of painstaking investigation, Pennycuick finally gathered enough evidence to bring a charge of murder against a young American immigrant, Ernest Cashel.

Cashel was tried, convicted and sentenced to be hanged in Calgary on December 15, 1903. Five days before the sentence was to be carried out he was visited in the N.W.M.P. guardroom by his brother John from Wyoming. During the visit John Cashel managed to pass two revolvers to his brother who escaped later that evening. John Cashel was quickly arrested but his brother, the convicted murderer, remained at large for several weeks. The hunt for Ernest Cashel became a sensational story and public attention was focused upon it throughout Canada. He was finally recaptured only a few miles from Calgary and hanged on February 2, 1904.

A Ukrainian homestead in Alberta.

Almost a third of the settlers who arrived between 1896 and 1914 were from continental Europe – Galicians, Germans, Finns, Swedes and Russians. Many did not speak English and the police had to employ interpreters to explain Canadian laws and customs to them. No criteria were used in selecting immigrants other than their ability and willingness to take up land. Some had religious beliefs which posed special problems for the police. During 1899 several thousand Doukhobors arrived to take up homesteads.

They proved excellent farmers, but in 1902 a fanatical element among them began the first of many protest marches to show their hostility to Canadian laws. More than a thousand of these settlers started out from Yorkton in winter weather without adequate food or clothing. They reached Minnedosa, Manitoba, in November. Here the N.W.M.P. detachment, under a young Danish-born N.C.O., Corporal Christian Junget, which had accompanied the marchers, forced them onto trains and returned them to Yorkton.

One of the most onerous tasks associated with settlement was the prevention and fighting of prairie fires. In dry years these could be serious, sweeping across the country and destroying everything in their path. It fell to the Mounted Police to encourage settlers to plough fire breaks around their property and take other precautions. Many settlers, however, were apathetic and failed to take precautions until the danger arose. The result was a steady toll in livestock and human lives.

In October 1905 a large fire blown by gale-force winds began sweeping across the prairie from Red Deer towards Battleford. Constable Conradi from Battleford was on patrol when he noticed the fire approaching. He asked the rancher, at whose place he had stopped for dinner, if there were any settlers in its path. He was told that there was a family with ten children, but they were too far away to be reached in time. Conradi felt he must try, and galloped off.

On arriving at the farm, he found the family, frightened and desperate. Frantically he helped the farmer finish ploughing a fire-break. Pails were filled with water and blankets soaked, but the fire came racing on. It jumped the fire-break and headed for the slough where the wife and children had taken refuge. Seeing that they would be suffocated by the thick smoke, Conradi ran through the flames, grabbed the two youngest children and led them all to safety.

Settlers came with all their worldly goods to start life anew on the Canadian Prairies. The Government offered 160 acres free to anyone who would settle on it.

His hair was singed, his clothing scorched and his hands and arms badly burned. His horse was so badly injured it had to be shot the next morning. For his pluck and endurance he was promoted to Corporal.

The Frank Slide. At 4.10 A.M. on April 29, 1903, a gigantic wedge of limestone from Turtle Mountain in the Crow's Nest Pass crashed down on the town of Frank, killing seventy persons.

Mounted Police reinforcements were quickly rushed to the area to lead the rescue operations and evacuate the remaining townspeople. The local N.W.M.P. detachment shown here was temporarily converted into a hospital for the injured.

Headquarters of "D" Division of the Royal North-West Mounted Police at Fort Macleod, Alberta.

The rush to register homesteads on Doukhobor lands at Yorkton, 1907. Almost from the moment they arrived in Canada, the Doukhobors posed a difficult policy problem for the Mounted Police. A small minority of them, firm in their religious beliefs, refused to conform to Canadian laws. In 1907 the Government decided that they must give up their practice of holding land communally. Those that refused had their lands declared vacant. These lands were then opened to other settlers.

Perry Takes Over

At the age of sixty Commissioner Herchmer volunteered his services for the South African War. With him went 178 other members of the Force. On August 1, 1900, he was succeeded by Superintendent A. B. Perry. As Commissioner for the next twenty-two years, Perry was to command the Force during its greatest period of change. While Herchmer had turned it into a police force, Perry was to lead that force over the constitutional and political hurdles that would see its services extended to every part of Canada.

The new commissioner took command just as the Force's future seemed very uncertain. Both the Gold Rush and the South African War had drastically reduced its strength on the prairies. Of more concern, however, was the development of provincial autonomy for the Territory. The first elected legislative assembly for the N.W.T. had met in 1888. In 1892 it had been given a measure of responsibility over local affairs, but the federal government had retained control over the administration of justice. Once the Territory became autonomous, this control would pass to the new provincial governments. The question for Perry was whether the Force could adjust to the new constitutional arrangement, or whether it would be relegated to the Yukon and the Arctic as merely a frontier police.

The inauguration of the Provinces of Alberta and Saskatchewan took place in September 1905. The federal authorities agreed to retain the R.N.W.M.P. on duty until the new provincial governments had had an opportunity to meet and decide their future policy. Under the government of the N.W.T. the Force had been responsible for enforcing territorial ordinances, criminal laws and federal statutes. With the change, the responsibility for administering provincial and criminal laws would pass to the provincial attorneys general. Unless the federal and provincial authorities agreed to cooperate, there would now be a multiplicity of police forces. The provincial governments could organize their own law enforcement agencies. The federal government, on the other hand, would have to have some means of enforcing the laws under its jurisdiction. In 1894 the N.W.M.P. Act had been amended to provide for the Force's use by the provinces, under contract.

Fortunately the citizens of the two new provinces were well-satisfied with the Force's past services. Their representatives in Parliament were usually among the first to defend it, whenever the question of its future arose. Many of them had grown up with the Force. If anything they tended to take its presence for granted, inhibiting any desire to replace it with a local organization. The federal government, meanwhile, was anxious to assist the new

provinces with their growing pains. In April 1906 Commissioner Perry went to Red Deer and Regina to meet with the respective provincial authorities to discuss the whole question of the Force's future.

The result of these negotiations was a five-year agreement for retaining the services of the Force in the provinces. Under the contract the Force was required to maintain a minimum of two hundred and fifty men in each province. The Force itself would remain a federal one, but, insofar as the administration of criminal laws and provincial statutes was concerned, it would come under the direction of the local attorney general. In return each province agreed to pay the federal government seventy-five thousand dollars annually.

Headquarters Staff, Regina 1909. Standing, l. to r.: Veterinary Surgeon J. F. Burnett, Inspector R. S. Knight, Adjutant.
Seated: Assistant Commissioner J. H. McIllree, Commissioner A. B. Perry, Surgeon G. P. Bell.

Commissioner Perry was born at Napanee, Ontario, in 1860. He was among the first class of cadets to graduate from the Royal Military College, Kingston, winning the Governor General's gold and silver medals. The future commissioner served briefly as a lieutenant in the Royal Engineers in England before accepting an appointment as an inspector in the N.W.M.P. in 1882. He succeeded Herchmer as Commissioner of the Force on August 1, 1900.

Perry found that the arrangement between the two governments worked very well at first. The provinces received a cheap but efficient police force. The annual cost of the Force between 1900 and 1914 averaged almost one million dollars. The contracts were renewed in 1911, but the Commissioner was unable to get a significant increase in the authorized strength. With the rapid growth in the population, he found it impossible to meet all the demands for the Force's services.

In 1911 Perry complained that the average constable now had an area of about two thousand square miles to patrol. One constable reported that patrols to some parts of his district were so infrequent that a settler mistook him for a sewing machine salesman. The incidence of crime also rose substantially. During 1905 the Force had handled 4,647 criminal cases. By 1912 this number had almost trebled to 13,394. In addition there were more frequent demands for men to police strikes, provide jail guards and handle emergencies like the explosion at the Hillcrest mine in 1914 which took over 180 lives. All these difficulties, however, were soon overshadowed by the gathering clouds of war in Europe. Canadians were soon locked in a bitter struggle that would last for four years. By the time peace was restored, the Force was faced with new conditions that would profoundly change the course of its future history.

R.N.W.M.P. contingent at the coronation of His Majesty King George V, 1911. Commissioner Perry (centre, with sword raised), flanked by Lord Kitchener on his right and the Duke of Connaught on his left, inspecting the Force's coronation contingent at the Chelsea Barracks in London.

The Living Legend

The romantic and heroic image of the Mountie is as old as the Force itself. Its origin lies not in the deeds of the North-West Mounted Police, but in the already well-developed romantic conception of the North American frontier. The stage was set in 1873 for a role of legendary dimensions. It only remained for the Force to ride onto the plains to assume the archetypal part of the noble horseman whose heroic mission is peace, order and justice. In part, the legendary figure was a projection of the conservative attitudes of the Upper Canadian loyalist tradition.

The legend grew quickly in literature. By the turn of the century the scarlet-clad hero had made his appearance in the writings and novels of Roger Pocock and Sir Gilbert Parker. A younger audience was established in 1897 when the adventurous escapades of the dauntless Mountie began to appear in *Boys' Own Paper*, a popular magazine for boys published in Britain. In the first two decades of the twentieth century he became a well-established literary figure. In scores of novels written by J. O. Curwood, R. Stead, R. S. Kendall, P. H. Godsell, C. L. Douthwaite and many others, the fearless and intrepid Mounted Policeman pursued the wrongdoer and upheld justice (the R.C.M.P. still receives letters from citizens who assume that the Force's motto is "Get Your Man"). Artists like Charles Russell added to the romantic lustre of the image.

These novels and stories were read widely, especially in North America and the British Isles. Interestingly enough, the Mountie is almost entirely absent from the literature of French Canada during this period. The literary hero prepared the way for the most popular medium for the legend, the movies.

Probably the first motion picture featuring the Mounted Police was *Riders of the Plains* made in the United States by the Edison Moving Picture Company in 1910. Other Mounted Police films followed with increasing regularity. In 1919 the famous Western star Tom Mix donned a red tunic in an epic of the Canadian West. During the 20s and 30s Mounted Police movies became very popular and the legendary hero rode across the silver screen in mile after mile of film.

Some of these were made by Canadian producers, but Hollywood was the most successful exploiter of the legend in films like *Cameron of the Mounted*, *The Trail of '98*, *Eskimo*, *Rose Marie*, *Susannah of the Mounties*, *Heart of the North*, *The Country Beyond*, *King of the Royal Mounted*, *North West Mounted Police*, to name just a few. They were followed in the postwar period by *Pony Soldier*, *Saskatchewan*, *The Canadians*, and *Mrs. Mike*, which one reviewer familiar with the Force's history suggested should be renamed Mrs. Tripe.

As time passed the hero of literature and films bore little resemblance to the real thing. Commissioner MacBrien, who took over the command of the Force in 1931, felt that the romance of the West

---

Song of the Mounted Police
BY KORN KOBB, JUN.

I'm away, I'm away, o'er the prairie so wide;
The saddle's my home, and my horse is my bride;
On, on, my good nag, we have got our release,
For your master is one of the mounted police.

We heed now no bailiffs, we care not for duns,
We'll be far from their clutches before many suns;
They may sue us, and welcome, our minds are at peace,
For we're safe in the ranks of the mounted police.

We'll tame the rude savage, we'll order, ordain,
And we'll chase the wild buffalo over the plain;
All riots and rows at our advent shall cease,
And we'll show them who's who with the mounted police.

In the far nor-west land, when our sabres we draw,
Our chiefs shall be judges, our edicts be law;
And those who conspire 'gainst Her Majesty's peace,
Shall get but short shrift from the mounted police.

Uncle Sam, if he's wise, will be mute as a mouse,
And Riel keep mum, if he's got any nous;
And the land shall wax fat, and bring forth and increase,
And men shall say "bless them," those mounted police.

Then hurrah boys, hurrah! for our wild life and free!
The care of a Province our pastime shall be;
Our steeds feel the impulse, their juices increase –
Make way there in front for the mounted police.

The romance of the Mounted Police began before the Force had even reached western Canada. This poem appeared in the Ottawa Daily Citizen *while the first recruits were preparing to leave for Lower Fort Garry. In what is certainly the first piece of Mounted Police literature, the unknown author foretells a carefree, heroic life of adventure, taming the "rude savage" and chasing the "wild buffalo over the plain."*

had gone far enough, that the Force should project a new image as a modern, efficient law-enforcement body. As a start he suggested the dropping of the word "Mounted" from the title of the Force. From the protests that greeted this suggestion, it was apparent that Canadians cherished the legendary Force and would not give it up easily. Although the myth was sometimes an encumbrance, the Force came to realize that it reflected a very positive image, and certainly one that made excellent public relations.

Not everyone has accepted the image uncritically. Its simplicity tends towards mindlessness and a naiveté that defies reason. Nevertheless, attempts to undermine it have had little effect and its critics are soon

Probably the best known of many poems written about the Force is the "Riders of the Plains." It was first published in the Saskatchewan Herald *in 1878, the first newspaper in the Northwest Territories. Although the poem is signed "W.S.," it is believed to have been the work of Constable T. A. Boys, who served from 1875 to 1878. Again it shows that the heroic image of the Mounted Policeman fearlessly carrying out his duty on the lawless frontier had developed quite early.*

"The Riders of the Plains"

NORTH-WEST MOUNTED POLICE, CANADA

Oh! let the prairies echo with
  The ever-welcome sound –
Ring out the boots and saddles,
  Its stinging notes resound.
Our horses toss their bridled heads,
  And chafe against the reins –
Ring out – ring out the marching call
  For the Riders of the Plains.

O'er many a league of prairie wide
  Our pathless way must be;
And round it roams the fiercest tribes
  of Blackfoot and of Cree.
But danger from their savage bands
  Our dauntless hearts disdain –
The hearts that bear the helmet up –
  The Riders of the Plain!

The thunder storm sweeps o'er our way,
  But onward still we go;
We scale the weary mountain's range,
  Descend the valleys low;
We face the broad Saskatchewan,
  Made fierce with heavy rains –
With all its might it cannot check
  The Riders of the Plains.

We track the sprouting cactus land,
  When lost to white man's ken,
We startle there the creatures wild
  And fight them in their den;
For where'er our leaders bid,
  The bugle sounds its strain,
In marching sections forward go
  The Riders of the Plains.

The Fire King stalks the broad prairie,
  And fearful 'tis to see
The rushing wall of flame and smoke
  Girdling round rapidly.
'Tis there we shout defiance
  And mock its fiery chains –
For safe the cleared circle guards
  The Riders of the Plains.

For us no cheerful hostelries
  Their welcome gates unfold –
No generous board, or downy bed,
  Await our troopers bold.
Beneath the starry canopy
  At eve, when daylight wanes,
There lie the hardy slumberers –
  The Riders of the Plains!

But that which tries the courage sore
  of horseman and of steed,
Is want of blessed water –
  Blessed water is our need.
We'll face, like men, whate'er befalls,
  Of perils, hardships, pains –
Oh! God, deny not water to
  The Riders of the Plains!

We muster but three hundred
  In all this "Great Lone Land,"
Which stretches from Superior's waves
  To where the Rockey's stand;
But not one heart doth falter,
  No coward voice complains,
That far too few in numbers are
  The Riders of the Plains.

In England's mighty Empire
  Each man must take his stand:
Some guard her honored flag at sea,
  Some bear it well by land.
Its not our part to face her foes –
  Then what to us remains?
What duty does our country give
  To the Riders of the Plains?

Our mission is to plant the right
  of British freedom here –
Restrain the lawless savages,
  And protect the pioneer.
And 'tis a proud and daring trust
  To hold these vast domains
With but three hundred mounted men –
  "The riders of the Plains."
                W.S., N.W.M.P.

Cobourg, July, 1878.

forgotten. In 1919 Lasky Studios of Hollywood produced a film called *Tyrant Fear* in which a Mounted Policeman was shown drinking in a brothel. Such an occurrence was not unusual in the early days of the Force, but protests in Canada led Famous Players to withdraw the film, and in Britain it was censored. Fifty years later, in *Vixen*, a sergeant was shown in a sexual encounter with a promiscuous young married woman. While *Vixen*, like *Tyrant Fear*, will soon pass into oblivion, *Rose Marie* lives on.

Literary critics have fared no better. The romance has flourished while defamatory tracts like C. D. Dwight's *Life in the N.W.M.P.* (1892) and R. Greave's *The Case of Constable Shields* (1940) have passed into obscurity. Attacks in the press or in Parliament have momentarily seemed to tarnish the image, but they too are soon forgotten. The romantic figure continues to fulfil some deep need to escape from reality, and the image remains widely accepted as a symbol of Canada itself.

One of the first comic strips to feature the Mounted Police started in the Toronto Evening Telegram in 1934. For once, the forests and plains of the West are set aside as Corporal Keene and Constable O'Hara coolly and courageously battle the forces of Darkness in the urban underworld. The following year the Chicago American began publishing a more familiar comic strip series, "King of the Royal Mounted" by Zane Grey.

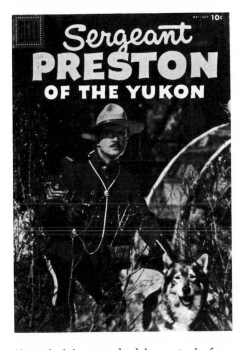

Typical of the comic book heroes is the fast-
acting, straight-shooting Sergeant Preston
with, of course, his faithful and intelligent
canine friend.

© 1973 Sergeant Preston of the Yukon, Inc.

In 1936, the hearts of millions of movie-goers throbbed at the sight of Nelson Eddy, his arms around Jeanette MacDonald, singing "Indian Love Call." Like many movies of the period Rose Marie reflected little of the nature of the real Force, past or present. During the 1930s hardly a year went by when a member of the Force was not sent to Hollywood to act as a technical adviser on the production of one picture or another. Senior officers in Ottawa winced at the licence taken by the movie makers, but agreed to their requests for technical assistance in the hope that the advisers might have some restraining influence. The governments of the day encouraged this, mindful of the advertising value of the films and their potential for attracting tourists.

4575-10

Taken for 6563-15

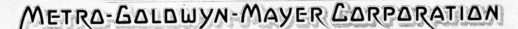

METRO-GOLDWYN-MAYER CORPORATION

ARS GRATIA ARTIS

S·T·U·D·I·O·S
CULVER~CITY
CALIFORNIA

OFFICE OF FIRST VICE-PRESIDENT
LOUIS B. MAYER

October 19, 1935

343685 OCT 25 35

Major General Sir James MacBrien
Commanding Officer
Royal Canadian Mounted Police
Ottawa, Ontario
Canada

My dear General MacBrien:

Many thanks for your wire of the 16th, advising that we may retain the services of Inspector Grennan for a further period. As I told you in my telegram, his advice and assistance in connection with our production of "Rose Marie" is invaluable to us, and essential for the authenticity of scenes in which the Royal Canadian Mounted Police appear.

We are making every effort to have "Rose Marie" a picture which will be correct in the smallest detail, and I am deeply grateful for your kind cooperation.

With kind regards,

believe me

Sincerely yours,

L B Mayer

LBM:S

Noted

NO AGREEMENT OR ORDER WILL BE BINDING ON THIS CORPORATION UNLESS IN WRITING AND SIGNED BY AN OFFICER

(Above) Rose Marie's great box office success prompted a spate of films on the Mounted Police. Susannah of the Mounties appeared in 1939. It starred Randolph Scott and the popular child actress Shirley Temple, shown here to the right of centre.

(Left) World War II failed to dull the public's romantic attachment to the Mounties. Here Alan Ladd is shown on location in the Rocky Mountains in 1954 for another epic of the West, Saskatchewan.

Reproduced courtesy of Universal Films (Canada)

The world première of Cecil B. DeMille's
North West Mounted Police *took place
in Regina in October 1940. Madeleine
Carroll, Robert Preston and Preston
Foster were on hand for the event. Canadian history is rewritten as Gary Cooper,
the Texas Ranger, arrives in time to win
the girl, Madeleine Carroll, and the Riel
Rebellion.*

Newspaper cartoonists have tended to treat the Force in a lighter vein.

(Opposite) The Force became a subject for musical composition long before Rose Marie. These waltzes were written about 1878 by the father of Inspector L. N. F. Crozier.

"... do you wish to exercise your search warrant... or join the library and let me find it for you?"

"Come out with your hands in the air — but don't hurry — I'm being paid time and a half."

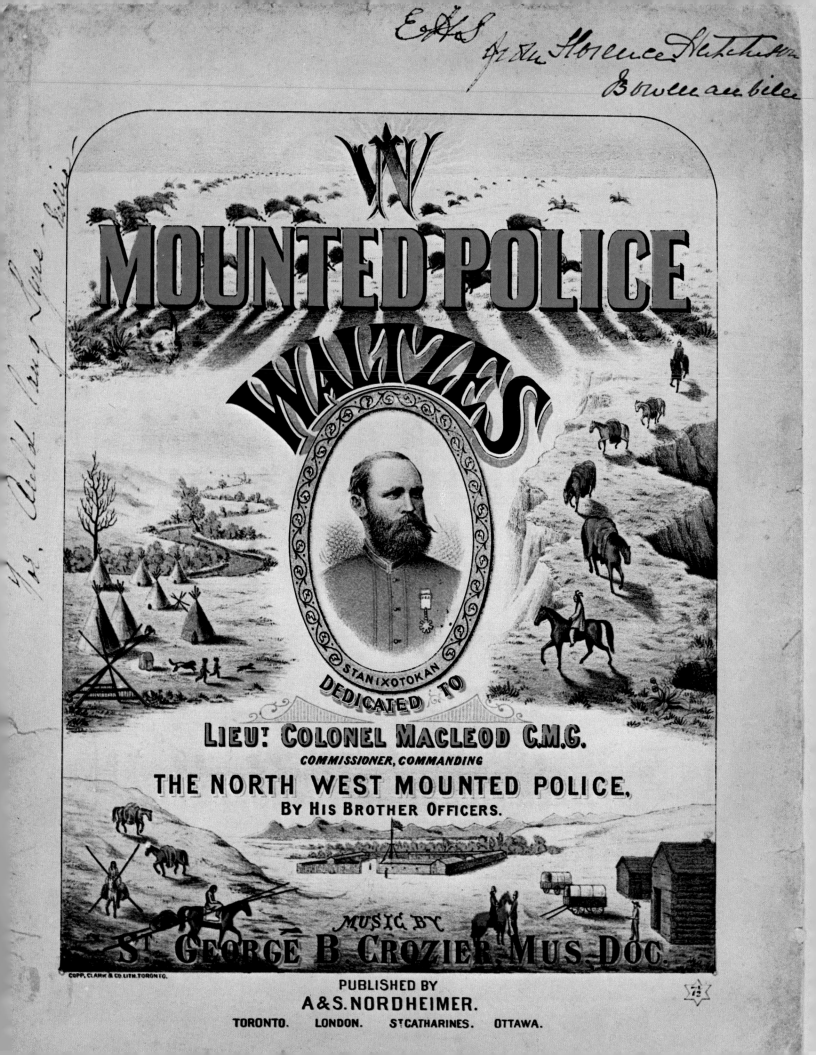

North to the Arctic Frontier

While the Force in Alberta and Saskatchewan was adjusting to the new demands of rural and urban settlement, a new frontier was slowly opening to the north where its former role as a frontier police would continue. In this northern wilderness, the N.W.M.P. was once again to be the advance guard of settlement and civil authority. As on the plains, its task was the establishment of law and order, the protection of the native peoples and the assertion of Canadian sovereignty. In meeting this new challenge the Force was fortunate in being able to draw upon its earlier experience, and its now well-established traditions of service, duty and discipline.

The territory purchased from the Hudson's Bay Company by Canada in 1870 extended in the east from Labrador across Hudson Bay westward for over two thousand miles to Alaska. From the United States border at its southern edge it rolled north across the Saskatchewan prairie through the subarctic forest of the Middle North to the barren shores of the Arctic Ocean. Still largely unexplored, this enormous empire was increased further in 1880 when Britain transferred to Canada its title to the Arctic islands lying north of the continental mainland. The most northerly of these, Ellesmere Island, extended the Dominion's sovereignty to within a few hundred miles of the North Pole.

The Force's jurisdiction extended throughout this vast domain as part of the Northwest Territories; but the Canadian Government was preoccupied with the settlement and development of the fertile lands of the Saskatchewan and little or no attempt was made at first to assert its authority farther north. The northern extremities were left to the enterprise of the fur traders and the zealous missionaries who followed them. In the Yukon a few miners eagerly dug for gold in creeks and rivers; occasionally officers of the Geological Survey penetrated the remote wilderness to map the mountains and coast lines.

By the 1890s, however, it was becoming apparent that the North could no longer be ignored. Steps would have to be taken to protect the territory's sovereignty and its resources. As the primary means for establishing Canadian authority, the Government turned to the Mounted Police. During the next thirty years the Force was to carry Canada's flag to every corner of these northern regions – to the Yukon, down the Athabaska and Mackenzie Rivers, along the shores of Hudson Bay and, finally, in the last thrust to the Arctic islands of the far north.

In this period of the Force's history it is frequently the actions of individuals that stand out. Its record in the North is the story of men struggling to survive in a hostile environment which demanded courage, physical endurance and resourcefulness. It is a story of high adventure, of individual tragedy, and drama where men loom larger than in real life.

Until the coming of radio and aircraft, the Force's pioneers in the North were totally isolated during the long cold arctic winters. To survive they had to learn from the Indians and Eskimos how to hunt, to travel with dog sleds and to live off the land. It was a tough, dangerous existence, requiring extraordinary men, and it was a tribute to the Force that such could be found in its ranks. To the public, the figure of the mounted policeman struggling in some northern setting against insurmountable odds to carry out his duty was to become a familiar image; but in the North there is more truth than legend in the tales of the Mounted Police.

The Yukon—Constantine Raises the Flag

The first significant discovery of gold in the Yukon occurred in 1886 on Forty Mile Creek, a tributary of the Yukon River, a few miles from the Alaska border. The discovery brought an influx of seven hundred miners, mostly Americans, who were soon prospecting and working on numerous creeks in the area. The commercial centre of this mining activity was the settlement of Forty Mile on the Yukon River. William Ogilvie, the Canadian government surveyor who visited the Territory about this time, reported a total absence of any constituent authority. The only law in force, he found, was that laid down by the "miners meetings" which settled disputes and regulated the activities of the miners. In 1893 Bishop William Bompas, a Church of England missionary, complained to Ottawa that the whites were demoralizing the local Indians with liquor. Bompas called for a police force to control the liquor traffic.

The Government realized that the establishment of Canadian authority would soon be a necessity. Therefore, they decided to send an officer of the N.W.M.P. to investigate and report on conditions in the Yukon. The man chosen for this task was Inspector Charles Constantine. A dignified man with a neatly trimmed goatee, Constantine was a man of considerable physical stamina and energy who already had a reputation as one of the Force's troubleshooters. He had come as a child to Canada, in 1854, from his native Yorkshire, in England. As a militia officer he went west in 1870 with the Red River Expedition. Later, he commanded the Manitoba Provincial Police before his appointment as an inspector in the N.W.M.P. in 1886.

Constantine spent the two months of July and August 1894 carrying out his reconnaissance of the Yukon. He left Victoria, B.C., by steamer in June of that year accompanied by Staff Sergeant Charles Brown. The two men entered the Yukon from Dyea in the Alaskan panhandle, climbed over the Chilkoot Pass and continued by boat down the Yukon River to Forty Mile.

Although it was a sort of "no man's land," Constantine found the Yukon generally peaceful and law abiding. He made every effort to meet and talk with the various groups in the Territory. Bishop Bompas introduced him to the Indians. He discovered them to be well-disposed towards the British, largely because the Hudson's Bay Company had treated them better in the past than had the American traders.

His main concern was the miners. In the absence of any established authority the miners had instituted their own laws with the "miners meetings" acting as a form of court. Constantine found that they were quite unfamiliar with Canadian laws and "very jealous of what they considered their rights." The authority of the Dominion, he reported, would have to be introduced firmly and the "miners meetings" discouraged.

The Inspector found little evidence of excessive drinking, but the liquor traffic was beginning to assume "large proportions," and needed to be controlled. In the saloons in Forty Mile whites could buy good quality liquor for fifty cents a drink. Distribution was controlled by a "whisky gang" which imported the liquor duty-free from Alaska. More than three thousand gallons, he learned, had entered the Territory in this manner during 1894 alone. The Indians, he reported, "make out of molasses, sugar and dried fruit a liquor known locally as Hoochi-moo." Much to the indignation of the miners and traders, Constantine collected more than three thousand dollars in customs duties. Leaving Brown behind, in August 1894 he began the long journey back to Ottawa to report his findings and recommend the despatch of a force of forty or fifty men to the territory to maintain law and order.

Within a few months Constantine was on his way back to the Yukon. Acting upon his report the Government decided to establish a detachment under his command at Forty Mile. His party consisted of Inspector D. Strickland, a surgeon and seventeen noncommissioned officers and constables – half the number he had suggested. On this occasion the interior was reached by the longer but less arduous route up the Yukon River from its mouth on the Bering Sea. The group left Seattle, Washington, on the

steamer *Excelsior* on June 5, 1895. A month later they reached St. Michaels on the west coast of Alaska. Here they transferred to river boats for the more than one-thousand-mile journey up-river. Plagued by flies and excessive heat the party finally reached their destination on July 24, 1895, and began unloading the supplies on the banks of the Yukon River close to the mouth of Forty Mile Creek.

Constantine at once set to work to build a post. A work force under Strickland continued up the river looking for suitable timber for logs. The others began clearing the land and laying out the site. Constantine praised the efforts of those under him. The men worked hard throughout the long sub-arctic summer days to complete the post before winter. By November eight substantial log buildings with sod roofs had been constructed. In the tradition of the

Inspector Charles Constantine, seated third from left, with members of the first Yukon detachment of the N.W.M.P. at Regina, May 1895, prior to their departure for the North. When gold was discovered on the Klondike a year later, Staff Sergeant Murray Hayne, seated fourth from left, staked a claim on Bonanza Creek. But while those around him struck it rich, Hayne's claim yielded only a few hundred dollars. In 1899 he published an account of his experiences in the North in a little known book entitled Pioneers of the Yukon. Hayne died suddenly at Fullerton in 1906 and was buried on the rocky shores of Hudson Bay. Unaware of his death, Ottawa a few months later promoted him to the rank of inspector.

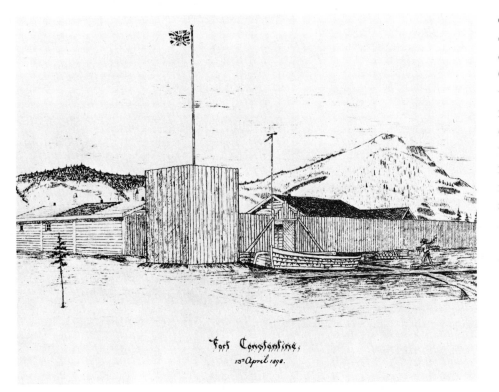

Fort Constantine,
13° April 1898.

Fort Constantine. Built in 1895 on the banks of the Yukon River a few miles from the Alaskan border, Fort Constantine was the first N.W.M.P. post in the Yukon. In August the following year two prospectors, Tagish Charlie and George Carmack, passed through its gates to register the claims that would start the great rush to the Klondike. The post was abandoned in 1901.

Force, the post was named Fort Constantine after its builder. Proudly, Constantine announced his position as the "most northerly military or semimilitary post in the British Empire." That winter the temperature dropped to 73 degrees below zero, and the men began wearing the native parka, "a shirt without an opening in front, made of the skin of the Siberian reindeer," as part of their dress.

As soon as he was established in the new post, Constantine set about making his authority known. As the representative of the Dominion Government, he was invested with the powers of a justice of the peace, land agent, custom's officer, postmaster and Indian agent, among others. The

only opposition to his authority came from the mining fraternity. A dispute arose over a claim on Glacier Creek. As in the past, it was settled by a meeting of the miners' "court." When the new owner arrived at Fort Constantine to register his claim, the inspector refused to recognize it, and the miner left the post uttering threats and "breathing defiance." Constantine immediately sent Inspector Strickland with ten men to Glacier Creek to warn the miners that their actions were contrary to Canadian laws.

The show of force by Strickland soon quieted the malcontents and prevented any organized resistance. Although the miners at first resented the introduction of customs duties and Canadian laws, most of them silently accepted the change. The "miners meeting" had worked better in theory than in practice. The enforcement of the mining regulations by the police brought a systematic and impartial approach to the question of recording claims, over which there had been many disputes.

By the summer of 1896 the Force had made its authority felt throughout the Yukon. There was little crime, but Constantine had succeeded in making it clear to the miners and settlers that they were in Canadian territory where Canadian laws would prevail. As it happened the Force's presence was to be most fortunate. The Yukon was about to become the scene of the most dramatic gold rush in history.

Ascending the Chilkoot Pass, 1898. In the winter of 1897/98 thousands of gold-hungry men and women made their way from the seaports on the Alaskan coast over the Chilkoot and White passes to Dawson. At Sheep Camp on the American side of the Chilkoot the hopeful throng assembled and packed their supplies for the final backbreaking climb. A landslide here in April 1898 killed seventy-two persons.

Inspector R. Belcher who was on duty at the summit of the pass brought his men down to assist with the recovery and identification of the bodies.

The Klondike Gold Rush

One day towards the end of August 1896 Fort Constantine had a visitor. His name was George Carmack, and the purpose of his visit was to register a mining claim. A few days earlier, on August 17, 1896, Carmack with two Indian companions, Skookum Jim and Tagish Charlie, had made a rich strike of coarse gold on Bonanza Creek, a tributary of the Klondike River which flowed into the Yukon about fifty miles upstream from Forty Mile. The three men became wealthy overnight. The strike yielded three dollars a pan. Ten cents would have been considered good.

The discovery was to be the most momentous event in the history of the Yukon. Constantine reported that the strike looked like being as good as that in California in 1849. Almost overnight Forty Mile became deserted, as men stampeded up-river. By November hundreds of claims had been registered along the Klondike and its creeks. Many of the latter began to acquire colourful names like "Eldorado," "Last Chance," "Gold Bottom," "Hunker" and "Too Much Gold."

News of the strike spread rapidly throughout the Yukon and Alaska. The best claims were staked by those already in the North who were able to reach the Klondike in the winter of 1896/97. Because of the isolation and poor communications, reliable news of the find did not reach the outside

N.W.M.P. detachment at the summit of the Chilkoot Pass, 1898. At the summit of the passes the gold seekers entered Canadian territory. A party of Mounted Police under Inspector Robert Belcher raised the Union Jack at the top of the Chilkoot in February, 1898. The detachment consisted of a few tents and a hastily improvised customs shed. Everyone who came over the pass came under the scrutiny of the police. Customs duties were collected, liquor seized, travel restrictions enforced and undesirables or known criminals refused entry.

until the summer of 1897. Its full significance was not realized until the first successful miners began arriving at the west coast ports of Seattle and San Francisco with their sacks and suitcases full of gold. Constantine estimated that three million dollars in gold was taken out in 1897. The following year this figure was more than doubled.

Once the sensation-hungry press had flashed the news around the world, the great rush to get to the Yukon began in earnest. At the magic word "gold," tens of thousands left their families and jobs and started for the Klondike in the hope of finding a fortune. Most of them took the short route from the Pacific Coast ports of the United States and Canada to Skagway or Dyea on the Alaskan Panhandle. Ahead of them was an exhausting climb with their supplies over the Chilkoot or White Passes to Lakes Lindemann and Bennett at the headwaters of the Yukon River. Here they waited until the spring breakup for the long and often dangerous journey down-river. Their immediate objective was Dawson at the mouth of the Klondike River. As the centre for the gold diggings, Dawson grew in two years from a half a dozen log huts to a booming town of over twenty thousand persons.

The Gold Rush drastically changed the problem of policing the Yukon. To oversee the incoming stream of humanity, police the widely scattered goldfields as well as the growing settlements, was going to take more men and a greater organization than the Government conceived possible. To administer civil authority in the Territory, Ottawa decided to appoint a commissioner for the Yukon. The man chosen for this part was James Morrow Walsh, the former superintendent who had retired under a'cloud in 1883 over the handling of Sitting Bull. Walsh was reappointed a superintendent in the N.W.M.P. and placed in charge of the Force in the Yukon. Thus the Force was in effect divided into two commands. Through the Commissioner of the Yukon, the members there came under the control and administration of Clifford Sifton, the Minister of the Interior.

Once Ottawa realized the full implications of the gold strike, men were rushed north to reinforce Constantine's small detachment. By the summer of 1897 his original command of nineteen had been increased to ninety-nine men. At Regina Herchmer was called upon to recruit an additional one hundred constables to meet the new demand. In November 1898 the total strength in the Yukon reached 285. In addition, the Government organized the Yukon Field Force, a military battalion of over two hundred men which assisted in maintaining control by carrying out guard and escort duties.

Superintendent Samuel Benfield Steele. As Commanding Officer of the N.W.M.P. in the Yukon in 1898, Steele administered the law with a firm hand. Horrified by the lawlessness on the United States side of the border, he worked a staggering nineteen hours a day to organize a police force which would uphold the Canadian system of justice he so fervently believed in. Steele was born in Simcoe County, Ontario, in 1851, the son of a retired captain of the Royal Navy. Joining the militia as a young man, he served during the Fenian Raids and on the Red River Expedition of 1870. He was one of the experienced N.C.O.'s who entered the N.W.M.P. in 1873 from "A" Battery of the Royal Canadian Artillery. Steele rose from the ranks to become an outstanding officer. During the Boer War he served with the Lord Strathcona Horse in South Africa. In World War I he raised and commanded the 2nd Canadian Division, attained the rank of Major General and was later knighted.

To police the new influx of miners, the Force now had to deploy its men over a large area. In the summer of 1897 Constantine moved his headquarters from Forty Mile down to the new centre of operations at Dawson. Here a new post was constructed called Fort Herchmer. Wherever a new discovery was made or a settlement sprang up, a detachment was quickly established. In February 1898 Superintendent S. B. Steele arrived to relieve Constantine. Later that year the Force was reorganized into two divisions, "B" at Dawson under Steele and "H" at Tagish under Superintendent Z. T. Wood. By 1899 the two divisions were operating more than thirty detachments, scattered from Stikine River in Northern British Columbia to Forty Mile more than five hundred miles to the north.

As happened earlier on the plains, the Mounted Police were for a time the only effective organized civil authority in the Yukon. Until relieved by the officials of other Government departments it continued to perform the variety of duties for which Constantine had been made responsible in 1895. Frequently, where there were no adequate regulations or laws, it had to impose controls for the general well-being of the community. Perhaps the most important of these, at the height of the Rush in 1898, were the restrictions placed on travel in the Yukon.

Lake Bennett. Once over the Chilkoot and on the Canadian side, the gold seekers gathered at Lake Bennett to wait for the opening of navigation on the Yukon River. When the ice cleared in May 1898, a motley fleet of boats began the long voyage downstream to Dawson.

When Superintendent Steele arrived from Skagway at the foot of the Chilkoot Pass in February of that year, he found thousands of men waiting to pack their supplies over the pass. The summits of the White and Chilkoot passes marked the boundary between the United States and Canada. Steele immediately took steps to see that permanent detachments were maintained at the summits. It was bitterly cold, the men had to live in tents, but the Union Jacks were raised and all who came over the passes were made aware that they were entering Canadian territory where Canadian laws were enforced by a well-organized police force. Later, when it appeared that there might be food shortages in Dawson, Steele issued a proclamation stating that no one would be allowed to enter the Yukon unless he had two months' provisions and five hundred dollars, or six months' provisions and two hundred dollars.

At Lake Bennett Steele found ten thousand persons waiting for navigation on the Yukon River to open. A motley collection of boats were being constructed in readiness for the trip down-stream. Before reaching Dawson they had to overcome several natural hazards, including Miles Canyon, Whitehorse Rapids and Five Fingers Rapids. Many of the boats were fragile and their crews inexperienced. After several boats had been overturned and their occupants drowned, Steele decided to impose restrictions to save the travellers from their own folly. Henceforth boats were inspected and required to be registered.

Main Street, Dawson, 1898. On the Yukon River at its junction with the Klondike was Dawson, the gold rush capital. Originally consisting of just a few log cabins, it grew almost overnight into a bustling, high-spirited town of dance halls, gambling houses, banks and churches, boasting its own electricity and telephone system. Food shortages in the winter of 1897/98 sent prices skyrocketing. Eggs, Inspector Harper reported, were eighteen dollars a dozen. The inhabitants were often wild and boisterous, saloon licences cost twenty-five hundred dollars, but Steele found that any man, woman or child could walk in any part of the town at night and be as safe as if they were on Sparks Street in Ottawa.

Women and children had to disembark and walk around dangerous sections of the river, and experienced pilots were used over the more difficult rapids.

The Rush naturally attracted a certain number of criminals, especially thieves, prostitutes and gamblers. Most of those who came, however, were honest and hardworking. Steel reported that "in proportion to the population crime is not very prevalent." Dawson was, of course, a wild, rough town by Southern standards, but one was still as safe on its streets as in any other part of Canada. There were few serious crimes. Petty theft was the most common offence largely because of the large number of persons who ran out of money and were destitute. Constantine complained of three hundred such individuals in 1897. Those convicted spent their time on the woodpile behind the Dawson jail, which like so many other services was run by the Mounted Police.

The orderliness was in part due to the effective network of detachments and patrols which the police quickly established. There were few places criminals could hide, and the only routes in and out of the territory were closely watched. Known criminals were often refused entry at the passes. With the officers appointed justices of the peace, the police held considerable authority with which to enforce the law.

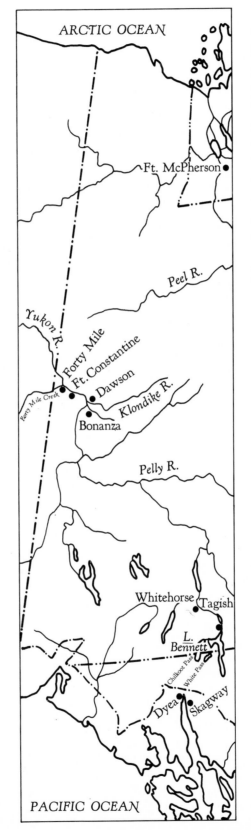

The police had less success with prostitution and gambling, however. Steele and his successors soon realized that it would be impossible to eradicate these activities. In the excitement of the gold rush, Dawson demanded a more open society than would have been tolerated elsewhere. There were scores of prostitutes in the town. At first the police carried out token raids on the brothels from time to time and fined the girls fifty dollars, or one month's hard labour. Later they were moved across the river to Lousetown where the law turned a blind eye to their business as long as they conducted it in an orderly fashion. Gambling, too, was permitted providing the house did not receive a percentage.

By September 1899, when Superintendent A. B. Perry relieved Steele, the gold rush had passed its peak and the population was gradually declining. Many of the miners were leaving in search of new El Dorado's, and the creek beds where thousands had dug were taken over by large mechanized mining operations. The need for a large police force declined too, but the strength of the Force was not reduced immediately. For a dispute had arisen with the United States over the position of the boundary with Alaska, and the Government was reluctant to reduce the Canadian presence in the Territory until the border question was settled. By 1910, however, the Yukon had become a quiet backwater. The two police divisions were amalgamated into one with headquarters in Dawson, and the strength in the area reduced to sixty men as the Force turned its attention to new frontiers.

Lower Labarge Detachment. ". . . on the marge of Lake Labarge/I cremated Sam Magee." Lake Labarge, the setting for Service's poem, was part of the Yukon river system over which the gold seekers travelled to reach Dawson. The detachment shown here was built at the lower end of the lake in 1898 as part of the network of police posts along the route to the Klondike.

"H" Division Headquarters, Whitehorse, 1900. In 1899 the headwaters of the Yukon River were bypassed by a railway built from the coast over the White Pass to Whitehorse. As a rail and steamboat terminus, Whitehorse soon became the main settlement in the Upper Yukon. As a result "H" Division headquarters was moved the following year from Tagish to the new town site. In 1943 the headquarters for the entire Yukon command was transferred from Dawson to Whitehorse.

Fort Herchmer, Dawson, December 1900. With the discovery of gold on the Klondike, the Force's headquarters in the Yukon was moved from Fort Constantine upstream to the new town of Dawson. Construction of the new post began in the summer of 1897. It was named Fort Herchmer after Commissioner L. W. Herchmer. The buildings shown here, centre, were grouped in the familiar fashion around a barrack square. On summer evenings the "B" Division band used the square to entertain the citizens of Dawson.

Bonanza Detachment, Yukon, January 1, 1904. New Year's Day complete with a good Spanish sherry, cigars, the post mascot and pinups.

George O'Brien was among those attracted to the Yukon by the lure of gold. O'Brien, an Englishman, was an ex-convict who had recently been released from Dartmoor Prison. On Christmas Day 1899 he and a companion, Robert Graves, ambushed and cold-bloodedly shot, on the Yukon Trail near Minto, three men who were on their way to have Christmas dinner with a friend. Stripping their victims of their valuables, O'Brien and Graves pushed the bodies through a hole they cut in the ice of the Yukon River.

Although the bodies were not discovered until several months later, the disappearance of the men touched off a long and painstaking investigation by the Mounted Police. Eventually a web of circumstantial evidence was uncovered which led to the arrest and conviction of O'Brien for murder. He was hanged in the Dawson Jail on August 23, 1901. His companion, Graves, was never found, but evidence suggested that O'Brien had killed and disposed of him also. The Force received widespread praise for the manner in which the evidence was gathered and presented in the O'Brien case.

Edouard LaBelle. In 1902 the Yukon was startled by news of another case of brutal murder. Three French Canadians on their way to Dawson were shot and robbed. The bodies were then weighted with stones and thrown into the Yukon River. When the corpses were discovered a few weeks later, the Mounted Police began another long and diligent investigation. The evidence pointed to two men, Victor Fournier and Edouard LaBelle, who had been seen with the victims leaving Whitehorse. Fournier was arrested in Dawson. The hunt for LaBelle extended to the United States. He was finally apprehended in Wadsworth, Nevada, and returned to the Yukon. The two men were convicted and hanged at Dawson in January 1903.

The murder cases in the Yukon received widespread publicity in North America and did much to enhance the growing popular image of the determined, dauntless and incorruptible "Mountie."

North to the Arctic Shores

As on the prairies, the opening up of Canada's northern frontier was preceded by the establishment of law and order. Although attention was focused upon its dramatic role in the Yukon, the Force had already begun to extend its activities into the subarctic forests of Canada's Middle North, the Athabaska country, the Mackenzie River system and the Keewatin District west of Hudson Bay. By the close of the nineteenth century these areas were being frequently penetrated by traders, trappers and prospectors. As a result there was a growing need for more effective control to protect the native people, enforce liquor laws and administer hunting regulations.

A patrol was made to York Factory on Hudson Bay as early as 1890. Three years later another patrol extended the Force's influence into the Athabaska country. In 1897 Inspector A. M. Jarvis with two men reached Fort Resolution on Great Slave Lake. Later that same year permanent detachments were established at Fort Chipewyan, Athabaska Landing and Lesser Slave Lake.

This movement northward was slowed, however, by the demand for men to police the gold rush. It was not until conditions in the Yukon began to return to normal that the movement accelerated once again. Through a network of detachments and patrols, the Force gradually extended its

authority through the forest belt to the barren shores of the Arctic Ocean. By the end of World War I the entire northern mainland had been effectively brought under Canadian jurisdiction.

The renewed thrust northward began in 1903. It was prompted by the dispute between Canada and the United States over the location of the Alaskan boundary. When the judicial council arbitrating the case decided in favour of the American claim, Ottawa became apprehensive that the activities of American whalers along Canada's Arctic

coasts might lead to further loss of territory. As a result Superintendent Constantine, Sergeant F. J. Fitzgerald and four constables were ordered to proceed to Fort McPherson, near the mouth of the Mackenzie River, to explore the need for posts in the Western Arctic.

Upon arrival at the settlement, Constantine obtained, from the local mission, quarters for a detachment. He then returned south leaving the rest of the men to spend the winter there.

Whaling vessels at Pauline Cove, Herschel Island about 1900. At the end of the nineteenth century, Herschel Island became a favourite wintering site for the whaling fleets which hunted in the Beaufort Sea. Reports that the idle crews spent the winter months debauching the Eskimos on the island led to the establishment of a police post there in 1903. At the time it was the most northerly in Canada and the first Mounted Police post in the Arctic Ocean.

In 1918 Constable A. Lamont died from typhoid which he contracted while nursing the explorer Vilhjalmur Stefansson through an almost fatal attack of the same disease.

Sergeant Fitzgerald meanwhile continued on down the Mackenzie River to Herchel Island in the Arctic Ocean, reaching there on August 7, 1903. The sergeant's visit was prompted by reports that the whalers who wintered on the island had been debauching the Eskimos with liquor. Fitzgerald rented two sod huts (one for storage) from one of the whaling companies and settled down to spend the winter – with only four sheets of note paper to write on.

He found very little liquor but succeeded in making it clear to the American whalers that henceforth the practice of supplying liquor to the natives must cease, Canadian laws must be respected, and customs paid on all goods landed. In 1905 the detachments in the Mackenzie and Athabaska country were organized as "N" Division with headquarters at Athabaska Landing.

Members of "M" Division under Superintendent J. D. Moodie at Fullerton, 1904. Their task was to introduce Canadian law to the Hudson Bay coast and the vast territory lying west of it.
Back row, l. to r.: Constables Verity, Seller, Heaps, Sergeant Nicholson, Constables Stothert, Jarvis.
Centre: Sergeant Donaldson, Constables Russell, MacMillan, Special Constable Moodie.
Front: Interpreter Lane, Staff Sergeant Hayne, Superintendent Moodie, Inspector Pelletier, Sergeant Major Dee, Interpreter Ford, Mike the Husky.
Foreground: Sergeant McArthur.

Thousands of miles away on the other side of the country, Superintendent J. D. Moodie and a party of five men were preparing to leave Halifax on the S.S. *Neptune* for Hudson Bay. Moodie's task was to police the whalers using the area and establish a post from which Canadian authority could be extended westward into the District of Keewatin. The site chosen for the new post was Fullerton on the west coast of Hudson Bay facing the southern tip of Southampton Island. The harbour here was a frequent wintering spot for the whaling vessels. The *Neptune* arrived at Fullerton on September 23, 1903. Moodie and his party unloaded their supplies and hastened to erect the detachment buildings before the freeze-up. During the winter one of the men went insane, and in the small cramped quarters his maddened screams were a great strain on the nerves of the others.

Leaving three men behind, Moodie returned eastward on the *Neptune* in the summer of 1904 to report his findings to Ottawa. He was sent back almost immediately with reinforcements and orders to extend his activities throughout the entire Hudson Bay region, which was to be designated "M" Division. This time his party sailed from Quebec City on September 17, 1904, on the C.G.S. *Arctic* commanded by Captain J. E. Bernier.

Superintendent John Douglas Moodie, born in Edinburgh, Scotland, was appointed an inspector in the N.W.M.P. in 1885. Much of his service was to be spent under hardship and privation in remote parts of Canada. In 1897 he was given the task of exploring an overland wagon route to the Yukon from Edmonton. With six men Moodie disappeared into the mountains north of Fort St. John, B.C., in September. Over a year and seven hundred arduous miles later his party emerged from the wilderness at Selkirk in the Yukon. Although a magnificent feat of endurance, his journey showed the impracticality of an overland route. More than forty years later the Alaska Highway would follow in Moodie's footsteps.

During the second winter at Fullerton, Moodie sent out several patrols, including one which completed the five-hundred-mile return trip to Baker Lake, and another which carried mail to Churchill and back, a distance of eleven hundred miles. In contrast to the hardship of the first winter, the second one passed "quickly and pleasantly." To keep their spirits up, the men organized weekly concerts and dances on the *Arctic*, wintering in the harbour.

In March 1905 the post was visited by an Eskimo from the Norwegian ship *Gjoa*, wintering off King William Island. For centuries men had been searching for a northern sea route between the Atlantic and Pacific Oceans. The *Gjoa*, under Captain R. Amundsen, was soon to be the first ship to navigate the Northwest Passage. Amundsen, who was short of sled dogs, had sent the Eskimo to ask the Mounted Police for help. Moodie replied by sending him ten of the animals.

To extend its control over the area covered by these two new divisions, the Force began operating a system of regular winter patrols by dog teams. In February 1906 Constable L. E. Seller inspected whaling operations in Repulse Bay and Lyon's Inlet, more than five hundred miles north of Fullerton. A year earlier, Corporal H. G. Mapley, with two constables and a guide, left Dawson in the Yukon on the first annual winter patrol carrying mail over the Mackenzie Mountains to Fort

Eskimos at Fullerton 1904.

R.N.W.M.P. patrol Dawson to Fort McPherson on the Peel River January 24, 1910. Starting in 1904/05 an annual winter patrol was made from Dawson in the Yukon to Fort McPherson near the Arctic coast, a distance of almost five hundred miles. The patrol in 1909/10, shown here, was led by Constable W. J. Dempster. It left Dawson with seventy pounds of mail on December 27, 1909, and arrived at Fort McPherson thirty-two days later.

McPherson. Mapley's party departed from Dawson on December 27, 1904. Discovering a short route through the mountain ranges, they reached Fort McPherson on February 2, 1905, having covered the 475 miles in just over a month.

The most spectacular patrol of this period was that led by Inspector E. A. Pelletier. This young French Canadian officer was given the task of establishing a link between "N" and "M" Divisions through the almost unknown country east of Great Slave Lake. With a corporal and two constables, Pelletier left Athabaska Landing in June 1908. Travelling by Hudson's Bay boat, the party crossed Lake Athabaska and continued down the Slave River to Fort Smith. Here they transferred to two canoes, and, with three months' supply of food, began the long and difficult journey eastward.

Their route took them across Great Slave Lake, over the height of land and down the Hanbury and Thelon Rivers to Baker Lake. They traversed scores of portages and were constantly attacked by hordes of insects. Pelletier reported seeing muskox and vast herds of migrating caribou. The first part of their journey ended at Chesterfield Inlet on August 31, 1908, when they were met by a whale boat sent from Fullerton. Later that winter Pelletier continued on southward by dog team to Churchill, Norway House and Gimli, completing a patrol of over three thousand miles.

One function of these patrols was to gather information about the North which could be used by other Government departments. Copious reports were forwarded to Ottawa on weather conditions, fish and game, soil, potential travel routes, timber and migratory birds.

Another frequent subject was the Eskimo. These people were greatly admired by the Mounted Police for whom they acted as guides. The members learned from them many skills which enabled them to survive in the harsh arctic environment. Returning from a patrol to Herschel Island in 1907, Inspector A. M. Jarvis composed an interesting description of the Eskimos:

> *They are quite religious, holding services on Sunday and doing no work on that day. There is no missionary here. Their religion they carry into their every day lives. They neither beg nor steal, and slander is unknown among them. They are as near "God's Chosen People" as any I have ever seen. After my experiences of this world, I could almost wish I had been born an Esquimaux.*

The Lost Patrol

In 1911 the Force's record of patrols in the North was marred by a tragic misadventure. Every winter since Corporal Mapley had inaugurated the run, a patrol had been made between Fort McPherson and Dawson. The man chosen to lead the patrol in the winter of 1910/11 was Inspector Francis J. Fitzgerald. Accompanying him were Constables G. F. Kinney, R. O. H. Taylor and Special Constable Sam Carter, whom Fitzgerald had hired as guide. The five hundred-mile trip usually took a little over a month to complete by dog team; the patrol had become something of a routine duty. Both Fitzgerald and Carter were experienced northern travellers, so no one felt any particular concern as the party pulled out of Fort McPherson on December 21, 1910, and disappeared into the vast snow-covered wilderness.

"M" Division headquarters R.N.W.M.P., 1907. In 1906 a post was erected at Churchill that became the headquarters for the Hudson Bay region until 1917. Through a regular winter patrol to Norway House and Split Lake, the new post gave "M" Division overland communication with Regina.

On February 20, 1911, an Indian arrived in Dawson from Fort McPherson. Questioned for news of Fitzgerald's party, the Indian informed Superintendent A. E. Snyder, the Commanding Officer in Dawson, that the patrol had left Fort McPherson late in December on schedule. If this was the case, Snyder reasoned, something must have gone wrong. Fitzgerald should have arrived in Dawson by the end of January.

Patrol under Corporal W. J. Dempster (far left), about to leave Dawson February 28, 1911, to begin the search for the lost patrol.

Snyder immediately telegraphed the news to Headquarters in Regina and began organizing a search party. As he had anticipated, the Commissioner instructed him to send out a patrol to find out what had happened to Fitzgerald. The search party left Dawson on February 28. It was commanded by Corporal W. J. Dempster who had made the patrol to Fort McPherson several times himself.

Dempster sped over the mountain passes but found no sign of Fitzgerald until March 12 when a faint trail was discovered on the Little Wind River. Later that night he located a camp which the patrol had used. Nearby were empty corned-beef cans and a piece of a flour bag marked "R.N.W.M.P. Fort McPherson." The next day the searchers found another camp used by Fitzgerald. Dempster now realized that Fitzgerald must have failed to find a way through the mountains and had turned back.

The corporal felt relieved by these discoveries. Fitzgerald, he reasoned, should have returned safely to Fort McPherson by now. On the following day, however, he passed three camps in fifteen miles. His anxiety returned immediately. If Fitzgerald was only travelling five miles a day, something must be very wrong. He was soon to realize the truth. On March 16 the searchers discovered an abandoned toboggan, harness and dog bones from which the meat appeared to have been stripped and eaten. It was now clear that the patrol was very short of food and was struggling to reach Fort McPherson.

The trail became clearer now and for four more days Dempster followed it down the frozen river. Each day their goal was getting closer, fifty miles, then forty miles. It began to look as if Fitzgerald had made it. Then on March 21, the searchers realized their worst fears. Only thirty miles from Fort McPherson, Dempster spied a blue handkerchief, the signal of distress, fluttering from a tree on the river bank. Pushing through the trees he found the bodies of Kinney and Taylor side by side. Kinney had died from starvation and exposure. Taylor had hastened his own end by shooting himself with his rifle, which was still clutched in his emaciated hands.

From the evidence around them, it appeared that Fitzgerald and Carter had left the two weaker men with the last of the food and set out in a desperate effort to reach Fort McPherson. Judging from the length of time the two bodies had been there, Dempster realized that Fitzgerald's heroic gesture had failed. Somewhere ahead he knew he would find two more bodies.

The next morning only twenty miles from Fort McPherson they came upon the final scene in the tragedy. The guide had evidently died first. His hands were across his breast, and Fitzgerald had placed a handkerchief over his face before lying down to die himself.

Handwritten diary entry:

> 48 Below   Sunday Feb 5th
> fine with strong S E wind
> Left camp at 9.15 am. moored one hour
> and camped about 8 miles further down
> Just after noon I broke through the
> ice and had to make fire, found one
> foot slightly frozen.
> Killed another dog tonight, have only
> five dogs now and can only go a
> few miles a day, everybody breaking
> out on the body and skin peeling off
> 8 miles

Handwritten will:

> All money in Despatch Bag
> and Bank, clothes etc I leave
> to my dearly beloved Mother
> Mrs John Fitzgerald Halifax
> God Bless all
>
> F. J. Fitzgerald
> R.N.W.M.P

Inspector Francis Joseph Fitzgerald. Fitzgerald joined the Force as a constable in 1888. Prior to the fatal patrol of 1911, he had established an outstanding reputation for service in the North. In 1897 he had accompanied Superintendent Moodie on the epic thirteen-month overland journey from Edmonton to Dawson. Six years later he had been responsible for establishing the first Mounted Police post in the Arctic Ocean at Herschel Island.

(Top) *The Last Entry in Inspector Fitzgerald's Diary, Sunday, February 5, 1911. The patrol continued for about a week after Fitzgerald made this last entry, before succumbing to starvation and exhaustion.*

(Above) *Will of Inspector F. J. Fitzgerald. When the bodies of the missing patrol members were brought to Fort McPherson, a scrap of paper was found in Fitzgerald's pocket upon which, shortly before his death, he had scratched his last will and testament with a charred stick:*
All money in Despatch Bag and Bank, clothes etc I leave to my dearly beloved mother Mrs. John Fitzgerald Halifax God Bless all.

F. J. Fitzgerald R.N.W.M.P.

Canadians were shocked when news of the patrol's fate reached the outside in April 1911. Commissioner Perry immediately ordered a full inquiry into the circumstances surrounding its loss. His findings summarized the cause of the calamity as follows: (1) the small quantity of provisions taken, (2) want of an efficient guide, and (3) delay in searching for the lost trail.

In fact, although a fine and gallant officer, Fitzgerald had shown a distinct lack of judgment in organizing the patrol and the mistakes had been costly. The guide was unreliable, and in his desire to make a fast time Fitzgerald had lightened the toboggans by reducing the rations well below that normally considered necessary. An excerpt from his diary, which was found with the bodies of Kinney and Taylor, tells the story:

Tuesday, January 17 . . . Carter is completely lost and does not know one river from another. We have now only ten pounds of flour and 8 pounds of bacon and some dried fish. My last hope has gone, and the only thing I can do is return, and kill some of the dogs to feed the others and ourselves, unless we can meet some Indians. We have now been a week looking for a river to take us over the divide, but there are dozens of rivers and I am at a loss. I should not have taken Carter's word that he knew the way from Little Wind River.

Funeral of the lost patrol. The members of the patrol were buried on March 28, 1911, at Fort McPherson, the settlement they had struggled so hard to reach. The four coffins were placed side by side in a single grave over which a farewell salute was fired. The burial service was read by the Church of England missionary, the Reverend C. E. Whittaker.

Murder in the Barren Lands

While Canada and its allies were engrossed in a struggle against Germany, patrols of the R.N.W.M.P., investigating reports of murders among the Eskimos, were bringing the elements of law and order to the last corner of the Arctic mainland. In 1913 rumours reached Fullerton Detachment that two explorers, Mr. H. V. Radford and Mr. T. G. Street, had been murdered at Bathurst Inlet. There had been no news from the two men since they had crossed the Barren Lands a year before to visit the Eskimos along Coronation Gulf. Immediate action was delayed by lack of communication, but in July 1914 a patrol under Inspector W. J. Beyts left Halifax for Hudson Bay to begin the search for the two men. After moving up Chesterfield Inlet, Beyts established a post at Baker Lake in the winter of 1914/15 as a base from which to commence the investigation farther north.

To the west meanwhile, there were rumours of the death of two Roman Catholic priests, Fathers Rouvière and LeRoux, who had last been heard of in 1913 when they had left Great Bear Lake to work among the Eskimos of the Coppermine River. To learn of their fate, a patrol under Inspector C. D. La Nauze left Fort Norman on the Mackenzie River in July 1915. After months of searching, La Nauze's party eventually rendezvoused at the mouth of the

Coppermine River with Corporal W. V. Bruce who had patrolled along the Arctic coast by ship from Herschel Island. The results of their investigation showed that the two priests had been murdered near Bloody Falls on the Coppermine River in November 1913. Two Eskimos were arrested and taken to Herschel Island to stand trial.

Inspector Beyts on the other hand had been less successful. He had made two attempts to reach Bathurst Inlet, but had to turn back each time because of the scarcity of game for dog feed. In September 1916 the investigation was taken over by Inspector F. H. French. Accompanied by Sergeant Major T. B. Caulkin and Eskimo guides, French set out on one of the longest and most arduous patrols in the annals of the Force. Travelling over two thousand miles through the Barren Lands,

Sinnisiak and Uluksak (seated foreground), awaiting trial at Edmonton, August, 1917, for the murder of two Oblate priests on the Coppermine River in 1913. The two Eskimos were arrested following a long investigation in the Great Bear Lake region by a patrol led by Inspector C. D. LaNauze (middle row, second from left). It was recognized early that criminal law would have to be enforced among the Eskimo in a manner which they could understand.

They were found guilty, and their sentence was commuted to life imprisonment. They were later released after serving a short period of their sentence in the Mounted Police guardroom at Fort Resolution.

encountering many hardships, living for a time on raw meat, French returned to Baker Lake in January 1918. Although four years had passed, his investigation showed that Radford and Street had been murdered on the shores of Bathurst Inlet in June 1913 and their bodies thrown into the sea.

Murder on the Belcher Islands. In August 1920, Inspector J. W. Phillips and Sergeant A. H. Joy (shown here third from left), left Moose Factory by boat to investigate reports that an Eskimo had been murdered on the Belcher Islands in Hudson Bay. Their subsequent enquiries revealed that an Eskimo named Ketaushuk had gone insane and threatened to kill anyone who crossed his path. His neighbours called a council meeting and decided that Ketaushuk must be killed at the first opportunity, to protect the rest of the band. The deed was duly carried out by an Eskimo named Tukautouk.

Acting as Coroner, Phillips constituted a jury from the whites present. After hearing the evidence the jury found that Ketaushuk had been "killed for the common good and safety of the band." It went on to recommend that "owing to the primitive existence and total absence of all knowledge of law" no criminal charge be laid.

These wartime patrols brought the entire northern mainland under Canadian authority. By 1919 the Force had twenty-five detachments policing the northern frontier with a strength of over seventy men. These included fourteen detachments in the Yukon under "B" Division at Dawson, and nine under "G" Division at Edmonton – Athabaska, Coppermine, Fort Fitzgerald, Fort Resolution, Fort Simpson, Fort McPherson, Grouard, Peace River and Herschel Island. On the shores of Hudson Bay two more, Fullerton and Port Nelson under "F" Division, completed the northern arm of the Force. It was a small band with which to police Canada's vast northern domain, but it was sufficient to ensure the enforcement of Canadian laws and the maintenance of Canadian sovereignty. Such was not yet the case in the Arctic islands farther north.

Guarding the Arctic Islands

North of the Canadian mainland lie the many scattered islands of the Arctic Archipelago, usually referred to today as the Eastern Arctic. Their total area covers over four hundred thousand square miles. The largest, Baffin Island, is almost as big as the Province of Saskatchewan. Ellesmere, the most northerly, is only five hundred miles from the North Pole. For most of the year they are swept by the blizzards of the long Arctic winter and locked fast in the frozen seas which surround them. The northern islands were so bleak and desolate that not even the Eskimos had settled there. In 1931 the entire population of the area consisted of only 75 whites and 2,436 Eskimos.

The first Europeans to visit this region were probably the Vikings almost one thousand years ago. After the Norsemen left, the islands disappeared from historical records until the arrival of the English explorer Martin Frobisher on the coast of Baffin Island in 1576. Frobisher was followed during the next three hundred years by many explorers, mostly British – Hudson, Davis, Ross and Franklin, to mention just a few. Each explored some new area and added to the geographical knowledge of the territory. In 1874 the Canadian government notified Great Britain of its desire to acquire sovereignty over these islands. Six years later, on July 31, 1880, the British government formally transferred its claim and title to them by Imperial Order-in-Council to Canada.

At first Canada did nothing to assert its sovereignty over the region. Towards the end of the nineteenth century, however, the islands were increasingly visited by whaling vessels and scientific expeditions from many nations. In 1882 a United States expedition under Lieutenant Greely established a scientific station on Ellesmere Island. More important was the Norwegian expedition of 1898 to 1902 under Otto Sverdrup. The Norwegians explored west of Ellesmere and mapped the islands of Axel Heiberg, Amund Ringnes and Ellef Ringnes. Sverdrup claimed the islands by right of discovery and endeavoured to persuade the governments of Sweden and Norway to proclaim their sovereignty over them.

These developments alarmed Canadians and resulted in the Government's sending a series of expeditions northward to protect Canadian sovereignty. The first of these, in 1903, in the *Neptune* under Mr. A. P. Low of the Geological Survey carried Inspector Moodie to Hudson Bay. In 1906/07 another expedition in the C.G.S. *Arctic*, commanded by Captain Joseph Bernier, visited Baffin Island, sailed west along Lancaster Sound, taking formal possession of the adjacent islands and enforcing Canadian fishing regulations. On his next voyage north in 1909, Bernier erected a tablet on Melville Island pro-

Margaret Agnes Clay. Mrs. Clay was one of the first wives of members of the Force to accompany her husband to an isolated northern post. In 1924 her husband, Staff Sergeant S. G. Clay, was transferred to the tiny settlement of Chesterfield Inlet on Hudson Bay. As on his earlier postings in the Mackenzie River District, Mrs. Clay accompanied her husband to the new assignment. The Clays had no children. On September 19, while her husband was away on patrol, Mrs. Clay was attacked by dogs and one of her legs was badly bitten. To save her life, it was decided that the leg would have to be amputated. There was no doctor, or adequate medical facilities. The operation was performed by the priest from the nearby mission. Although it was expertly done, Mrs. Clay did not recover from the shock. Her husband returned several weeks later to find that the harsh northern life had taken his young wife's life.

claiming Canadian sovereignty over the whole archipelago from longitude 60° W. to 141° W. up to latitude 90° N. Other Canadian expeditions followed, but no attempt was made at permanent occupation by Canadian authorities.

By the end of World War I Canadian sovereignty over the islands no longer seemed in doubt. Suddenly, however, in 1920 a new challenge appeared. A year earlier a Danish expedition led by Knud Rasmussen had visited Ellesmere Island. The Danes and the Greenland Eskimos were reported to have killed large numbers of muskox which were protected under Canadian law. When Ottawa asked the Danish authorities to stop the Greenlanders from hunting on Ellesmere, Rasmussen replied that he considered the island a "No Man's Land." The answer startled Canadian officials, especially as the Danish government appeared to support Rasmussen's position. Concern increased over unconfirmed newspaper reports that another Danish expedition planned to settle on Ellesmere.

The need to affirm Canadian sovereignty over the islands, particularly Ellesmere, now became an urgent matter for the government. The earlier proclamations, it was realized, had not secured undisputed recognition of Canada's claims. The islands would have to be permanently occupied by Canadian authorities, and Canadian laws enforced. To achieve

this, the government decided to establish a number of police posts, and in 1921 plans were started to outfit the *Arctic* for northern service once again.

In the meantime Staff Sergeant A. H. Joy left Montreal in July 1921 on the Hudson's Bay ship *Baychimo* to establish a post at Pond Inlet on the north coast of Baffin Island. Joy was invested with several powers which enabled him to act as a representative of the Canadian Government – those of justice of the peace, coroner, customs officer and postmaster. The immediate objective of his despatch to Baffin Island was to investigate reports that a Newfoundland trader, Robert Janes, had been killed by Eskimos at Cape Crawford.

Bache Peninsula Detachment, Ellesmere Island. This photograph was taken shortly after the flag-raising ceremony which officially opened the post on August 9, 1926. The party of Mounted Police was under the command of Inspector C. E. Wilcox, second from right. With them are Government officials, members of the crew of the S. S. Beothic, and Eskimo Guides. Bache Peninsula was the most northerly Mounted Police post ever established.

Joy's involvement in this case illustrates clearly the varied role of the Mounted Police in the Arctic. As a police officer the staff sergeant investigated the circumstances of Janes's death, disinterred the body (Janes had been buried for over a year) and conducted an autopsy. Returning with the remains by sled to Pond Inlet, Joy held an inquest in his capacity

as coroner. As a justice of the peace he issued the warrants for the arrest of the accused, executed the arrests as a police officer and finally as a justice of the peace again held the Preliminary Inquiry. Every step in the proceedings, for which Joy was commended, was precisely carried out.

In 1922 the *Arctic*, under Bernier (now almost seventy years old), returned to northern service once again. Leaving Quebec City in July with Inspector C. E. Wilcox and eight men, the ship called in at Pond Inlet, where ice conditions prevented it from unloading supplies, before continuing on to the south shore of Ellesmere Island. Here a site for a detachment was chosen at Craig Harbour.

After unloading the materials and stores for the post, the *Arctic* returned south, leaving Wilcox, one N.C.O. and five men isolated until its return a year later. "The sun was last seen on October 25," reported Wilcox. One hundred and nine days of darkness followed, with intense cold and gale force winds sweeping the coast.

Each summer for the next three years the *Arctic* returned north to bring supplies and establish new detachments – Pangnirtung on the east coast of Baffin Island in 1923, Dundas Harbour on Devon Island in 1924. The following year an attempt was made to erect a post at Bache Peninsula on the east coast of Ellesmere Island only fifty miles from Greenland, but the ice was too thick and the ship had to turn back. In 1926 Bache Peninsula was finally reached, this time on the S.S. *Beothic*. The detachment buildings were erected on the shore beneath the towering coastal cliffs, and Staff Sergeant Joy was left in charge with two constables.

From these new detachments the members of the Force began systematically to patrol the neighbouring territories. By 1929 Canada was in undisputed control of the entire Eastern Arctic. Most important in this respect were two patrols by Joy and one by Constable Anstead across Ellesmere and the disputed islands to the west. On his first patrol Joy left Bache Peninsula in March 1927 accompanied by Constable Garnett and three Eskimos. They travelled

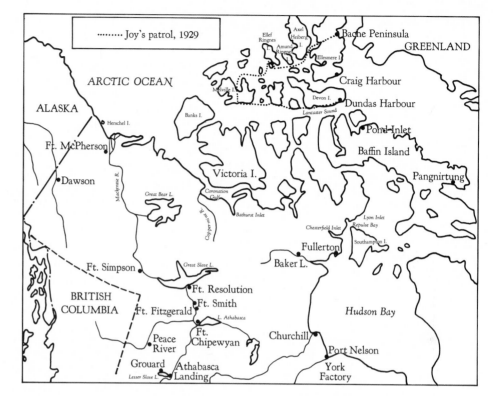

west across Ellesmere, then turned southwest, visiting Axel Heiberg, Amund Ringnes and Ellef Ringnes Islands, which had been claimed by Sverdrup. Two years later, with Constable Taggart and one Eskimo guide, Joy patrolled the Sverdrup Islands again from Dundas Harbour to Bache Peninsula, an outstanding patrol of over 1,700 miles in 81 days. At one point the party were attacked in their igloo by a polar bear. The same year Constable Anstead from Bache Peninsula explored Greely Fiord and the northeast coast of Axel Heiberg Island. With these patrols and Sverdrup's death in 1930, the dispute over the territory came to an end.

The establishment of posts in the Eastern Arctic was the final chapter in the Force's role as a frontier police. Since the March West in 1874 it had assumed the task of introducing the stable elements of law and order to most of the unsettled areas of Canada. As the policing arm of the Dominion Government, it had followed each phase in the opening of the frontier, protecting Canadian sovereignty and extending Canadian laws and authority. By the time it reached the Arctic shores, this task had become only a minor part of its work. Elsewhere the Force had been undergoing fundamental changes in responsibilities and character.

Northern justice. An itinerant magistrate,
seated, holds court in the open to try an
Eskimo charged with theft at Port Harrison
in 1935.

The Band and the Musical Ride

The Sound of Music

The distinction of forming the first musical group in the Force is usually attributed to two talented performers who improvised a "combo" on the March West to entertain their comrades. Their instruments were a fife and a large tin dish, with a spoon for a drumstick.

In 1875 Commissioner French asked the Government for money to purchase instruments to organize a band similar to those of the Dublin and London metropolitan police forces. A band, he felt, would provide entertainment during the long winter months and add some pageantry to official ceremonies. His request was refused.

The would-be musicians of the early Force could not be deterred, however, by the lack of Government funds. At a meeting at Swan River Barracks in February 1876 the men decided to organize a band themselves, at their own expense.

The first instruments were brought from Winnipeg by dog sled. The band made its debut on Queen Victoria's Birthday, May 24, 1876, under the eye of the first bandmaster, Sergeant Major T. H. Lake.

"D" Division band, Battleford 1885. The Battleford band was led by Sergeant Fred Bagley (centre, holding sword). Two of its members were killed in the North West Rebellion shortly after this photograph was taken. Bagley joined the Force as a bugler in 1874. He was an enthusiastic musician and during his service organized more than one band to entertain the men and the local settlers.

Assembled around the post's flagstaff, it struck up the solemn strains of "God Save the Queen." Later that year it travelled to Fort Carlton, where it excited the curiosity of the Indians at the signing of Treaty No. 6. In 1877 it was a part of the colourful assembly at Blackfoot Crossing for the signing of the Blackfoot Treaty.

In the years that followed bands were organized from time to time at various posts. They were voluntary groups, the men giving of their own time and money to entertain themselves and the community. Many a holiday parade, ball or other festivity in the small Western towns was enlivened by the melodious sounds of the local Mounted Police band.

In 1938 Commissioner Wood decided to establish a permanent full-time band. Its organization was placed in the hands of Staff Sergeant J. T. Brown, formerly Director of Music for the Governor General's

Foot Guards. The band, consisting of thirty-seven members, made its debut in 1939 during the visit of Their Majesties King George VI and Queen Elizabeth. It set the course for future bands, playing at state functions, entertaining visiting dignitaries and touring Canada and the United States, performing in high schools, concert halls and exhibition grounds.

A second band was formed at Regina in 1949 under the direction of Staff Sergeant C. C. Bryson. It was disbanded ten years later when the Force decided to concentrate all of its musical resources in one band at Ottawa. In recent years the band has been an important part of the Force's community relations program. On cross-country tours it has annually appeared live before audiences totalling hundreds of thousands of persons. One recent highlight was its visit to Osaka, Japan, for Expo '70 where it performed under the direction of Inspector W. Bramwell Smith, who succeeded Superintendent E. J. Lydall as Supervisor of Music in 1967.

"B" Division band leading the May 24 parade at Dawson, 1902. Most of the miners who entered the Yukon during the gold rush were Americans. On July 4 they congregated in Dawson to celebrate Independence Day. The Canadians responded by holding parades on May 24 and July 1, Dominion Day, to show their own patriotism and remind the citizens of Dawson that the Yukon was still a part of the British Empire.

(Left) Each change in the daily routine at the early police posts in the West was preceded by a specified bugle call. The sound of the bugle was the signal to work, eat, rest or sleep. The day started with "Reveille" at 5.30 A.M. to 6.30 A.M., according to the season of the year, and ended with "Lights Out."

The Force's "Regimental March," composed by Dr. Charles O'Neill in 1952, embodies the early Regimental Bugle Call of the N.W.M.P.

(Above) N.W.M.P. mounted band, Regina 1890.

(Left) R.C.M.P. band 1967. During Canada's Centenary the band under the direction of Superintendant E. J. Lydall covered more than ten thousand miles to perform before Canadians in all parts of the country, including the Arctic.

The Mounted Tradition

Since equitation was discontinued for recruits in 1966, the mounted traditions of the Force have been kept alive solely by the R.C.M.P. Musical Ride. The horse, the scarlet tunic and the lance of the Ride are among the last links with the Force's early history and traditions, living reminders of the romance of the frontier.

Like the bands of the Force, the Musical Ride developed from a desire by the men to amuse themselves, display their riding ability, of which they were very proud, and entertain the local community. The coordinated series of figures which form the basis of the musical ride were developed from traditional cavalry drill movements. The performance of these was usually accompanied by music. In addition, the riders frequently displayed their expertise at tent pegging, jumping, roman riding and other mounted sports.

Musical ride. "The Charge of the N.W.M.P. Musical Ride" as drawn by Frederic Remington for Harper's Weekly *in 1887.*

The first known display of riding was given in 1876 by a troop trained by Sergeant Major Robert Belcher. With the building of a riding school at "Depot" Division, Regina, in 1886, it became possible for extensive mounted training to continue during the winter months. Shortly after the riding school was erected, a musical ride was given in several performances under the direction of Inspector W. G. Matthews, former Riding Master and Adjutant of a British cavalry regiment, the 3rd (King's Own) Hussars.

The Musical Ride as a regular form of public entertainment dates from 1904 when a troop trained by Inspector Frank Church performed at the Winnipeg, Brandon, Qu'Appelle and Regina Fairs. It was enthusiastically received by the Western crowds who appreciated expert horsemanship. Commissioner Perry quickly realized its value as a means of promoting good public relations.

After the move to Ottawa in 1920, the musical ride appeared for the first time in eastern Canada. During much of the twenties and thirties two rides were in operation, one at Regina, the other at Ottawa. With tours of Canada and the United States, the R.C.M.P. Musical Ride had become an established attraction in North America by the outbreak of war in 1939.

The war curtailed its activities, but in 1948 it was reorganized and soon re-established its old popularity. The Ride quickly became a familiar sight again throughout Canada and the United States. It also travelled to the United Kingdom and Bermuda. More recently it appeared at Expo '70 in Osaka, Japan, under the command of the Officer in Charge of Equitation, Inspector P. J. C. Morin.

During recent years only black horses have been used on the Ride. In 1943 the Force established a breeding ranch at Fort Walsh in Saskatchewan. This was transferred to Pakenham, Ontario, in 1968. The horses raised for the Musical Ride are of no established breed, but derive from crossing thoroughbred stallions with selected grade-thoroughbred mares. The objective is to raise a horse of from 15.3 to 17 hands, weighing from 1,100 to 1,350 pounds. One mare raised by the Force, "Burmese," sired by the famous English race horse "Faux-Pas," was presented to Her Majesty the Queen in 1969. Burmese has since been ridden by Her Majesty at the annual Trooping of the Colour in London.

The Musical Ride today is performed by a troop of thirty-two men. Each tour is preceded by months of intensive training and rehearsal. The lances carried are of male bamboo, approximately eight feet in length, with a red-and-white pennon. The shabracks, or saddle cloths, are of royal blue and yellow, the regimental colours of the Force. On them appear the fused letters " **MP** " which have been the registered horse brand of the Force since 1887. The Ride performs a variety of intricate movements at the trot and the canter. Some of these are: "The Bridal Arch," "The Star," "The Wagon Wheel," "The Maze" and "The Dome." The final movement is "The Charge" at full gallop down the arena. With the sound of the trumpet the troop re-forms for the March Past and ceremonial salute to the guest of honour.

(Right) R.C.M.P. Musical Ride – the
Dome. (Far right) A member of the
Musical Ride. (Below) The R.C.M.P.
Band.

(Left) Lansdowne Park, Ottawa, 1920. The Musical Ride appeared for the first time in Eastern Canada in 1920. During the years that followed it became a familiar sight at the Central Canada Exhibition in Ottawa and the Canadian National Exhibition in Toronto.

The international reputation of the Musical Ride was firmly established after its first appearance in Madison Square Garden in November 1934.

(Above) It's not all glamour and romance.

In recent times the Musical Ride has usually been performed by a troop of thirty-two men. These are all volunteers. Some have never ridden before. They are transferred from regular police work and given a course in equitation before being assigned for a tour of duty with the Ride.

(Left) World's Fair, 1939. The Ride and the Band, foreground, appeared together at the New York World's Fair, June 1939.

Members of the Musical Ride performing at "N" Division, Ottawa, 1949.

Tentpegging with swords and lances has been a traditional pastime of mounted regiments for centuries. Requiring perfect timing and coordination of horse and rider, it is still performed from time to time by members of the R.C.M.P. Musical Ride.

The Metamorphosis of the Mounties

Wherever I went I found but one opinion – the force should be continued, that it would be a calamity to discontinue this magnificent force, which rendered such conspicuous service to Western Canada ever since it was organized in 1873.

N. W. Rowell (Durham)
Minister Responsible for the R.N.W.M.P.
House of Commons, May 12, 1919

I think it would have been a great deal better . . . had they disbanded the old Mounted Police and allowed them to retire with the credit they had already established for themselves.

W. H. White (Victoria, Alta.)
House of Commons, June 7, 1920

The other morning I saw ninety-five of these men, mounted, pass my house on Metcalfe Street (Ottawa). They are a fine body of men, but it occurred to me that they could be more usefully employed planting potatoes than riding around in red coats in Ottawa, Montreal, or any of our eastern cities.

F. S. Cahill (Pontiac)
House of Commons, June 7, 1920

I hope the minister will see the childishness of taking men from the plains of the west and sending them down to the breakers of the Atlantic. . . . I speak for 73,000 people in Cape Breton, and I can say that they will not appreciate any such intrusion. If the government sends the Mounted Police down there those men will not only be unappreciated but they will be regarded as intruders and trouble will ensue.

R. H. Butts (Cape Breton)
House of Commons, June 7, 1920

Our redcoat in the West is a great deal more respected than any Dominion policeman in plain clothes. As we have to maintain the Northwest Mounted Police why not combine the two forces and avoid duplicate expenses.

W. D. Cowan (Regina)
House of Commons, June 7, 1920

Speaking as a representative of Labour, I believe that there is no other organization that causes so much friction in our communities as the Northwest Mounted Police.

J. S. Woodsworth (Winnipeg North Centre)
House of Commons, April, 1922

By the outbreak of war in 1914 the Royal North-West Mounted Police had established a nation-wide reputation for the role it had played in the orderly development of western Canada. In so short a time it seemed the vast open plains had matured into peaceful and prosperous provinces. It was an achievement of which Canadians were proud. The Mounted Police, it was widely believed, had had a vital hand in the fulfilment of this great task. Already the Force's deeds and its heroes were becoming a part of the legend of the West, a source of adventure and romance for the novelist and the early producers of motion pictures. To many it was a visible symbol of the country's orderly progress, a distinctly Canadian institution in which Canadians could take pride.

As the war years passed, the question of the Force's future became a matter of increasing uncertainty. With no more frontiers to tame, what possible role was there left for a semimilitary mounted police force? True, the Arctic regions still lay largely wild and unorganized, but policing the North would require a small force of little more than one hundred men. Had the Mounted Police served its usefulness, or could it find a new role in postwar Canada? This was the problem which confronted the Government and the Commissioner in the turbulent years which immediately followed the Armistice of 1918.

In the debate on its future, many felt that like the frontier the Force should be allowed to pass away with its honour and glory intact, to become a proud memory in a closed chapter of the past. To others, who cherished its record, there was a strong feeling that somehow it must be preserved and a new role found. But what was this to be? Was it to be confined to the North, transformed in the aftermath of war into a regular military unit, or would it become the nucleus of a new federal police force? The answers to these questions were to be determined in large part by the conditions to be found in postwar Canada. The Mounted Police was to be cast in a new mould. It was to retain much of its honour and tradition, but the organization and duties were to be very different from those of the small force of men who had marched across the plains in 1874.

Wartime Duties

On June 28, 1914, a terrorist shot and killed the Archduke Franz Ferdinand, the heir to the Austrian Empire. The assassination, which went almost unnoticed in Canada, took place in Sarajevo, the capital of Bosnia, an Austrian province in the Balkans. Believing the murder to have been the work of Serbian nationalists, Austria declared war on Serbia on July 28. Frantic diplomatic negotiations followed, but one by one the great European powers were drawn into the con-

flict. On the morning of August 4, Germany violated Belgium's neutrality by invading Belgian territory. The British Foreign Secretary, Sir Edward Grey, promptly demanded Germany's withdrawal. When the British ultimatum expired at midnight, Canadians found themselves suddenly at war.

The Force was still very military in character and outlook, and the instinctive reaction of the members, at the outbreak of hostilities, was to volunteer for active service. Since native Canadians were not attracted to the Mounted Police, recent recruits had been largely British, often veterans of well-known Imperial cavalry regiments. By 1914 almost 80 per cent of the men in the Force came from one part or another of the British Isles. Patriotic feelings ran high. Many felt that their first duty was to defend the mother country. By 1915 the able-bodied among them would have been fighting in the mud of France. Much to their chagrin, however, the Government had other plans for the Mounted Police.

The great rush for land in the previous decade had brought almost two hundred thousand Austrian and German nationals to the provinces of Alberta and Saskatchewan. Following the declaration of war, most of these settlers became enemy aliens. In the first few months of hostilities, no one was certain how their attachment to the "old country" would cause them to react. In the still neutral United States, Ger-

man-Americans were openly sympathizing with the Fatherland's struggle.

Anxious to avoid internal discord, Ottawa decided that the enemy alien population of the prairies would have to be carefully watched. Within a few days of the commencement of hostilities, Parliament passed the *War Measures Act*, which gave the authorities special powers to ensure the internal security and defence of the country. These included provisions for the registration and detention of aliens, the censorship and control of the means of communication, and the arrest of anyone endeavouring to leave Canada to join the military forces of an opposing nation.

Under the circumstances, the Government decided that the Mounted Police would have to remain on the prairies. Just over fifty recruits were granted their discharge to rejoin their regiments in Britain. The remainder would have to curb their patriotic desire to fight, at least for the moment. In addition to continuing normal duties, the Force took on the task of maintaining close surveillance over the enemy alien population and enforcing the Government's emergency regulations. To carry out the work, its authorized strength was hurriedly increased by five hundred to a total of twelve hundred officers and men. By September 1914, Divisions had begun registering Austrian and German nationals and confiscating weapons in their possession.

The first car. The change from horse to mechanized transport began in 1915 with the purchase of a seven-passenger model 55 McLaughlin. It was used to carry prisoners from the guardroom at "Depot" Division to the Regina Jail. By 1920 the Force had acquired thirty-three motorcars and trucks, and twenty-eight motorcycles. Horses continued to be used for regular patrols in some areas, however, until the 1930s.

In the first anxious months of the war, a few loyal Canadians, zealous in their desire to help, saw, or thought they saw, espionage rings and saboteurs plotting behind the door of every German settler. By September 1915 the Force had examined over 2,300 cases, almost half in the Regina area, concerning the conduct of enemy aliens. Its investigation resulted in 396 aliens being interned and another 326 being placed on parole. Those interned were handed over to the military authorities for confinement in detention camps at Brandon and Lethbridge. To protect the region from civil disorder, a reserve force of 147 men and 5 officers was organized at Regina under Superintendent G. S. Worsley. It was held in readiness to be rushed to any trouble spot on the prairies, should a disturbance occur.

After a few months it became apparent that active support for Germany and Austria existed only among a very small minority of settlers. The great majority of those from central Europe, whatever their private opinions, were peacefully occupied establishing themselves in their new homeland. With the few troublemakers removed, Commissioner Perry was able to inform Ottawa confidently, by 1916, that there was no further danger of unrest from internal sources.

One area of continuing concern was the international boundary. Shortly after the war began, a system of mounted patrols was organized along the border from Lake of the Woods to the Rocky Mountains. In the early months of the war a few Germans were caught trying to reach the United States in order to return home and fight. The main threat to peace, however, came from south of the line. In 1916 Ottawa received reliable information from American police sources that pro-German elements in the United States were planning to raid Canadian territory and create unrest among the settlers of German and Austrian origin. The information was substantiated by the discovery of a secret dispatch from the German Foreign Office to the German Ambassador in Washington ordering the sabotage of the Canadian Pacific Railway.

Boundary Patrol, Boissevain, Manitoba, 1917. The fear of a border raid by pro-German elements from the United States in 1916 led to the hasty mechanization of patrols along the nine-hundred-mile boundary from Ontario to British Columbia. In May of that year cars were supplied to the posts at Assiniboia, Boissevain, Cardston, Coutts, Emerson, Lethbridge, Shaunavon and Weyburn.

It was alarming news. The nine hundred-mile boundary was difficult to secure. A border raid would embarrass the Canadian Government, and threaten the orderly conditions in the West. Sir Robert Borden, the Prime Minister, decided the Mounted Police would have to concentrate as far as possible its entire efforts upon safeguarding the frontier.

With the consent of the provincial authorities, the Force was hurriedly relieved of its provincial police responsibilities in Alberta, Saskatchewan and Manitoba. The system of border patrols was reorganized and made more efficient by the purchase of a number of motorcars and motorcycles. Fortunately, the danger lasted only a few months, and passed without incident. With the entry of the United States into the war in April, 1917, the border threat disappeared and with it an anxious period in the history of western Canada came to an end.

The End of Provincial Policing

By 1914 there were signs that the provincial authorities were no longer entirely satisfied with the contractual arrangement under which the Mounted Police carried out its duties in Alberta and Saskatchewan. In 1911 both provinces had renewed their contract with the federal Government for another five years. The following year the boundaries of Manitoba were extended northward, and under an agreement with that province the Force took over provincial police responsibilities in the new area, which was known as New Manitoba.

There was no change in the terms of the contract as far as Alberta and Saskatchewan were concerned. In return for the services of the Force, each province paid Ottawa seventy-five thousand dollars annually. Under the agreement the Mounted Police was required to enforce all criminal laws, administer provincial statutes and maintain common jails. The sum paid by the provinces did not meet the costs of these services. The deficit was taken up by the federal Government. In the years before the war the total annual expenditure for the Force rose to almost one million dollars.

The dissatisfaction in Regina and Edmonton was partly a result of the provinces' desire to break the remaining colonial ties with Ottawa, and gain greater control over the administration of justice. In the days of territorial government on the prairies, the Mounted Police had carried out its duties with little interference from the local authorities. In 1905 the constitutional responsibility for law and order passed to the new governments of Alberta and Saskatchewan. Although the Commissioner then became nominally responsible to the provincial attorneys general for the enforcement of criminal and provincial laws, there was in practice little change as far as the control of the Force was concerned. It remained a federal body and its direction and distribution were still to a large extent determined by Ottawa through its commanding officer.

Military Training Class, Regina 1917. In preparation for war service special classes were held at Regina in 1917 in cavalry field tactics and the use of military weapons.

In December 1913 Premier Scott of Saskatchewan informed Prime Minister Borden, the federal Minister in charge of the Force, that the province would not renew its contract for the Force's services when it expired, as Saskatchewan wanted more control over policing and intended to establish its own provincial force.

The desire for a change in the system of policing in the two provinces also resulted from the Force's own rather rigid view of its role in Alberta and Saskatchewan. The Force, as Commissioner Perry often pointed out, was a "Mounted Police," not a "Civil Police." Its task was the policing of the unsettled parts of

the provinces. Once areas became incorporated, its services were withdrawn and law enforcement was left to the new municipalities. It was encouraged in this policy by the federal Government which showed no desire to extend its duties or meet the cost of increased police services. The withdrawal of the Mounted Police from settled areas, however, left the provincial authorities without adequate means of enforcing provincial laws just at a time when the towns and villages were undergoing a rapid growth. To fill the vacuum, both Alberta and Saskatchewan organized additional policing agencies.

Perhaps the best example of the Force's failure to meet the changing needs of policing in the provinces was in regard to the enforcement of provincial liquor regulations. Prohibition in the 1880s had been a bitter experience for the Mounted Police, a lesson

Alberta's Farewell to the Royal Mounted
By Elizabeth Bailey Price

THE Royal North-West Mounted Police are no more! In answer to their numerous petitions, they have at last been accepted for war service in France—at a moment in the world's history when their weight and experience may turn the tide of battle.

On April 29th, they were tendered Alberta's official farewell at Calgary, and that day will go down in the Canadian histories of the future as an epoch ending date.

Only forty-four years before, in 1874, the Mounted Police arrived in Southern Alberta to be the guardians of law and order. On April 29th, 1918, their work done, their places taken by the less spectacular provincial police, the remnant of the world's greatest and most famous police force departed—not disbanded. They are bound for France on an even greater mission of establishing law and order than that which brought them west in '74.

Perhaps you will say that the above is not absolutely accurate; that the Royal North-West Mounted Police, as a body, still does exist, for its patrols still stretch over the frozen reaches of the north, along the mighty Peace and Mackenzie Rivers, through the Yukon. Also you may say that their departure from Calgary—"Fort Calgary" of the early days—is only an incident in an epoch-forming event. Again you may be right. But to the person born in the west, whose first recollections are the "Sun-dances" of the Blackfeet and the

The ranks divided as Mrs Macleod, widow of Col. Macleod, founder of the first mounted force in Alberta, proceeded to the platform. The men in the picturesque police uniforms are now on their way to France

by hostile Indians and whiskey smugglers.

What more fitting tribute could be paid to the success of the venture that prompted the organization of this force which made the west safe for habitation than that at the farewell at Calgary there should be, as the guard of honor, a troop of Sarcee Indians?

Headed by Chief Big Belly and minor chief Jim Skylark, mounted and dressed in full tribal regalia, the natives proudly escorted the last of the mounties to the Calgary City Hall, and thence to the

case, the gift of Calgary. Spe made by Mayor other officials.

But something had been overlooked. Chief Big Belly apparently had been slighted. A pleasing smile stole over his face when His Worship called him to the front of the platform. He, too, was given a cigarette case.

Major Fitz-Horrigan whose thirty years in the force marks him as a conspicuous man in any company, replied on behalf of the departing mounties. His clear voice rang forth:

"When the news flashed across the water that our army had its back against the wall and that more men were urgently required—although our little band would have preferred to go as a unit—they responded to that urgent message. We go as reinforcements to Canadian mounted troops in France. We would have all been there long ago but have been urged to stay. The Duke of Connaught, when here on his farewell tour, personally asked us to stay.

"There are Oxford and other university men in our number and the majority would have honored the King's commission in any branch of the service. We have volunteered to go overseas in any capacity, no matter what or where duty calls—to serve in the ranks."

From the City Hall they proceeded to the C. P. R. station. There the last of the famous red-coated riders of the plains boarded the transcontinental

in law enforcement never to be forgotten. Criticism had been heaped upon it from all sides, followed by a corresponding loss in public trust and confidence. There had been a great sigh of relief in 1892 when the prohibitory permit system had been replaced by licensed bars. Enforcing liquor laws was just the kind of "civil policing" from which Perry believed the Force should remain aloof. Their enforcement, he in-

formed Prime Minister Borden in 1916, undermined both efficiency and morale.

By 1914 prohibition had become a major social and political issue in Alberta and Saskatchewan. Spurred on by the Women's Christian Temperance Union and the Temperance and Moral Reform Society a new crusade had begun to "Banish-the-Bar" and rid the provinces of the corrupting influences of John Barleycorn.

The Canada Weekly of May 25, 1918, illustrates the widespread belief of the time that the end of provincial policing and the entry of the Force into the war marked the end of its history as a law enforcement body.

An Alberta Provincial Police motorcycle patrol. Bootlegging in the province became a serious problem for the police during Prohibition. The bootleggers were well organized and often armed.

Honour Guard of the Saskatchewan Provincial Police under Assistant Commissioner Tracey at Regina in 1922 for Lord Byng, the Governor General. The Saskatchewan Provincial Police originated with a small force of provincial constables organized about 1911 under Chief Constable C. A. Mahoney of the Attorney General's Department to enforce the Provincial Liquor Act and carry out certain other duties. It was hurriedly reorganized and expanded in order to relieve the Mounted Police of its provincial police responsibilities on January 1, 1917. Like the Alberta Provincial Police, its internal organization and administration were to a considerable extent influenced by the earlier force. The service dress of its members consisted of khaki breeches and tunic, brown boots or leggings, and a broad-brimmed felt hat with the left side distinctly fastened-up.

Once again the police found themselves caught in the struggle between the prohibitionists and their opponents. Whatever action they took was inevitably criticized by one party or the other. In 1915 the provincial government closed the bars in Saskatchewan. The same year the citizens of Alberta voted in a plebiscite 58,295 to 37,209 in favour of prohibition. Under the new regulations which followed, the police were left with the unpopular task of preventing bootlegging among the substantial segment of the population which was still determined to quench its thirst regardless of the law.

With the Mounted Police reluctant to enforce liquor regulations, particularly in urban areas, both provinces had by 1912 formed small forces of provincial constables. Their initial task was to administer liquor regulations.

Gradually, however, they took on other provincial police duties. In doing so they began to run into conflict with the Mounted Police over the exercise of their authority. Perry informed Ottawa of the growing friction in 1914, stating that the existence of two provincial police forces in each province resulted in a system of policing which would eventually become unworkable.

In the end it was the war conditions which hastened the curtailment of the Force's provincial police duties. Alberta and Saskatchewan agreed to renew their contracts in 1916, but only for one year. Before the year was up Ottawa had received the alarming news of a possible border raid by pro-German agitators in the United States. In October 1916 Borden decided that the Mounted Police must concentrate its efforts upon protecting the boundary. He instructed Perry to explain the serious situation to the provincial authorities and ask them to consent to an early termination of the agreements. On January 1, 1917, the Force was relieved of its provincial police duties in Saskatchewan and Manitoba by the Saskatchewan Provincial Police and the Manitoba Provincial Police. The transfer of responsibility to the Alberta Provincial Police was delayed until the following March 1. After more than forty years the role of the Mounted Police as the guardian of law and order on the western plains had come to an end.

The Development of a Federal Police Force: The Dominion Police

In 1868 an Act of Parliament, 31 Vic. Cap. 73, authorized the appointment of police constables under the control and direction of the federal Government. Shortly after, a small protective force was formed which became known as the Dominion Police. Its first duties consisted of the protection and supervision of Government buildings in Ottawa. In addition, it provided bodyguards for Government leaders and from time to time carried on secret service investigations. In the early days these were primarily concerned with the intrigues of Irish Fenians in Canada and the United States. By 1878 the force had a strength of seventeen men. From 1880 it was commanded by a Commissioner of Police who was responsible to the Minister of Justice.

Later it took over the guarding of the naval yards at Halifax and Esquimalt.

In the decade before the war, the duties of the Dominion Police were broadened to include investigations into counterfeiting, thefts from post offices, and the white slave traffic. Most important of all, however, was the organization under its control, in Ottawa, of a central repository for the storage of criminal records and fingerprints. The Fingerprint Bureau, as it became known, was the beginning of a national police service to aid police forces across Canada in the investigation of crime.

In Canada and abroad, the system of identifying criminals by means of fingerprint impressions was gradually becoming accepted. Law enforcement agencies throughout the country were encouraged to forward to Ottawa copies of the fingerprints of anyone charged with a criminal offence. At the

Dominion Policemen outside the Parliament Buildings in Ottawa, 1909. From 1868 to 1920 the Dominion Police were responsible for guarding the Parliament Buildings, Rideau Hall and other government-owned property in Canada's capital. The Dominion Policemen who performed these duties continued to carry them out after they were transferred to the R.C.M.P. in 1920. There was, in fact, little visible change when the new federal force took over. They adopted R.C.M.P. insignia, but the former Dominion Policemen continued to wear the dark blue uniform and helmet shown here until the early 1930s, at which time their uniforms were replaced by the familiar red tunic and breeches of the Mounted Police.

Fingerprint Bureau they were then indexed and filed for future reference. This system came into general use throughout the R.N.W.M.P. in 1911. With criminals becoming increasingly mobile, the Fingerprint Bureau enabled police forces in any part of the country to quickly identify known criminals.

Under wartime conditions the responsibilities and activities of the Dominion Police were expanded. As well as supervising the efforts of local police forces in enforcing the provisions of the War Measures Act, it coordinated the gathering of intelligence on subversive elements which posed a threat to the country's internal security. By the end of the war it had reached a strength of just over 150 men. This figure did not include about 30 special agents employed on secret service investigations. In 1917 a separate temporary body, also known as the Dominion Police, was organized by the Government to enforce the Military Services Act.

In spite of wartime expansion, the Dominion Police remained primarily a guard service for government-owned buildings. The enforcement of federal statutes and the surveillance of subversive organizations was still largely carried out by municipal and provincial police forces. As a federal force it did not maintain a network of police offices throughout Canada. In Ottawa an inspector and half a dozen constables conducted a very limited number of investigations of offences under the federal statutes. Another inspector and four constables staffed the Fingerprint Bureau.

Sir Arthur Percy Sherwood. As Commissioner of the Dominion Police, Sherwood encouraged Foster with his plans for establishing the fingerprint system in Canada. During World War I he was in charge of Canada's expanded secret service operations. His law enforcement career began in 1879 as Chief of the Ottawa City Police. In 1885 he was appointed Commissioner of the Dominion Police, a position he held until his retirement in 1919.

Although from time to time the Dominion Police hired special agents to carry out secret service operations, it relied for its security intelligence primarily upon the information forwarded to Ottawa by local police forces as well as by immigration and customs officials. The special agents frequently came from American detective agencies like Pinkerton's.

Postwar Reorganization of Federal Policing

As the war came to an end social and political divisions appeared in Canada which were to change fundamentally the earlier system of federal policing. In 1917 the Prime Minister decided that conscription for military service had become a necessity if the war was to be brought to a quick and successful conclusion. Compulsory service was a controversial issue. To avoid racial division, Borden invited all parties to form a coalition government. Opposed to compulsory military service, Sir Wilfrid Laurier, the Liberal leader, and his French-speaking supporters refused. The Prime Minister succeeded, however, in gaining the support of the Liberals outside Quebec, and in October 1917 the Union Government was formed of Conservatives and English speaking Liberals. In the new cabinet Borden retained the Prime Minister's office, but the Presidency of the Privy Council, the department responsible for the Mounted Police, passed to N. W. Rowell, the leader of the Ontario Liberals. Along with the split over conscription there appeared a growing agitation from within the labour movement (encouraged by the success of the Russian Revolution and the British Labour party), against unemployment, low wages and the lack of union rights.

The father of Canada's National Fingerprint Bureau, Inspector Edward Foster.
While guarding an exhibit at the St. Louis
World's Fair in 1904, Constable Edward
Foster of the Dominion Police met Detective J. K. Ferrier of New Scotland Yard
who had come to the United States to speak
on fingerprinting.

What Ferrier had to tell him about the
accuracy of fingerprints as a means of
identification had a profound effect on the
Canadian from Stittsville, Ontario. He
returned home determined to encourage the
adoption of the fingerprint system in
Canada. In spite of opposition and official
apathy, Foster's advocacy of the system
finally resulted in the establishment of the
Fingerprint Bureau. Promoted to the rank
of Inspector, he was responsible for the
organization and management of the new
service until his retirement from the
R.C.M.P. in 1932.

Dominion Police Fingerprint Bureau,
Ottawa, 1912. In 1906 the recently formed
Chief Constables' Association of Canada
appointed a committee to urge the federal
Government to establish a national bureau
for the storage of fingerprints or other
criminal records gathered by police forces
across the country under the Identification
of Criminals Act.

The fingerprint system was finally
sanctioned by Order-in-Council on July 21,
1908. Three years later photography was
also authorized as a means of identification.
When the Fingerprint Bureau opened in
1911 it was one of the first establishments
of its kind in the world. With a modest
accumulation of just over two thousand
records, it occupied offices on Wellington
Street in Ottawa facing the Parliament
Buildings. In 1920 its operation was taken
over by the Royal Canadian Mounted
Police.

With discontent and tension
mounting, the cabinet decided
towards the end of 1918 that
federal policing must be expanded
and strengthened to give the
Government more direct control
over secret service investigations
and to meet any possible break-
down in public order. In December
of that year an Order-in-Council
was approved dividing Canada,
for the purpose of federal policing,
into two parts. The western
provinces, including a small por-
tion of Ontario adjacent to Manitoba, were placed under the
jurisdiction of the R.N.W.M.P.
The Dominion Police, meanwhile,
was to confine its activities to the
eastern half of the country.

Some of the badges and buttons of the Dominion Police.

The Mounted Police was quite unprepared for the extension of its responsibilities. In April 1918 the Government had finally acceded to the men's long-standing desire to serve overseas. Authority was given for the Force to recruit for active service, and on May 12 officers and 726 N.C.O.'s and constables sailed for Europe to join the Canadian Cavalry Brigade. The recruits among them were used to reinforce the regiments already in the field, while the older members were organized in England into "A Squadron, R.N.W.M.P."

Drumheller Detachment, Alberta, 1919.

During the summer another opportunity for overseas service occurred as a result of the Government's decision to join the allied intervention in the Russian Civil War. In August a cavalry squadron of 6 officers and 184 men, later known as "B Squadron, R.N.W.-M.P.," was recruited for service with the Canadian Expeditionary Force to Siberia. By November the Force was reduced to those who were too old, medically unfit, or performing duties too important for them to be allowed to leave. This left a total of 303 men, many of these serving at isolated posts in the North. Eighty-seven detachments were closed in 1918, leaving 10 divisional posts and 26 detachments still in operation. More than half of these were located in the Yukon and Northwest Territories.

Under the Order-in-Council the new duties of the Force were defined as (1) the enforcement of federal laws, (2) the patrolling and protection of the international boundary, (3) the enforcement of all measures passed under the War Measures Act, (4) generally to aid and assist the civil powers in the preservation of law and order. The Order-in-Council also authorized that the Force be brought up to its full strength of twelve hundred men as soon as possible. Another provision ended the widespread belief that the Force would soon be disbanded. The Mounted Police's future, the order stated, was assured "as the basis of a Permanent Federal Police Force or as one of the Mounted Units in the Permanent Force of Canada."

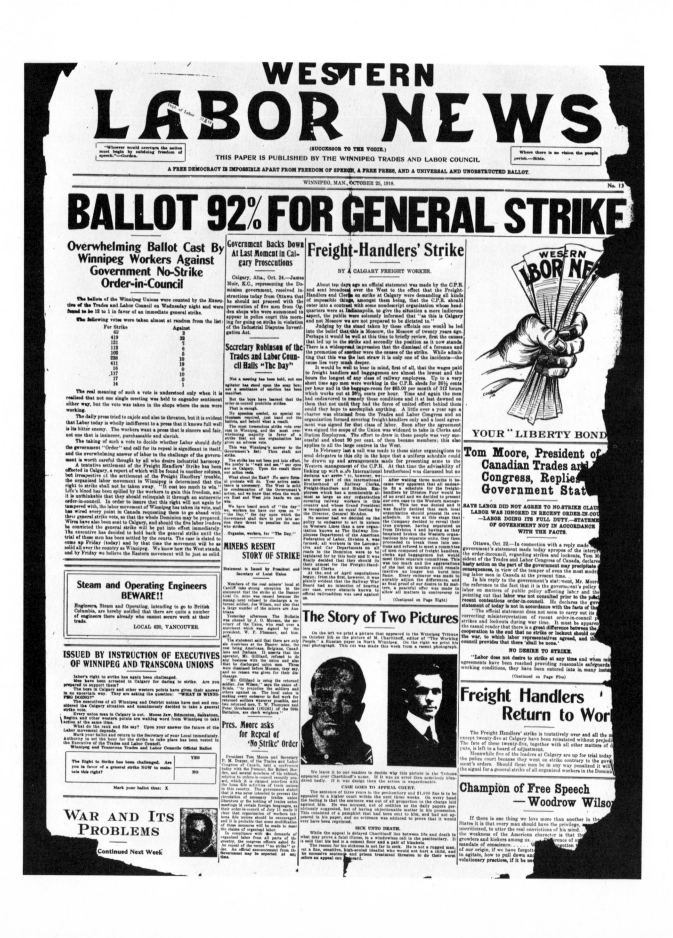

The Western Labour News *announces the decision of the members of the Winnipeg trade unions to call a general strike. The events which followed were to be the most significant in the history of the Force since its early days on the frontier. Controversy over the Government's action in transforming it into a federal police force was to last for many years.*

Debate centred on the secret service operations of the new force, and the plan to use it in aiding the civil authorities in maintaining order during industrial disputes. T. A. Crerar, the leader of the Progressive party, spoke for many Westerners when he called upon the Government to confine the duties of the Mounted Police to the North and leave the maintenance of law and order entirely to the provincial authorities. Mackenzie King, the Liberal leader, felt that in the event of disorder the civil powers should rely upon the militia. After his party took office in 1921, the reserve squadrons which had been organized to aid the civil authorities were reduced.

The most determined foe of the changes of 1920 was J. S. Woodsworth, the former Methodist minister who had been arrested as a strike leader in 1919. In 1921 he was elected to Parliament as the Independent Labour party member for Winnipeg North Centre. Woodsworth represented the views of a small minority of trade unionists and socialists who thought they saw in the new force the beginnings of a police state and a means by which the authorities would obstruct their movement for social justice and the rights of labour.

Newton Wesley Rowell 1867–1941. As the minister in charge of the Force from 1917 to 1920, Rowell was responsible for its reorganization as the Royal Canadian Mounted Police. Leader of the Ontario Liberals, he joined the Union Government of Sir Robert Borden in 1917. He was later Chief Justice of Ontario and Chairman of the Rowell-Sirois Commission.

An active recruiting campaign began early in 1919 to bring the Force up to strength. This was aided by a substantial raise in remuneration for all ranks, which showed the new importance the Government placed on the police. A constable's pay rose from $1.25 to $1.75 a day. Steps were taken to obtain the early release of the two overseas squadrons from military service. The men of "A Squadron" began arriving from Europe in March. By July 1919 both contingents had returned to police duties.

The extension of responsibilities necessitated a redistribution of the Force throughout western Canada. Some of the earliest divisional posts like Fort Macleod, Calgary and Battleford were reduced to detachments in the reorganization. Seven new divisional districts were created with their headquarters at Winnipeg, Regina, Prince Albert, Lethbridge, Edmonton, Vancouver and Dawson. Over seventy detachments were opened, from Fort William in Ontario to Port Alberni on Vancouver Island.

One aspect of the Force's new duties was the organization of a secret service throughout the western provinces to gather intelligence on subversive and seditious elements. Rowell was alarmed by the radical and revolutionary stance of some of the union leaders. The Government regarded the expansion of the secret service as vital. In February 1919 eighty thousand dollars was allocated for this purpose and the Force's undercover agents began the difficult job of infiltrating the One Big Union and other labour organizations who were suspected of planning to overthrow constituted authority.

Internal security was to be one of the most controversial of the new tasks assigned to the Mounted Police. To assist the Force in carrying out this work, Rowell laid down some important guidelines: the responsible leaders of organized labour, he informed Commissioner Perry, were opposed

Winnipeg General Strike. The strike in Winnipeg was the climax of the labour unrest of 1918/19. On Saturday, June 21, 1919, strikers assembled in front of the City Hall on Main Street to hold a parade. Earlier the Mayor had issued an order banning such demonstrations and a proclamation warning all those who took part that they did so at their own risk. As the demonstrators gathered the Riot Act was read.

To prevent the strikers from parading, two troops of Mounted Police rode north up Main Street, scattering the crowd to the sides of the road. As they returned south towards Portage Avenue (a), a few shots were fired at them and some of the crowd began to pelt them with bricks, slabs of concrete and bottles. Several of the men were injured, and three were pulled or knocked off their horses and set upon by the rioters.

The two troops regrouped and returned north. Believing that the three dismounted men would be killed, the order was given to draw revolvers. Turning left down William Street towards City Hall (b), a warning volley was fired over the heads of the gathering. When this failed to have effect, a second volley was fired low into the crowd which then began to disperse (c).

It was an ugly and tragic event which none regretted more than those members of the Force who took part in it. As policemen they believed that their primary objective should be the maintenance of the constituted order it was their sworn duty to uphold.

a

b

c

The Prince of Wales visits Regina. During his tour of Canada in 1919 the popular Prince of Wales, later King Edward VIII, visited the headquarters of the R.N.W.M.P. at Regina. He is shown here, centre, with Commissioner Perry on his left. The following year he became the first Honorary Commissioner of the Royal Canadian Mounted Police.

to Bolshevik propaganda, and were endeavouring to eradicate it from their organizations. The rank and file among the workers, he continued, who expressed approval for communist ideals did so without really understanding their true aim and character. Finally, there was a very small hard core, he believed, who had imbibed the doctrine of a class war and were committed to social and political revolution. It was this group alone that he singled out for investigation and prosecution whenever possible.

As strike followed strike in 1919, the federal authorities became increasingly concerned about the preservation of public order. Discontent centred on Winnipeg, where in May the Trades and Labour Council called a General Strike in sympathy with a local union that had been denied the right to bargain collectively. With the economic life of the city at a standstill, and sympathetic strikes breaking out across the country, the federal and provincial authorities decided to step in and bring the strike to an end. On June 17 several of the strike leaders were arrested. Four days later violence erupted on the downtown streets when two troops of Mounted Police attempted to break up an illegal parade. One civilian was killed in the ensuing melee, and about thirty persons, including sixteen Mounted Policemen, were injured.

From Sea to Sea: The Royal Canadian Mounted Police

The traumatic shock produced by the Winnipeg General Strike settled the future of the Royal North-West Mounted Police as Canada's federal police. One thing that troubled the authorities in Ottawa about the course of the strike was the sympathy for it among the city police in both Winnipeg and Vancouver. In Winnipeg the police commission had finally dismissed the city force, replacing it with volunteer special constables. Uppermost on Rowell's priorities was the need to maintain order and constituted authority. If local police forces could not be depended upon, a more reliable alternative must be found.

Usually in Canada, when public order appeared threatened, the municipal or provincial authorities called upon the militia to aid the civil powers. In 1919, however, the Government felt that the militia was not sufficiently reorganized, following the recent war, to continue this function. Instead it turned to the Mounted Police. In doing so it looked to its unique character as a semimilitary organization, whose discipline and traditions made it a dependable arm of authority. On July 14 an Order-in-Council increased its statutory strength to twenty-five hundred men. Shortly afterwards steps were taken to organize mounted troops at strategic locations across western Canada, where they were held in readiness

"Beyond the Law," by Franz Johnston, A.R.C.A., O.S.A. One of the original Group of Seven, Johnston based this scene upon the actual manhunt which took place near Fort MacMurray, Alberta, in 1915. When found by his pursuer, the fugitive-murderer had shot himself to avoid arrest.

to assist the civil authorities if required.

With the necessary steps taken to protect the rule of law, Ottawa turned to the task of re-organizing the federal police services. Commissioner Perry was one of the principal architects of the changes which followed. In August he was summoned to the capital for top-level discussions with Rowell and Borden. Following the meetings he was asked to submit his recommendations upon the future of federal policing. His subsequent proposals had two main provisions: (1) the absorption of the Dominion Police by the Royal North-West Mounted Police, (2) the extension of the jurisdiction of the Royal North-West Mounted Police throughout Canada as the sole federal police force.

The Commissioner's submission also recommended the establishment of four new divisions in eastern Canada, each with a reserve squadron of 160 men to aid the civil authorities in the event of disorder; the transfer of the Force's headquarters from Regina to Ottawa; and the organization of an expanded secret service within the new body, removing the dependence upon local police forces and American detective agencies for maintaining internal security.

In November 1919 Parliament amended the R.N.W.M.P. Act to incorporate Perry's recommendations. The reorganization would give Canada a strong centralized federal police force, placing the responsibility for federal law enforcement almost entirely in the hands of one well-organized and respected body. The new arrangement contrasted with the system of federal law enforcement developing in the United States. In Washington the responsibility for administering laws under the jurisdiction of the Federal Government was divided among separate agencies like the Federal Bureau of Investigation and the United States Secret Service who were under the control of individual Government departments.

One proposal that the Government did not accept was the Commissioner's plea that the title of the Force should remain unchanged. Instead, it was decided to call the new body the Royal Canadian Mounted Police, preserving something of the past, but recognizing its new status. When the legislative changes came into effect by Order-in-Council on February 1, 1920, the old R.N.W.M.P. ceased to exist. Shortly after, Perry and his staff left the spacious and orderly surroundings of the Regina Barracks for the bureaucratic labyrinth of Ottawa and the cramped offices of their new headquarters above a hardware store in the city's business district. The move marked

"N" Division summer camp beside the Ottawa River at Rockcliffe, 1921. In March 1920 four troops under Inspector R. L. Cadiz arrived in Ottawa from Regina to establish a new command which was designated "N" Division. Its first home was the exhibition buildings at Lansdowne Park. In 1925 it moved into permanent quarters on the site of the old rifle ranges at Rockcliffe, where it had earlier camped during the summer months.

the end of an era in the Force's history. The old association with western Canada was left behind. In meeting the challenge of the future, however, the traditions of its frontier heritage were to be a vital asset.

Pageantry and Ceremony

(Above) H.M. Queen Elizabeth II, the Honorary Commissioner of the Force, attending celebrations on Parliament Hill, Ottawa, on July 1, 1967, to mark Canada's Centenary.

(Right) A member of the R.C.M.P. Detail on duty outside the Canadian Pavilion at Expo '70 in Osaka, Japan.

(Below) His Excellency the Right Honourable Roland Michener, C.C., C.D., Governor General of Canada, leaves Government House, Ottawa, with a mounted escort of the R.C.M.P.

SPORTS ON THE OCCASION OF THE VISIT OF THEIR EXCELLENCIES THE GOVERNOR
GENERAL AND COUNTESS ABERDEEN, CALGARY OCT. 12, 1894.

The ceremonial appearance of the Mounted Police began in the small settlements of Western Canada. On Royal Tours, state occasions and as Canada's representatives overseas, they have since become a widely recognized component of the ritual life of the country.

N.W.M.P. escort for the Governor General, the Earl of Aberdeen.

The Evolution of the Modern Force

The primary weakness of law enforcement in the Dominion is the multiplicity of individual and independent police departments. . . . In every little city and town, and, I suppose, in large ones too, there are at least four separate police authorities, all under different control, operating with different machinery, without any real reference to each other. There are the city or town police, under the control of the council or Police Commission, the county constabulary, under the Sheriff, the Provincial Police operating from the Attorney General's Department of their particular provinces, and the Royal Canadian Mounted Police.

Chief Constable Crabb,
Welland Police Department,
Addressing the annual meeting
of the Chief Constables'
Association of Canada,
July 1924.

The decades which separated the two world wars were to be the most influential years in the development of the Royal Canadian Mounted Police as it is today. The period was a time of rapid social and technological change which profoundly affected the methods of law enforcement throughout Canada. With the continued urbanization of the population, municipal police forces were expanded. As highways began to thread their way across the land, new provincial forces were established and the existing ones reorganized to meet the increasing mobility of the community.

A greater degree of cooperation between law enforcement agencies at home and abroad became a necessity to combat organized crime. Radio, the telephone and the motor car became essential elements in police operations; ballistics, forensic science, photography, fingerprinting, a normal and accepted part of criminal investigation. In addition, the responsibilities of the police grew, as new laws were enacted at every level of government to meet the needs of an increasingly complex society. By the outbreak of war in 1939 law enforcement in Canada had attained a degree of organization, specialized skill and technical application that was almost unknown twenty years before.

The expansion of police forces took place at all three levels of government – federal, provincial and municipal The result was often an overlapping of responsibility and a duplication of effort by individual forces which tended to lower the effectiveness of the system of law enforcement as a whole. The poorer provinces and the smaller municipalities were increasingly incapable of providing the equipment, training and scientific resources necessary for an efficient police force. The period witnessed, therefore, the start of a movement in many areas to centralize or amalgamate police services.

In two decades these developments were to alter radically the character of the R.C.M.P. In 1920 it was just a small federal force with a special role on Canada's northern frontier. Eight years later it returned to provincial policing under a contract with the government of Saskatchewan. In 1932 similar agreements were reached with all of the remaining provinces except Ontario, Quebec and British Columbia. During the same year the Force took over the responsibilities of the Preventive Service of the Department of National Revenue. In 1935 it began municipal police work for the first time in the town of Flin Flon, Manitoba. No less significant was the development under its administration of a system of national police services to assist law enforcement agencies throughout the country. By 1939 the modern role of the R.C.M.P. in Canada had fully evolved. Although this role would continue to develop in the years ahead, it would undergo little fundamental change.

Federal Policing

While patrols of the R.C.M.P. were consolidating the Dominion's authority in the Arctic, the main body of the Force was engaged in a wide variety of duties throughout the country as Canada's federal police. These included the enforcement of federal statutes and the provision of assistance to a number of federal Government departments. Members of the force soon found themselves supervising race track betting, inspecting explosives, protecting migratory birds, guarding post offices and escorting train loads of harvesters to the prairies. A small amount of criminal code work was carried out where the Dominion Government was the aggrieved party, or the offence took place on federal property. As the federal force, however, it escaped the responsibility of enforcing the unpopular prohibitory liquor laws which were in force in most provinces, and which did so much to undermine public confidence in the police at this time.

Commissioner Cortlandt Starnes. Born in Montreal in 1864, Starnes through his mother's family became the first Commissioner of French Canadian ancestry. Upon the outbreak of the rebellion in 1885, he went west as a lieutenant in the 65th Mount Royal Rifles. The following year he was appointed an inspector in the N.W.M.P. Starnes took over the command of the Force on April 1, 1923, upon the retirement of Commissioner Perry. As Commissioner he played an influential part in the negotiations which led to the R.C.M.P.'s assuming provincial police duties in Saskatchewan in 1928. Upon retirement in 1931, he had completed over forty-five years of service, one of the longest periods on record.

One important task from which it was shortly relieved, at least for the time being, was that of assisting provincial authorities in maintaining order during industrial disputes. In 1921 the Force was called out to support local authorities in policing a number of strikes, including serious ones at Thorold, Ontario, and Saint John, New Brunswick. Following the Liberal victory in the federal election of that year, this policy was changed. The new Prime Minister, W. L. Mackenzie King, believed that local authorities should return to the practice of calling upon the militia for assistance. The change was welcomed by the R.C.M.P. Although it was to return to this task in the thirties under the Conservatives, it brought the Force a great deal of criticism and established a legacy of mistrust which has lasted over the years. The change enabled the Government to reduce its strength the following year by over 25 per cent, down to approximately twelve hundred men. This resulted in the abolition or reduction of the mounted squadrons at Brandon, Fort Macleod and Ottawa.

A number of requests for assistance from provincial authorities at this time clearly showed the change in criminal activity brought about by the automobile and the need for a reorganization of the system of policing in many parts of the country. As an example, in 1921 a gang of armed motorcar bandits began terrorizing the counties of Colchester and Pictou in Nova Scotia, somewhat in the manner of the movie *Bonnie and Clyde*. Using a car, they travelled back and forth across the countryside at night holding up lonely farms and appearing at one town after another to rob local stores and warehouses. Apprehending them seemed to be beyond the ability of the local town forces with their limited responsibility and jurisdiction. Lacking a provincial force, the Nova Scotia authorities telegraphed the Commissioner in Ottawa for assistance. With a police car, Sergeant Lucas and Constable Fahie set out on the trail of the elusive criminals. Gathering evidence as they went, the two men soon located the bandits' hideout and with the help of the Truro police brought their unlawful activities to an end.

The greater part of the Force's manpower during the twenties was engaged in the enforcement of federal statutes. The number of these gradually increased, and the following is just a partial list of those involved:

Air Board Act
Animal Contagious Diseases Act
Bank Act
Canada Shipping Act
Customs Act
Dominion Lands Act
Explosives Act
Food and Drug Act
Fugitive Offenders Act
Immigration Act
Indian Act
Inland Revenue Act
Leprosy Act
Militia Act
Opium and Narcotic Drug Act
Post Office Act
Radiotelegraph Act
Railway Act

While the Force was responsible for enforcing all federal laws, the circumstances of the time resulted in a special concentration on three particular statutes. These were the Customs Act, the Inland Revenue Act and the Opium and

Superintendent John Leopold. In keeping with Government policy, the primary target of the Force's security operations in the twenties and thirties was the investigation of the hard core of Communists who were committed to a revolutionary change in the political, economic and social life of the country. In 1931 the Government of Ontario decided to take legal action against the Communist party of Canada under Section 98 of the Criminal Code, a contentious measure which prohibited seditious conspiracy and unlawful associations. On August 11 that year a combined force of the R.C.M.P., Ontario Provincial Police and Toronto City Police raided a number of houses in Toronto and arrested several party officials. Eight of these, including the party's General Secretary, Tim Buck, were later convicted and sentenced to terms of imprisonment. The Government's action severely disrupted Communist activities in Canada for several years.

The key witness for the Crown was John Leopold, then a sergeant. Leopold's evidence revealed a remarkable story of undercover investigation. Posing as a house painter named Jack Esselwein he had successfully infiltrated the party's organization for over seven years. In Regina he had helped to organize a Communist front, the Worker's party. In 1927 party officials transferred him to Toronto. There he had plotted and planned with the very men who now faced him in the dock. In 1928 a chance incident exposed his real identity and he was expelled from the party. As the story of his exploits was brought before the court, the public became aware for the first time of the extent and capability of the Force's security operations.

An illicit still discovered in swampy land near Toronto. The unlawful distillation of alcohol under the Excise Act was a common offence in Canada during the prohibition years.

Narcotic Drug Act. With prohibition in one form or another in effect in most provinces, the smuggling of liquor and its illegal distillation were widespread. The elimination of smuggling was next to impossible considering the manpower available and the extent of the area to be policed. This included the lonely bays and inlets along the Atlantic and Pacific coasts, the St. Lawrence, the Great Lakes and the long land frontier with the United States. Enforcement was also complicated by the degree to which the smugglers were organized, often with international connections, and the extent of corruption within the federal Department of Customs.

One of the most sensational smuggling cases of the period took place near La Have, Nova Scotia, on the night of July 3, 1923, when Detective Sergeant J. Blakeney, Corporal W. A. Coldwell and Constable Fahie put out to sea in a small motorboat to intercept the schooner *Veda M. McKeown*. Earlier investigation had revealed that the ship carried a large supply of contraband liquor which was to be turned over on a prearranged signal to a party of bootleggers. Flashing the expected signal, the three policemen, dressed in plain clothes, succeeded in impersonating the anticipated buyers. Blakeney steered the motorboat alongside the schooner and boldly climbed aboard to haggle with the captain over the price of the cargo.

As the smugglers began to unload the ten-gallon kegs of rum over the side, Blakeney revealed his true identity. Much to the astonishment of the crew, the policeman announced his intention of seizing the ship and arresting the nine men aboard. For a few moments the crew were silent, weighing their chances of overpowering the three policemen. Blakeney stood his ground, however, and next day the ship was brought safely into port under his orders. In its hold were 1700 gallons of rum, 190 cases of Scotch whisky and 35 cases of gin.

Nowhere was the lack of unity among the police forces more apparent in the twenties than in the enforcement of the federal drug laws. The drug trade in Canada was first brought to the public's attention by a young deputy minister of labour from Ottawa, W. L. Mackenzie King. Sent to Vancouver in 1907 to investigate race riots, King discovered an extensive opium trade which grossed over $600,000 annually. His report "On the Need for the Suppression of the Opium Trade in Canada" became the basis of the Opium and Narcotic Drug Act of 1908. At first the Act prohibited only the importation and sale of opium. In 1911 it was amended to prohibit also cocaine and morphine. In addition, for the first time, the simple possession of the proscribed drugs was made an offence.

At first there was little public concern about the spread of these drugs, probably because in the beginning their use was largely confined to persons of Chinese origin. The penalties under the Act were light considering the extent of the trade. The maximum sentence provided was one year in prison or a fine of one thousand dollars. The law made no distinction between the large trafficker and the individual addict.

Following World War I public concern over the illegal use of drugs began to grow. Reports showed that the use of morphine and cocaine (and later heroin) among Canadians was rapidly increasing. The extent of the drug trade, its association with other forms of crime and the plight of the addicts was dramatically brought to the attention of the public in 1921 in a series of articles in *Maclean's* by Judge Emily Murphy. Gradually a movement for the suppression of the drug traffic gained momentum. Nevertheless, it was some time before this new concern was reflected in changes in the law and the attitudes of the courts. In the meantime, the police remained seriously handicapped in combatting a highly organized and lucrative criminal activity.

The main centres of drug use were Vancouver and Montreal. By 1921 the R.C.M.P. had established a drug squad in both cities. They were very small, less than half a dozen men working full time in each. Under the circumstances, the Commissioner soon decided to concentrate the Force's efforts against the leaders of the large drug rings, leaving the small pushers and addicts to the local police. The police methods were based upon the employment of paid informers and the use of undercover men who infiltrated the gangs and trapped them by acting as agents provocateurs. This latter practice was criticized by J. S. Woodsworth and other civil libertarians, but upheld by the courts as a justifiable means of police investigation.

An opium den on the coast of British Columbia, 1921. In 1922 the Vancouver Drug Squad estimated that over a hundred thousand ounces of opium and almost four thousand ounces of morphine and cocaine were being illegally used in the Vancouver area every month. Most of these drugs were smuggled into Canada from the Far East. Their value provided the drug rings with an income of over a million dollars annually. The wholesale price of opium was thirty to forty dollars a pound. By the time it reached the addict the price had more than trebled.

Although there were some outstanding successes, the Force's efforts had little effect at first upon the traffic as a whole. In Vancouver a few customs officers cooperated with the criminals, making it difficult to detect the drugs as they entered the country. The courts handed out light sentences which had no deterrent effect upon the ringleaders. In a typical case, a man was arrested in the act of smuggling a quantity of cocaine valued at over $200,000 on the open market. He pleaded guilty and was fined $500.

Investigations were also hindered by local police forces which acted independently and showed no desire to cooperate with the R.C.M.P. To make matters worse, the provincial authorities regarded the federal policemen as intruders in their own area of responsibility. Matters came to a head in 1923 when customs officers charged two members of the Force with trafficking in drugs. An inquiry completely exonerated them, but the resulting publicity and exposure paralyzed the Force's drug operations in Vancouver for more than two years.

In Montreal the drug squad was able to establish a working relationship with the local police forces but, while there was less conflict than on the West Coast, there was just as much frustration.

Although convictions were obtained against some of the ringleaders in the traffic, the fines levied upon them were quickly paid and they were soon back in business. One notable case in Montreal exposed the extent to which the drug rings were organized as well as the international scope of their activities. It all began with a luncheon appointment in the dining room of the Ritz Carlton Hotel one day in August 1923. Posing as a rich American, Sergeant C. C. Brown persuaded Don Miguel Maluquer y Salvador, the Spanish Consul in Montreal, who was already suspected of trafficking, to help him purchase a large supply of drugs from overseas and see that it passed through the customs house without any difficulty. To complete the deal, Brown had to go to Spain to arrange with the Consul's contacts for a shipment of alcohol (drugs were not available). When the booze arrived in Montreal, the wily policeman was able to trap the gang by using marked money. Don Miguel and his leading henchman, as well as the dishonest customs officials, were all successfully prosecuted.

By 1925 conditions began to swing in favour of the police. As the use of drugs appeared to grow, even among teen-agers, the call for stronger measures gradually gained public acceptance. The Act was amended to provide for heavier penalties and the courts moved to deter the convicted traffickers with stiffer sentences. The new

mood was brought sharply home to the criminal element in 1927 in the case of a wealthy Vancouver businessman named Lim Jim, a leading figure in the city's drug trade for many years. The Force finally secured sufficient evidence to press charges against him. Found guilty, he was sentenced to four years. The Crown appealed the sentence on the grounds that it was not severe enough. The higher court agreed and increased it to seven years, a long sentence by earlier standards, but a sign of what was to come.

With the courts behind them and better cooperation established with local police forces and customs officials (corruption in the Customs Department had earlier been the subject of a Royal Commission), the antinarcotics campaign began to have a noticeable effect in the thirties. A number of large rings were broken and their organizers given long prison sentences. The nature of the drug trade, meanwhile, underwent considerable change. The use of opium decreased. Its prominence in the trade was taken over by morphine and heroin. The association of drugs with one ethnic group also began to disappear, as traffickers and addicts were now largely Canadians of diverse European descent. Nevertheless, by 1935 the drug trade as a whole appears to have suffered a significant decline. At the outbreak of war four years later the illegal use of drugs in Canada was probably at its lowest point in two decades.

Much more important for the future of law enforcement in the country was the Force's return to provincial policing. In drafting the British North America Act the Fathers of Confederation had given little thought to the problem of policing twentieth century Canada. Under the constitution the criminal laws were legislated by the Dominion Government, but their enforcement as well as the administration of the system of justice was delegated to the provinces. Both federal and provincial governments meanwhile were empowered to initiate further legislation in the areas that were their responsibility. In addition the provinces delegated legislative powers to the municipalities within their jurisdiction. As each level of government assumed a law enforcement role, a tri-level system of policing developed.

The resulting lack of unity in law enforcement had not been a serious problem in the nineteenth century while the provinces remained relatively isolated and the urban communities small. After World War I the deficiencies in the system became readily apparent. Its critics drew attention to the overlapping of responsibility and the lack of cooperation between the independent police bodies. Noting that the activities of criminals were not confined by municipal or provincial boundaries, they called for a more unified and economical system of policing.

A Provincial and Municipal Force

The enlargement of the federal responsibilities of the Force in 1920 was more apparent than real. The creation of the R.C.M.P. had stemmed from the Government's concern over public order, internal security and the need for a Canadian presence in the Arctic. The new force was not intended to take over all federal law enforcement. This was still a duty of local police forces who continued to carry out an important and substantial part of the work. As a federal law enforcement body, the R.C.M.P. was at first little more than a token force. Throughout the twenties,

James Garfield (Jimmy) Gardiner. As Premier of Saskatchewan, Gardiner initiated the discussions which led to the policing of his province by the R.C.M.P. under a federal-provincial contract. The premier's economic proposals for sharing the cost of policing were eventually adopted by every province except Ontario and Quebec.

for example, its strength in the entire Province of Quebec never exceeded forty men. Nevertheless, a unified and systematic approach to federal policing on a nation-wide scale was taking place for the first time.

New Brunswick Provincial Policemen at Fredericton, 1929. Most of these men were later absorbed into the R.C.M.P. when that force took over the policing of New Brunswick in 1932. Among them is L. H. Nicholson who was Commissioner of the R.C.M.P. from 1951 to 1959.

At one time or another every province in Canada had its own provincial force. In some cases these started merely as small groups of constables under a magistrate or commissioner of police, with responsibility for enforcing certain provincial regulations, and they were later reorganized into permanent uniformed bodies. Of the following list only three are still in existence: the Newfoundland Constabulary, the Ontario Provincial Police and the Quebec Provincial Police. The remainder were absorbed by the R.C.M.P. when it took over the policing of their provinces:

Alberta Provincial Police	1912–1932
British Columbia Provincial Police	1858–1950
Manitoba Provincial Police	1871–1932
New Brunswick Provincial Police	1927–1932
Newfoundland Constabulary	1871–
Newfoundland Rangers	1935–1950
Nova Scotia Provincial Police	1930–1932
Ontario Provincial Police	1909–
Prince Edward Island Provincial Police	1930–1932
Quebec Provincial Police	1871–
Saskatchewan Provincial Police	1911–1928

The first to seek a change in the existing order was the Liberal government of Saskatchewan led by Premier James G. Gardiner. Writing to the Minister of Justice, Ernest Lapointe, in November 1926, Gardiner outlined the "impossible situation" which was developing in regard to the policing of the Province.

> *We have a condition which developed during the war, which leaves us with virtually three police forces, the R.C.M.P., the Provincial Police and the Municipal Police. The result is that there is overlapping, local friction, disagreement between different organizations, the appearance of too many uniformed men at every public gathering, (giving the appearance of a military occupation) and cost which, if continued, will develop a first class political issue.*

The Western leader sought a meeting with the federal minister to try and find an answer to the problems of policing the province. As the basis for discussion he suggested three possible solutions.

> *Firstly: A return to the arrangement previous to 1917 whereby we paid a certain sum to have the province policed by the R.C.M.P.*
>
> *Secondly: An arrangement whereby the Province be policed by the province under agreement whereby Federal work is paid for by the Federal Government.*
>
> *Thirdly: An arrangement whereby the R.C.M.P. confine their activities to the U.S. boundary and the north land, while the greater part of the settled portion of the province is policed by the Provincial Force.*

The Premier's request resulted in a series of meetings between provincial and federal officials over the next sixteen months. Commissioner Starnes, who played a leading role in the negotiations, agreed with the need for reorganizing the system. He informed Lapointe that a new arrangement could lead to greater efficiency at less cost to both parties. He was, nevertheless, startled by Gardiner's last two recommendations which would raise once again the question of the future of the Force. The Prairie premier hoped to obtain an agreement to share the cost of law enforcement based upon his second proposal. Lapointe and Starnes, however, stuck firmly to the position that any new arrangement must be negotiated upon his first proposition, that the R.C.M.P. should take over the duties of the provincial police. In the end the provincial authorities reluctantly agreed.

More than 150 members of the Alberta Provincial Police were absorbed into the R.C.M.P. when the latter took over the policing of the Province of Alberta on April 1, 1932.

Under the terms of the federal-provincial contract which resulted, the Royal Canadian Mounted Police took over the duties of the Saskatchewan Provincial Police on June 1, 1928.

Although under the seven-year agreement it would come under the direction of the provincial attorney general as far as the administration of justice was concerned, the Force would remain a federal one under the control of the Dominion Government. The terms called for the R.C.M.P. to maintain a minimum of 220 men in the Province and to enforce all provincial statutes, including the liquor laws, in addition to its federal responsibilities. It was further obliged to absorb into its ranks as many members of the disbanded provincial force as possible.

In return for these services, the Saskatchewan government agreed to pay Ottawa $175,000 annually, plus the costs of transporting and maintaining prisoners. This represented a saving of approximately 50 per cent of its former annual expenditure for its own force of about 140 men. The federal Government on the other hand soon discovered that it had seriously underestimated the costs of the provincial police work. When the province refused to budge from the terms of the contract, it had to meet the deficit from federal funds.

The agreement with Saskatchewan was a milestone in the history of law enforcement in Canada. Economic considerations were uppermost in the decision of the Saskatchewan government, but it is important to realize that the return of the Force to provincial policing might not have been possible without the confidence which

the people of the province had for it as a result of its earlier association with the territory. The Force's frontier past was still a vital influence in its modern evolution. As an example of cooperation between the federal and provincial governments, the contract was to be a lasting and highly successful venture. During the economic strain of the Depression in 1932, it became the model upon which similar agreements were reached with the provinces of Alberta, Manitoba, Nova Scotia, New Brunswick and Prince Edward Island.

The provincial contracts paved the way for the Force's entry into municipal policing. During the early thirties Headquarters received requests from a number of small towns seeking to have their community policed by the R.C.M.P. Constitutionally, this was not possible without a tri-level agreement between the municipal authorities, the provincial government and Ottawa. The first town to be policed under such an agreement was Flin Flon, Manitoba, on April 1, 1935. The five-year contract which was drawn up was based on those reached earlier with the provinces. In return for the three men who would police the community, the town agreed to pay $3000 annually.

By 1939 the Force's future role in provincial and municipal policing had been clearly defined. Only British Columbia, Ontario and Quebec remained outside the cooperative system for policing the provinces. The West Coast province would enter later. As to the other two, they had remained aloof from the movement to unify law enforcement under a federally controlled police force. Ontario had its own well-organized provincial force, and seemed unconcerned with the economic advantages to be gained. In Quebec the prewar resurgence of nationalism and the province's historic concern for preserving its own cultural identity left little possibility of a federal force ever carrying out provincial police duties in French Canada.

The extent of the Force's provincial police work, meanwhile, set the limits of its future municipal duties. Although towns in Ontario and Quebec indicated an interest in being policed by the R.C.M.P., the Government soon established a policy of restricting municipal contracts to those provinces where it was already the provincial force. In one notable exception, in 1942, the R.C.M.P. agreed to police the city of Hull, Quebec, in the hope that it might eventually take over law enforcement in the entire capital region. The Hull officials, however, withdrew from the negotiations at the last moment.

The Edmonton Journal of February 18, 1932, reports the final violent episode in the hunt for Albert Johnson. The case of the "Mad Trapper," as it was soon tagged by the press, was not particularly unusual, but it became sensational news in the first weeks of 1932. Newspapers in Canada and the United States carried daily accounts of its progress. Millions more followed the latest developments over the new medium of radio. The apparent drama and adventure on the continent's last frontier captured the public's imagination. Interest in the case has continued over the years as Johnson's real identity has never been satisfactorily explained. From the Force's point of view, the incident showed the need for aircraft and improved means of communication in the North.

National Police Services

In 1933 the R.C.M.P. completed sixty years of service. With the country caught in the midst of a depression, the Government decided against any formal celebrations to commemorate its Diamond Jubilee. The year was marked, nevertheless, by the appearance of two lasting features of the modern force. The first of these was the establishment at "Depot" Division in Regina of a museum to preserve and display its history and traditions. The second was the publication in July of that year of the first issue of the *Royal Canadian Mounted Police Quarterly.* Two years earlier Commissioner Starnes had retired. He was replaced by the man who was to be primarily responsible for forging the modern character and organization of the Force, Major General James Howden MacBrien.

Cornered By Pursuers, Wounded and Fighting To Last, Johnson Slain

Fugitive, in Last Desperate Stand, Badly Wounds Staff Sergeant E. F. Hersey—Rushed to Aklavik by Aeroplane—May Be Brought to Edmonton

TRAIL'S END FOR ARCTIC SLAYER COMES IN BATTLE NEAR YUKON BORDER

Bullet From Johnson's Rifle Shoots Radio Man in Knee, Chest and Elbow—Aeroplane Drones Overhead as Struggle Rages

Trail's end for Albert Johnson, elusive Arctic slayer, came Wednesday.

Cornered on the Eagle river, east of LaPierre House in the Yukon, Johnson, who was wanted for the slaying of one mountie and the wounding of another, dropped as a hail of lead from a police posse was pumped into his body.

Staff Sgt. Hersey

Before he died, however, he shot and critically wounded Staff Sergeant E. F. Hersey of the Royal Canadian Signals, Aklavik radio station. Hersey was rushed back by aeroplane to Aklavik and Capt. W. R. "Wop" May is standing by there until Dr. J. A. Urquhart decides if it is necessary to rush him over the 1,700-mile air route to Edmonton to get a bullet extracted from his chest.

The secret of Johnson's true identity died with him, and it may never be possible to clear up the mystery of who he was or where he came from.

Pictures purporting to be of him were published in several papers, including an Edmonton daily, but they have turned out to be of a respected resident of Princeton, B.C. No pictures of him exist, as far as is known at the present time.

Johnson's death came in a spectacular battle and he went down fighting.

Staff Sergeant Hersey and Trapper Noel Verville were in charge of the leading team of a posse following his trail. Suddenly they saw

Johnson Case Story Is Told Day to Day

Following is the story of the Albert Johnson case, told chronologically:

December 26, 1931.—Constable A. W. King visits Johnson's cabin and refused admittance. He went to the place as a result of complaints made by Indians that the man was pilfering their trap-lines.

December 31, 1931.—Constable King returned with Constable R. G. McDowell and King shot in the chest by Johnson.

January 10, 1932.—Second patrol in 15-hour gun battle fails to get Johnson out of his fortress.

January 19, 1932—Johnson gone when third patrol reaches cabin.

January 30, 1932 — Constable E. Millen killed by Johnson when fourth patrol finds him in second barricade.

February 3, 1932. — Capt. W. R. "Wop" May takes off for Aklavik with tear bombs, Constable W. S. Carter and more ammunition.

February 7 to 17, 1932— Capt. May makes several trips between Aklavik and posse.

February 17, 1932 — Posse comes on Johnson and kills him. Staff Sergeant E. F. Hersey wounded in battle.

Of lasting importance for the future was the expansion under the new commissioner's vigorous leadership of the Force's role as a national repository of criminal intelligence. The Fingerprint Section had grown by leaps and bounds during the twenties. With the help of other police departments it had by 1935 established the most extensive collection of fingerprints in the country. Meanwhile, regular cooperation with regard to the identifying of fingerprints had been established with the F.B.I. in Washington and other identification bureaus overseas. In 1934 the Criminal Code was amended to require the registration of all pistols and revolvers. As a result, on January 1, 1935, a Firearms Section was established at Headquarters as a central registry for licensed weapons.

Equipment seized at the hideout of a Vancouver counterfeiting ring in 1935. It was easier to pass counterfeit notes when chartered banks still issued their own currency and a wide variety of bills were in circulation. In this case five thousand good quality ten-dollar Bank of Montreal counterfeit notes were found ready for distribution to the Vancouver underworld.

Two top police reformers of the thirties, Commissioner Sir James H. MacBrien, left, and J. Edgar Hoover, Director of the United States Federal Bureau of Investigation. Both men laboured to modernize their organizations and turn them into national police services. Perhaps the most capable leader ever to command the Force, Mac-Brien had two valuable assets in his plans for expanding its duties and responsibilities: wide public respect as a war hero, and a degree of political influence which few if any of his predecessors had ever enjoyed. During his short period of office, the R.C.M.P. developed into the most important police force in Canada.

Another important national service was inaugurated in January 1937, with the organization of the Modus Operandi Section. Based upon a system developed at New Scotland Yard, it provided a national register, or "Who's Who," of habitual criminals – their characteristics, descriptions and methods of operation for the information of all police forces. On March 3 of the same year the first issue of the *Royal Canadian Mounted Police Gazette* made its appearance. Designed to disseminate information on current criminal activities, its circulation was restricted to accredited police agencies across the country. The pages of the *Gazette* carried up-to-date news on wanted criminals, important arrests, stolen property, missing persons and the movements of known offenders.

Rumrunning. Most of the efforts of the R.C.M.P. Marine Section in the thirties were directed towards the prevention of rumrunning off the coast of Prince Edward Island and Nova Scotia. The rum was brought to Canadian shores by ships of French or British registry from St. Pierre and Miquelon, Newfoundland and the West Indies. The "mother ships," as they were called, waited offshore beyond the three-mile territorial limit. Once darkness fell or fog closed in, smaller vessels put out from land to load up with rum and run it ashore where it was cached for distribution later. A cat-and-mouse game resulted between the smugglers and the police patrols, which endeavoured to intercept the rumrunners by maintaining a constant watch on the mother ships and breaking down their coded radio messages.

The rumrunning business was closely linked to the existence of prohibition in the Maritimes; liquor could legally be obtained only with a doctor's prescription. This increased the price for the drinker who had to pay for both the bottle and the prescription. Smuggled rum at five dollars a gallon was much cheaper. As it was usually 45 per cent overproof, it could also be watered down.

The police methods gradually began to disrupt the trade. More effective ship-to-air patrols were developed. A number of smuggling rings were broken by bringing conspiracy charges against the principals under the Criminal Code. The territorial limit was extended to twelve miles for ships of British registry, making it more difficult to smuggle rum ashore. What finally broke the back of the trade, however, was the end of prohibition and the opening of Government liquor stores.

a

b

c

(a) R.C.M.P. Fleur de Lis, one of the eleven ocean-going vessels taken over from the Preventive Service by the Force in 1932. In searching for rumrunners along the coast the ships were assisted at first by aircraft of the R.C.A.F. These were later replaced by the Force's own planes.

(b) A rumrunner, the Charles L, off Prince Edward Island. As police patrols became more effective, the smugglers gradually abandoned sail in favour of high-speed motor vessels.

(c) The M.V. Florann, left, and the M.V. Liberty hovering outside territorial waters off the coast of P.E.I. in July, 1937. Nine hundred gallons of rum which was run ashore from these vessels was later seized by the police.

Lord Bessborough, the Governor General,
presenting the R.C.M.P. with its first
guidon at Regina, April 13, 1935.

On-to-Ottawa trek. Under Prime Minister Bennett, the R.C.M.P. was once again used to assist local authorities in maintaining order during labour disputes. During the Depression, strikes and mass protests were all too frequent, often ending in violence.

In June 1935 relief camp workers in Vancouver decided to trek to Ottawa by train to dramatize their plight and press the Government into meeting their demands. By the time the train reached Regina, their numbers had swollen to over two thousand men. At this point Bennett instructed the R.C.M.P. to prevent the strikers from continuing eastward. The order was carried out. But when the Mounted Police and the Regina City Police attempted to arrest the strike leaders at a meeting in Regina's Market Square on July 1, a bloody riot ensued which left one city policeman dead and many police and civilians injured. A subsequent inquiry upheld the action of the police in trying to maintain order and placed the blame for the violence on the Communist party.

Bennett's action was critized by the provincial authorities who claimed that the federal Government had invaded the province's jurisdiction over the administra-tion of justice. Caught in the dispute between the two governments, Assistant Commissioner Wood, who was in command at Regina, chose to ignore Premier Gardiner's instructions and obey the orders from Ottawa. The incident illustrated the delicate constitutional position in which the Force can find itself under the federal-provincial agreement. Fortunately good sense prevailed, and that agreement was not jeopardized.

Police Service Dogs. As early as 1908 members of the Force had used privately owned dogs from time to time to assist them with their investigations. It was not until 1935, however, that the R.C.M.P. acquired its own dogs and organized a Police Service Dog Section. The first dog was a German shepherd named Dale of Cawsalta who had already been trained for police work by his former owner, Sergeant J. N. Cawsey. Dale's ability as a tracker was soon proven in a number of outstanding cases. He was soon joined by his son Black Lux and another German shepherd, Sultan. Satisfied with the value of dogs in search and rescue operations, Commissioner MacBrien ordered the establishment of a training school at Calgary in 1937 for dogs and their handlers. At first a number of breeds were tried, reinsenschnauzers, rottweilers, Doberman pinschers and others. Eventually the German shepherd became the accepted breed.

In addition to searching for missing or wanted persons, police dogs provided a valuable service in detecting illicit stills and caches of smuggled liquor.

*The Canadian Exhibit at the Chicago
World's Fair 1933. By the 1930s the
"Mountie" had become an established
tourist attraction and an inseparable part
of Canada's image abroad.*

Counting birds was one of the more unusual duties thrust upon the R.C.M.P. as the federal police force. In October 1932 it was made responsible for enforcing regulations under the Migratory Birds Convention Act. This included the protection of rare species and the periodic census of migrating birds.

In October 1938 an agreement was reached between Radio Station CKCK, Regina, and the R.C.M.P. for the broadcasting of police bulletins. Radio had been used from time to time before, but these broadcasts marked the official beginning of the use of the new means of communication by the Force.

The twice-daily bulletins reported stolen cars, missing or wanted persons, escaped prisoners and other information. As police cars and detachments were not at first equipped with radio, members arranged to visit farms, restaurants and service stations that had receivers. The public were also requested to listen to the bulletins and assist the police.

—Leader-Post Photo.

Where the Bulletins Come From

This is the radio transmitter at R.C.M.P. headquarters in Regina which played such a big part in finding the body of J. A. Kaeser, slain Moosomin farmer, last week. Mrs. Percy Trout, Sintaluta farm woman, heard a regular police broadcast of the Kaeser case and subsequently found the body near her home. Broadcasts are made at 10:35 and 3:50 each day, including Sunday, usually by Sergeant E. D. Fryett, shown at the microphone. The Leader-Post radio station is the outlet.

The first radio transmitter operated by the R.C.M.P. went into service in Winnipeg in 1940. During the war years more stations were built and cars and detachments equipped with two-way radios.

The R.C.M.P. contingent passing Canada House in London on the Coronation of His Majesty King George VI, May 12, 1937.

Surgeon Maurice Powers. In 1937 the R.C.M.P. opened its first crime detection laboratory at "Depot" Division in Regina. It was organized and directed by Dr. Maurice Powers, one of the first graduates in forensic medicine in North America. Powers had been appointed to the rank of Surgeon the same year. He first assembled his equipment in a vacant bedroom off the officers' mess, while more suitable accommodation was being prepared. With additional staff Powers soon expanded the lab's facilities, adding sections specializing in documents, toxicology, spectrograph analysis, firearms and toolmarks. A second scientific laboratory was opened at "N" Division in Rockcliffe in 1939.

Like the other services developed by the Force, the crime labs were intended to assist police forces throughout Canada. Surgeon Powers was killed, tragically, when the plane in which he was travelling crashed near Battleford, Saskatchewan in 1943.

One of MacBrien's primary concerns was the standard of training available to police officers, not only in the R.C.M.P. but throughout Canada. It was his hope that a National Training Centre or Police Academy could be developed under the Force's charge for the training of all policemen. In 1932, as a first step, recruit training was thoroughly overhauled. The old program with its emphasis on military drill and discipline was replaced by a six-month, two-part course that reflected the growing complexity and professionalism of police work. From first aid, judo, foot and mounted drill, firearms instruction and physical training, the recruit moved on to a second phase of instruction which included lectures on the Criminal Code and other statutes, criminal investigation, administrative procedures, public relations, fingerprinting, ballistics and other scientific aids,

as well as typing and the maintenance of motor vehicles. In keeping with the Commissioner's aim to make police work a career for well-educated men, recruiting standards were raised and the Force started the very progressive policy for the time of sending selected members to university for further education. Promotional examinations were introduced for noncommissioned officers and advanced training courses held for experienced men. These began to attract a number of police officers from other departments, but the training centre at Regina was never quite to realize MacBrien's hope for a national police college.

By 1939 the modern character of the R.C.M.P. had taken shape. From a small federal police force, it had been transformed in two decades into the principal institution for law enforcement in Canada. With the cooperation of the various levels of government, it had taken on provincial and municipal duties, bringing a more effective and economical system of policing to a large part of the country. In the North, it continued its traditional role as a frontier service. From coast to coast, meanwhile, it had expanded and consolidated its operations as the enforcement arm of the federal Government. As a means of communication, the horse had almost disappeared. It had been replaced

The funeral of Commissioner Sir James Howden MacBrien on March 8, 1938, was one of the largest ever seen in Ottawa. The more than mile-long cortege included Prime Minister W. L. Mackenzie King and R. B. Bennett, as well as military and diplomatic leaders. MacBrien was born at Myrtle, Ontario, in 1878, the son of a school inspector. He joined the N.W.M.P. as a constable on April 7, 1900. "I have been used to horses all my life," he wrote on his application forms. In February 1901, he took his discharge to enlist in the South African Constabulary. Returning to Canada in 1906, he secured a commission in the Canadian Militia and started out on a long and distinguished military career. During World War I he commanded an infantry brigade, received the D.S.O. and bar, was wounded at Vimy Ridge and rose to the rank of Major General.

Following the war he served for a time as Chief of Staff of the Department of National Defence. In 1931 he was appointed Commissioner of the R.C.M.P.

by radio-equipped motor vehicles aircraft and ships which logged millions of operational miles each year. With a total strength of over twenty-six hundred men, the Force's internal organization and divisional distribution had taken its modern form. Under its direction, a growing complex of criminal intelligence, scientific knowledge and technical services had been developed as an essential aid to the maintenance of law and order throughout Canada. As the war clouds gathered in Europe, the R.C.M.P. concluded the most significant period in its history since its formation and trek westward in 1874.

Air and Marine Services

Air Services

The advantages of aircraft as a means of patrolling Canadian coastal waters and establishing faster communications between the remote settlements of the North were realized quite early. In 1919 Commissioner Perry recommended the formation of an "Air Police Service" equipped with surplus wartime aircraft. The government was not prepared for such a novel idea, and nothing came of his suggestion. For the next eighteen years the Force depended upon commercial airlines or the R.C.A.F. when aircraft were required for emergencies, or special operations. The hunt for Albert Johnson, the Mad Trapper, in the Yukon in 1931/32 dramatically showed, however, the need for a police air service.

The first member of the Force to fly whilst on duty was Sergeant H. T. Thorne in 1921. Thorne spent several weeks travelling by dog team and train to reach Edmonton from Fort Providence in the Mackenzie District with a prisoner charged with murder. He made the return trip to Fort Providence in a Junkers aircraft of Imperial Oil in just four days, including overnight stops. Thorne's flight exemplified the great change that air travel would bring to life in the Canadian North.

The Force obtained its own aircraft largely through the efforts of Commissioner Sir J. H. MacBrien, who was himself a qualified pilot and an aviation enthusiast. In 1932 the R.C.M.P. took over the responsibilities of the Preventive Service of the Department of National Revenue. To assist the Force, MacBrien acquired the help of several R.C.A.F. planes. In cooperation with the Marine Section, these aircraft patrolled the Atlantic and Pacific coasts to prevent smuggling, particularly rumrunning.

This arrangement did not work satisfactorily and in 1936 the Department of National Defence decided it could no longer spare the aircraft and personnel. As a result, MacBrien decided the Force should purchase its own planes and establish an Air Section. The first planes, four DeHavilland Dragonflies, were obtained in 1937. On May 22 of that year the first official patrol by an R.C.M.P. aircraft was made by the Commissioner and two crew members from Ottawa to Toronto. A year later a Noordwyn Norseman was added to the fleet. The Air Section's usefulness was shown the same year when a Dragonfly succeeded in rescuing two fishermen who had drifted out to sea in an open boat off the coast of New Brunswick. In 1939 the flying personnel and the aircraft, with the exception of the Norseman, were transferred to the R.C.A.F. for the duration of the war.

The Air Section was not reorganized until 1946, when in addition to the Norseman the Force acquired two new Beechcraft and an ex-R.C.A.F. Grumman Goose. Later it was raised to the status of a division with its own commanding officer and headquarters in Ottawa. This was reorganized as Air Services Directorate on April 1, 1973.

The first fatal accident involving an R.C.M.P. aircraft occurred in 1958 when a Beaver, CF-FHW, crashed into a hillside while searching for a wanted man near Skaha Lake, British Columbia. This plane, the only one without the MP registration, formerly belonged to the British Columbia Provincial Police. Staff Sergeant S. S. Rothwell (the pilot), Special Constable R. E. Cormier and Constable R. W. Green were all killed.

In 1958 a cylinder cracked in one of the Force's Otters and its pilot, Corporal Carter, made an emergency landing on Highway 11 near North Bay, Ontario. After a new engine had been rushed from Ottawa, the plane took off down the highway and continued its journey.

The planes of the R.C.M.P. Air Services provide fast and convenient transportation to members of the Force whose duties take them to areas where commercial or charter services are not readily available. They carry out patrols in connection with the enforcement of the Customs and Excise Act, provide a means of transporting prisoners from outlying areas and are also used in search or rescue operations. In 1973 Air Services had twenty-one aircraft stationed at seventeen locations in Canada. In a year these planes flew more than two million air miles.

Commissioner MacBrien refueling near Rae, N.W.T., on his inspections of northern posts in 1933. The aircraft, a Fairchild 71, was provided by the R.C.A.F. The Commissioner covered over eleven thousand miles. By conventional means of travel in the North, it would have taken several months.

(Above) The four original Dragonflies of the R.C.M.P. Air Section at Toronto, June 1937. At this time the Department of Transport reserved the "MP" registration series for R.C.M.P. Aircraft. The crews for these aircraft were drawn from members of the Force who already possessed flying qualifications.

In 1946 the Air Section was reorganized with the purchase of two Beechcraft (opposite) and an amphibious Grumman Goose (left). C.F. M.P.H. is now on display at the R.C.M.P. Museum in Regina.

Air Division aircraft are maintained and serviced by R.C.M.P. personnel.

R.C.M.P. Beaver.

Aircraft are essential for modern police service in the north. (Right) R.C.M.P. Twin Otter on the ice at Grise Fiord, N.W.T. (Below) R.C.M.P. Otter. Since this photograph was taken the Force's long use of sled dogs as a means of transportation in the Arctic has come to an end. The last dog patrol was made in 1969 from Old Crow in the Yukon to Fort McPherson in the N.W.T.

Marine Services

The Force adopted water transport quite early in its history. In 1890 a sailing vessel, the *Keewatin*, was acquired to patrol Lake Winnipeg. A few months later it capsized in a storm with the loss of two of its crew, Corporal H. O. Morphy and Constable G. de Beaujeu. Morphy had been a prominent member of the Toronto Argonaut Rowing Club and had competed at the Henley Regatta in England.

During the early years in the Yukon, steam-operated boats were used on the Yukon River as patrol and supply transports. By 1919 four seagoing motor vessels had been taken on strength – the *Victory* at Herschel Island, the *Duncan* and the *Lady Borden* in Hudson Bay, and the *Chakawana* on the West Coast.

The Force's Marine Section came into existence in 1932 as a result of the takeover of the duties and vessels of the Preventive Service. The newly acquired fleet numbered approximately thirty-five ships, including eleven seagoing craft. Their primary duty was to prevent smuggling in the Gulf of St. Lawrence and on the east and west coasts.

N.W.M.P. Vidette, *the pride of the Yukon Fleet. Purchased in 1902 for three thousand dollars, the* Vidette *served for several years as a patrol and supply vessel on the Yukon River between Dawson and Whitehorse.*

Using radio and aircraft, an air/land/sea police patrol network was established which effectively reduced rumrunning and other forms of smuggling. With the outbreak of war in 1939, the Marine Section ships and some 155 officers and men were transferred to the Royal Canadian Navy.

The Marine Section was not reorganized until after hostilities ended in 1945. The new fleet was made up of former R.C.N. patrol vessels:

(1) 165-foot Bangor-type minesweepers. These were designated "Commissioner" class ships and named after former commissioners of the Force.

(2) 118-foot Fairmile antisubmarine chasers. These were designated "Fort" class ships after historic forts in the Force's early history.

(3) 50-foot harbour defence craft which became "Detachment" class vessels named after historic land detachments.

In 1947 Marine Section was constituted a Division with headquarters in Halifax, later transferred to Ottawa. Three years later a construction program was launched to replace the older vessels with modern ships designed for police operations. Their responsibility was the enforcement of the Customs and Excise Act, the Canada Shipping Act and other federal statutes as well as rescue operations. In 1973 Marine Services had thirty-three patrol vessels carrying out law enforcement duties in Canadian territorial waters in the Atlantic, the Pacific and the Great Lakes.

R.C.M.P. Chakawana. *Based at Prince Rupert, the Chakawana was used to patrol the coast of British Columbia from 1919 to 1921. The officer in command was Inspector A. C. Acland, far right.*

(Below) The R.C.M.P. cruisers Macdonald and Laurier ready for launching at Quebec City on August 20, 1936. These two vessels were especially designed and built for the Marine Section. The Laurier was christened by Madame Lapointe, wife of Ernest Lapointe, Minister of Justice, the Macdonald by Lady MacBrien, wife of Commissioner Sir J. H. MacBrien. Like the other Marine Section vessels, these two ships and their crews were transferred to the Royal Canadian Navy in 1939 for war service.

(Opposite) Uniform of the R.C.M.P. Marine Section 1932-39. Prior to World War II the personnel of Marine Section wore a naval type of uniform with their own distinctive rank insignia.

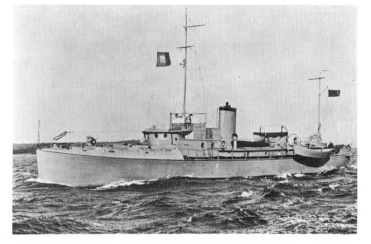

(Right) R.C.M.P. cruiser Adversus. The Adversus became the first R.C.M.P. ship to pass through the Panama Canal when she was transferred from Halifax to Vancouver in 1933.

The Adversus was lost at sea during World War II.

(Above) R.C.M.P.S. Irvine. Formerly H.M.C.S. Noranda, the Irvine was one of eight 168-foot diesel powered Bangor class minesweepers obtained from War Assets after World War II. For many years she patrolled the waters off the coast of Newfoundland and Labrador before being taken out of operational service in 1960.
(Right) R.C.M.P.S. Wood. The 178-foot steel-welded Wood was launched at Lauzon, Quebec, in October 1957. During Expo '67, the Wood carried out marine security duties at Montreal. She was taken out of operational service in 1970.

R.C.M.P. *patrol vessel* Advance. *A 35-foot high-speed motorboat on harbour patrol near Vancouver, B.C.*

(Top) R.C.M.P. Detachment-class boats
Tofino and Nanaimo patrolling Pacific
coastal waters.
(Above) Twelve-passenger Bell 212 heli-
copter acquired by the Force in 1972.
(Right) A patrol in Arctic waters off the
coast of Baffin Island.

R.C.M.P. *St. Roch*, Conqueror of the Northwest Passage

The *St. Roch* was built for the R.C.M.P. in 1928 at North Vancouver by the Burrard Dry Dock Company. She was designed as a supply vessel and floating detachment for service in the Arctic. The ship was named after a parish in the Quebec City constituency of the minister then responsible for the R.C.M.P., the Honourable E. Lapointe, Minister of Justice.

In 1940 Sergeant Henry A. Larsen, the ship's skipper, received orders to sail from Vancouver to Halifax by way of the Northwest Passage. For centuries explorers had sought a sea route across the top of North America. Many had sought to find a path through the icy Arctic waters but failed, often losing their lives in the attempt. The first to accomplish the feat was the Norwegian explorer, Roald Amundsen. In his ship, the *Gjoa*, Amundsen entered the passage from the Atlantic in 1903. He finally reached the Pacific Ocean in 1906, after spending three winters in the Arctic carrying out scientific experiments. The *Gjoa* was followed by the Hudson's Bay schooner *Aklavik*, which in 1937 navigated the most difficult part of the ice-bound route from Cambridge Bay in the western Arctic to Bellot Strait in the east, and return.

The navigation season in the Arctic Ocean usually lasts only for a few weeks each summer when the ice breaks up or recedes sufficiently to allow a ship to proceed. Ice conditions, however, can vary considerably from one year to another. The *St. Roch* left Vancouver on June 23, 1940. The first leg of her voyage ended at Walker Bay on the west side of Victoria Island where she spent the winter of 1940/41. During the summer of 1941 she continued eastward, but was frozen-in again for the winter at Pasley Bay. In the summer of 1942 Larsen picked his way among the ice floes and sped through the Bellot Strait to open water. The long voyage ended at Halifax on October 11, 1942, making the *St. Roch* the first vessel to navigate the Northwest Passage from the Pacific to the Atlantic Ocean.

In preparation for the return voyage the *St. Roch* was overhauled and her original 150-h.p. diesel engine replaced by a 300-h.p. unit. The westward voyage began from Halifax on July 22, 1944. On this occasion Larsen was fortunate in finding an ice-free route, and the 7,295 mile voyage was completed, without stopping, in the remarkably short time of eighty-six days. With her arrival at Vancouver on October 16, 1944, the *St. Roch* became the first vessel to navigate the long sea passage in both directions. Six years later she sailed from Vancouver to Halifax via the Panama Canal, earning the additional distinction of being the first vessel to circumnavigate the entire North American continent.

The *St. Roch*'s seagoing career came to an end in 1954 when the federal Government handed her over to the City of Vancouver. She is now the main attraction at the Vancouver Maritime Museum.

(Above) "*The St. Roch in the Ice,*" by P. J. Dunleavy.

Members of the St. Roch's original crew, with Inspector V. A. M. Kemp, at Herschel Island on the ship's maiden voyage in 1928.
Front, L. to r.: Mr. P. Kelly, Technical Adviser; Inspector V. A. M. Kemp, Officer Commanding Western Arctic Sub-District; Constable J. Foster, Engineer.
Middle: Constable M. J. Olsen, Second Mate; Constable H. A. Larsen, Skipper; Sergeant F. Anderton, in charge of police duties; Constable W. J. Parry, Cook.
Back: Constable R. W. Kells, Second Engineer; Constable T. G. Parsloe, Seaman; Special Constable F. Seeley, Radio Operator.

(Above) St. Roch in winter quarters, Tree River, N.W.T., 1930. To withstand the pressure of the Arctic ice, the ship's hull was built of Douglas fir covered with sheets of durable Australian gumwood. Accommodation on the 104-foot-long vessel was cramped. Larsen described her as "the most uncomfortable ship I have ever been in."

(Left) Larsen on winter patrol. During the months the St. Roch was frozen-in and unable to act as a supply vessel, the ship became a police detachment with the crew carrying out patrols and other police duties in the adjacent territory.

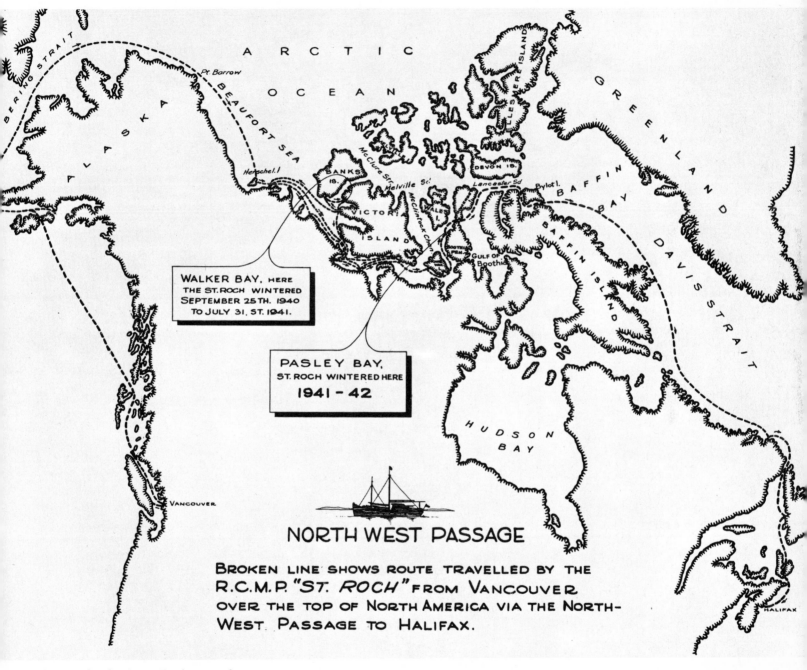

WALKER BAY, HERE
THE ST. ROCH WINTERED
SEPTEMBER 25TH. 1940
TO JULY 31. ST. 1941.

PASLEY BAY,
ST. ROCH WINTERED HERE
1941-42

NORTH WEST PASSAGE

BROKEN LINE SHOWS ROUTE TRAVELLED BY THE
R.C.M.P. "ST. ROCH" FROM VANCOUVER
OVER THE TOP OF NORTH AMERICA VIA THE NORTH-
WEST PASSAGE TO HALIFAX.

Route taken by the St. Roch on its first voyage through the Northwest Passage, 1940-42. News that the small eighty-ton ship had triumphed over the hazardous Arctic route boosted morale of Canadians during the dark days of World War II. The widely publicized event also served to reaffirm Canada's sovereignty in the North.

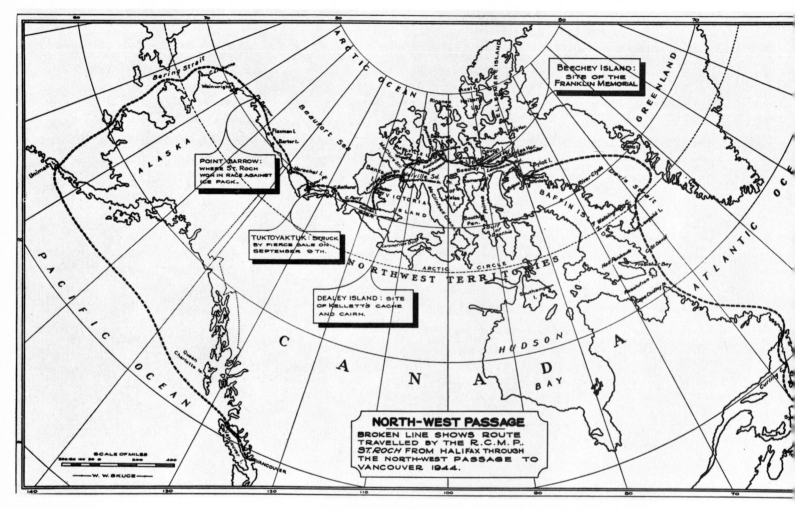

BEECHEY ISLAND:
SITE OF THE
FRANKLIN MEMORIAL

POINT BARROW:
WHERE ST. ROCH
WON IN RACE AGAINST
ICE PACK.

TUKTOYAKTUK: STRUCK
BY FIERCE GALE ON
SEPTEMBER 9TH.

DEALEY ISLAND: SITE
OF KELLETT'S CACHE
AND CAIRN.

NORTH-WEST PASSAGE
BROKEN LINE SHOWS ROUTE
TRAVELLED BY THE R.C.M.P.
ST. ROCH FROM HALIFAX THROUGH
THE NORTH-WEST PASSAGE TO
VANCOUVER 1944.

SCALE OF MILES

— W. W. SKUCE —

(Above) On the 1944 voyage the St. Roch took the northern route through Lancaster Sound.

(Right) The crew of the second historic voyage. Front, L. to r.: Constable J. M. Diplock, Seaman; Corporal G. W. Peters, Engineer; Corporal P. G. Hunt, Clerk and Seaman; Special Constable R. T. Johnsen, Second Engineer; Staff Sergeant H. A. Larsen, Skipper.
Back: Constable M. G. Owens, on transfer to Pond Inlet; Special Constable G. B. Dickins, Cook; Special Constable F. Matthews, Seaman; Special Constable J. S. McKenzie, Seaman; and Special Constable L. G. Russill, Radio Operator.

Henry Asbjorn Larsen. Larsen was
born in Fredrikstad, Norway, in 1899.
Before joining the R.C.M.P. in 1928 he had
served with the Royal Norwegian Navy and
the merchant marine. While a young boy
he dreamed of becoming an Arctic explorer
like his famous fellow-countryman, Roald
Amundsen. As the skipper of the St. Roch
on both of her voyages through the Northwest Passage, he was to realize these early
ambitions.

His exploits brought him many
honours as well as international recognition. Along with the other members of the
1940–42 voyage he was awarded the Polar
Medal. He became a Fellow of both the
Royal Geographical Society of Canada and
the Arctic Institute of North America.
In 1946 he was awarded the Patrons'
Medal (gold) of the Royal Geographical
Society of London. He was also the first
recipient of the Massey Medal of the Royal
Geographical Society of Canada. In 1961
he received the honorary degree of Doctor
of Laws from Waterloo University.

Larsen retired from the Force in 1961
with the rank of superintendent. He died
in Vancouver three years later.

The St. Roch leaving Halifax, Nova Scotia,
on her second attempt to navigate the
Northwest Passage, July 22, 1944.

Towards a Second Century

Police community relationships have a direct bearing on the character of life in our cities, and on the community's ability to maintain stability and to solve its problems. At the same time the police department's capacity to deal with crime depends to a large extent upon its relationship with the citizenry. Indeed, no lasting improvement in law enforcement is likely in this country unless police-community relations are substantially improved.

Task Force on the Police
The President's Commission on Law
Enforcement and Administration of
Justice, Washington, 1967

World War II

The R.C.M.P.'s preparations for war began long before its formal declaration by Canada on September 10, 1939. Once it became clear that conditions in Europe were drifting towards war, the Force began making plans for the additional responsibilities which would accompany the outbreak of hostilities. These would include the protection of vital installations, the prevention of sabotage, registration of enemy aliens, the identification of groups or individuals sympathetic to the enemy cause and the enforcement of the innumerable emergency regulations which would come into effect during wartime. At the same time, the Force would have to carry on with its regular police duties.

By 1938, R.C.M.P. undercover agents had penetrated the Nazi and Fascist organizations in Canada. The leaders of both groups were known to the police as well as their subversive intentions once the war started. Within forty-eight hours of the commencement of hostilities with Germany, several hundred Nazi sympathizers had been rounded up across Canada and placed under arrest. Under the Defence of Canada Regulations, these were later brought before impartial screening committees who decided which of them should be released or detained. Those considered a security risk were handed over to the Army authorities for internment. The work was complicated by thou-

sands of complaints by public-minded citizens who thought they saw spies at every corner. Each of these was, nevertheless, patiently and meticulously investigated.

A few months later, similar action was taken against the adherents of the Canada Fascist party following Italy's entry into the war. These precautions proved successful in preventing any serious incident of espionage or sabotage in Canada during the war on behalf of the hostile powers. Such was not the case with the Communists, however. Although at first opposed to the war, Communist leaders reversed their position and came out openly in support of the allied cause following the German invasion of Russia in 1941. Reorganized as the Labour Progressive party in 1943, party officials took advantage of the turn of events to establish a system of espionage. These activities were not brought to light until 1945 when a cipher clerk at the Russian Embassy in Ottawa, Igor Gouzenko, decided to defect. Gouzenko's disclosures revealed that key members of the party in Canada were part of a Russian espionage network. The recommendations of the Royal Commission which subsequently enquired into the espionage in Canada led to an expansion of the Force's security duties in the postwar years.

*President Roosevelt, Prime Minister
Winston Churchill and their advisers at
Quebec City 1944. The allied leaders held
conferences in the Quebec capital in 1943
and 1944 to map out postwar peace plans.
Police protection was provided on both
occasions by the R.C.M.P.*

The spy who came out of the sea. The uniform and effects of Lieutenant Janowski, a German officer who landed from a U-boat near New Carlisle, Quebec, in November 1942. Although he buried his uniform and dressed himself in civilian clothes, the German's conversation with a local hotel-keeper the next day aroused the latter's suspicions. Arrested by the provincial police, he was subsequently turned over to the R.C.M.P. for interrogation. Janowski was later used as a double agent in Canada and Britain. His effects are now on display in the R.C.M.P. Museum in Regina.

The war brought other responsibilities. From coast to coast there were vital installations which would have to be placed under constant protection. Early in 1939 with the assistance of the Department of National Defence, the Force began a survey of essential industrial plants, harbours, canals, bridges, dockyards and other vulnerable points. With the commencement of hostilities, special constables were recruited to guard these locations. The presence of the Force in the Canadian North, meanwhile, assumed new importance with the construction of the Alaska Highway and an oil pipe line from Norman Wells to Whitehorse. War conditions also engendered new criminal activities which had to be investigated.

These included the faking of thousands of ration books, black-marketeering, counterfeiting of National Registration Certificates and graft in Government contracts.

To handle the work, the R.C.M.P. had to adjust its man-power resources considerably. In the first place the ranks were depleted by the departure of the air and marine services personnel on active duty, as well as the volunteers for No. 1 Provost Company. To meet the need for protecting vital installations, nearly two thousand Special Constable Guards were enlisted. These were retired members or older men who were medically unfit for active service. The recruiting of regular members, however, came almost to a stand-still for the duration of the war.

A detachment of the R.C.M.P. marches into the Chateau Frontenac, site of the 1944 Quebec Conference, to take over security arrangements. To meet additional wartime duties like this, the Force utilized the services of the R.C.M.P. Reserve, a uniformed body of part-time volunteers who could be called up to assist regular members when needed.

As a result, an important change took place in the employment structure of the Force. In the past most clerical, typing and office work had been carried out by uniformed members. With the urgent need for more men on police work, these duties were gradually taken over by civilian employees, mostly women. It was not until 1946 that normal recruiting and training procedures commenced once again.

Postwar Developments

Apart from taking over police duties in numerous municipalities, and becoming the provincial force in British Columbia and Newfoundland, there has been little basic change in the responsibilities of the R.C.M.P. since the end of World War II. The emphasis of the postwar period has been upon the increasing use of technology, particularly in the field of communications, in the combatting of old and new patterns of crime. At the same time the Force has become more and more specialized in almost every phase of police work. These changes have been accompanied by a growing awareness of the necessity of maintaining good relations between the police and the public they serve. They have also been followed by the most rapid expansion of the Force's manpower and resources in its entire history.

Upon the return of members from war service in 1945, work was begun on the reorganization of the Force's air and marine services. During the same year Commissioner Wood inaugurated "Youth and Police," a countrywide community relations program. With its emphasis on crime prevention, the program was aimed at promoting understanding between the police and young people. Under the scheme members were encouraged to establish contact with local youth through lectures, visits to schools, film shows, as

Stuart Taylor Wood, C.M.G., Commissioner of the Force from 1938 to 1951, came from a distinguished military line that included President Zachary Taylor of the United States and John Taylor Wood, commander of the Confederate blockade-runner, the Tallahassee. Following the Civil War the Wood family emigrated to Canada, where the Commissioner's father, Zachary Taylor Wood, was appointed an inspector in the N.W.M.P. in 1885. Like his father, S. T. Wood attended the Royal Military College, Kingston. He received a commission as an inspector in the R.N.W.M.P. in 1912. During World War I he served as a lieutenant in "A" Squadron R.N.W.M.P. Commissioner Wood died in 1966.

well as by participation in sports and community activities.

As the use of the motor vehicle spread and society became increasingly mobile, the improvement of police communications

became vital. In 1949 the R.C.M.P. took the first step in creating its own nationwide radio system when its installations in Manitoba were enlarged to create a network that covered the three prairie provinces. Gradually the system was extended until two-way radios in most police cars, ships, planes, detachments and other posts became standard equipment. The year 1949 also saw the Force appointed Canada's representative at Interpol, the International Criminal Police Organization. This eventually resulted in radio communications being established with police organizations overseas. At its General Assembly in Frankfurt, West Germany, in 1972, Commissioner W. L. Higgitt of the R.C.M.P. was elected president of Interpol, the first time the office has been held outside of Europe.

In 1951 Commissioner Wood, who had commanded the Force during the difficult war years, retired to pension. He was succeeded by Assistant Commissioner L. H. Nicholson. The fifties saw the reappearance of an old problem for the R.C.M.P., a new outbreak of terrorist activities in British Columbia by Doukhobor extremists. In 1958 the first postwar crime laboratory went into operation at Sackville, New Brunswick. It joined those already in service at Ottawa and Regina. Additional ones were later opened at Vancouver in 1963, Edmonton in 1968 and Winnipeg in 1973. The year

(Above) Firearms identification. By comparing test bullets fired in the laboratory with a bullet found at the scene of a crime, it is possible for ballistics experts to identify the weapon which was used.

(Top Right) The simultaneous appearance of bogus Bank of Canada ten-dollar notes at Montreal, Toronto, Ottawa, Hamilton, Vancouver and other points over the 1949 Labour Day weekend touched off one of the biggest counterfeiting investigations in Canadian history. As soon as it was clear that a well-organized counterfeiting operation was under way, steps were taken to warn the public, but many of the bills found their way into circulation. Working with U.S. law enforcement agencies, the source of the money was eventually traced to Buffalo, New York, where a number of arrests were made. Meanwhile, the Toronto syndicate responsible for its distribution was exposed by an R.C.M.P. undercover agent posing as a member of the underworld. Of the more than half a million dollars printed, 325,000 were recovered before they went into circulation.

(Right) Members of the Scenes of Crime Section photographing tire impressions left by a suspected motor vehicle.

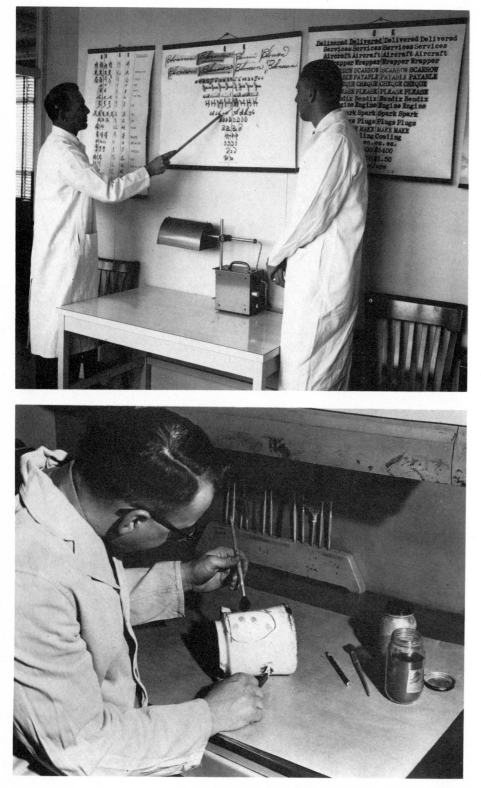

(*Above*) *With the help of witnesses a wanted person's facial features can be reconstructed through the use of a Facial Identification Kit.*

(*Left*) *Handwriting analysis in the Document Section of the R.C.M.P. Crime Detection Laboratory in Vancouver.*

Dusting for fingerprints.

also saw the installation of Telex equipment to the Force's growing communications system. A year later Commissioner Nicholson resigned following a dispute with the Minister of Justice over the policing of a loggers' strike in Newfoundland.

By 1960 the total strength of the R.C.M.P. had climbed to over sixty-five hundred. Included in this number were men and women under the new status of "civilian member" who carried out specialized duties but did not hold appointments as peace officers. As the need for professional and technical skills grew in police work, more and more emphasis was placed on education. University graduates were actively sought after by

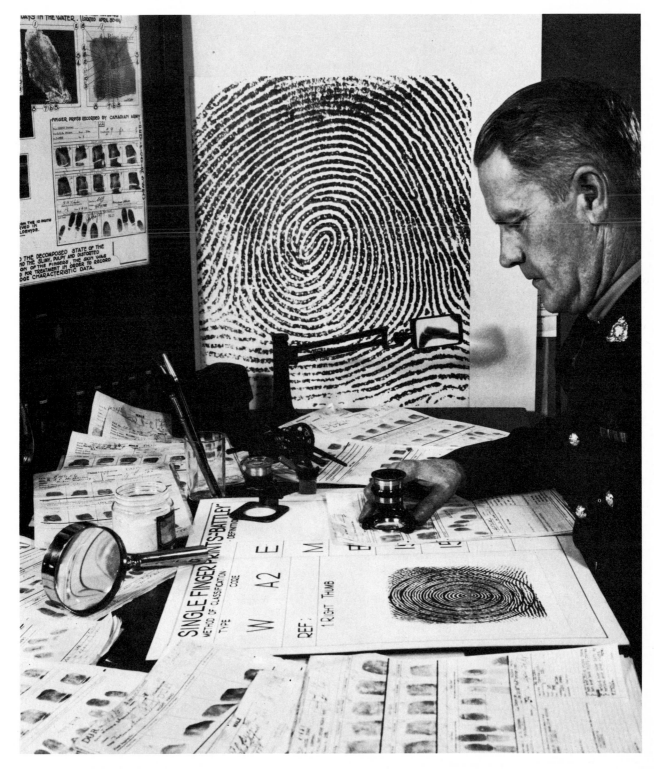

The Battley system of filing in the Single
Fingerprint Section provides a means of
identification when only a single or partial
impression is left at the scene of a crime.

(Left) Recruits practising on the revolver range.

(Right) Investigating a safe-breaking at Disbury, Alberta, 1959.

recruiting officers. An increasing number of serving members were selected for university education or provided with advanced training courses, both inside and outside of the Force. The sixties also saw the Force facing new problems posed by the radical elements of the New Left and the sudden increase in the use of illegal drugs.

Advances in communications continued to be the main theme of change, as the Force approached its Centenary. In 1967, a year which saw the R.C.M.P. widely involved in Canada's Centennial celebrations, including the provision of security measures for more than sixty visiting heads of state, wire photo facilities were added to its communications network. This enabled facsimiles of photographs, fingerprints and documents to be transmitted across the country in minutes. The same year also saw the official inauguration of plans for the Canadian Police Information Centre, a computerized information system designed to provide police forces throughout Canada with almost instantaneous data on stolen cars, wanted persons and other matters. The first phase of this program went into operation on July 1, 1972, when the Canadian Police Information Centre in Ottawa established contact with thirty-three terminals located in Ontario.

The Shape of Present Things

The Royal Canadian Mounted Police is organized today by authority of the R.C.M.P. Act. At its head is the Commissioner who is under the direction of the Solicitor General of Canada. As the federal police force, it is responsible for enforcing federal statutes throughout Canada. In addition, the Force has contract agreements with all provinces, except Ontario and Quebec, to enforce criminal and provincial laws. In these eight provinces it also provides police services for over one hundred and sixty municipalities. The Yukon and Northwest Territories, meanwhile, are policed exclusively by the R.C.M.P.

The headquarters of the Force is located in Ottawa, Canada's capital. The building complex there houses the administrative centre for its field operations and many support services. In the field the Force is still organized as it has been for a century into divisions, subdivisions and detachments. Today, there are more than seven hundred of the latter. Generally speaking, as the following list will show, a division embraces an entire province, with its headquarters in the provincial capital. These are designated by a letter of the alphabet as they have been since 1873:

(*Left*) A mounted member of the British Columbia Provincial Police. Under a contract with the provincial government the R.C.M.P. took over provincial police duties in British Columbia in August 1950. The accompanying absorption of the British Columbia Provincial Police brought to an end the history of a force that had its beginnings in 1858, a force that had struggled to bring law and order to the gold-rush towns of the province's mountainous frontier long before the N.W.M.P. came into existence.

(*Left*) *The original members of the New-foundland Rangers, which was organized in July 1935. Among them, sixth from the left, middle row, is Sergeant Major F. Anderton of the R.C.M.P. who was loaned to the New-foundland Government to assist in training the new force. The Rangers were raised to police the remoter areas of the colony, the coastal outports and the Labrador settlements. The towns and more settled parts of the island were already being policed by a much older force, the Newfoundland Constabulary.*

A year after Newfoundland joined Canada in 1949, the Rangers were absorbed by the R.C.M.P., who took over the policing of the entire province except the capital city of St. John's, where the Constabulary still remain on duty.

Division	Area	Headquarters
"HQ"	— —	Ottawa
"A"	Eastern Ontario	Ottawa
"B"	Newfoundland	St. John's
"C"	Quebec	Montreal
"D"	Manitoba	Winnipeg
"E"	British Columbia	Victoria
"F"	Saskatchewan	Regina
"G"	Yukon, Northwest Territories	Ottawa
"H"	Nova Scotia	Halifax
"J"	New Brunswick	Fredericton
"K"	Alberta	Edmonton
"L"	Prince Edward Island	Charlottetown
"N"	Training	Ottawa
"Depot"	Training	Regina
"O"	Western Ontario	Toronto

Since its establishment in 1873 approximately thirty-five thousand men have worn the uniform of the Force – a surprisingly small figure considering that uniformed strength in its centennial year is almost eleven thousand. This is explained, of course, by a comparatively rapid growth in the last two decades. To the total uniformed strength today must be added over one thousand civilian members and well over two thousand public servants.

(*Above*) *When Manitoba's Red River over-flowed its banks in 1950, flooding towns and farmlands, members of the R.C.M.P. assisted with the evacuation of thousands of residents and the organization of emer-gency measures to fight the rising waters.*

(*Top*) *The R.C.M.P. Detachment at Morris, Manitoba.*

The members of Dundas Harbour Detachment, 1949. With them are two Eskimo special constables and their families. As guides and interpreters, the Eskimos have contributed their own special skills to the R.C.M.P.'s activities in the Arctic since the earliest days.

Grise Fiord Detachment on Ellesmere Island, the Force's most northerly post in 1973 – closer to the North Pole than to Ottawa.

As almost the sole representative of the Canadian Government in the Arctic, the Family Allowance Act of 1944 added a new task to the Mounted Policeman's varied role of postmaster, customs officer, registrar of vital statistics and the like. These duties have now been taken over almost entirely by the individual departments concerned, who have their own representatives in the isolated northern settlements.

Baking bread in the coal stove at Pond Inlet Detachment in the 1950s. Most of the northern posts now have their own electricity supplies.

In 1950 the Force had 270 sled dogs which patrolled a total of 46,860 miles. Today the dogs have been replaced by the motor toboggan.

Special Constable S. M. Kyak, S.M. Eskimos have served the Force in the Canadian North for many years. In 1970 Special Constable Kyak became the first member of the Force to be awarded the Medal of Service of the Order of Canada.

The last dog patrol. The Mounted Police first used sled dogs in the winter of 1873/74 on a patrol from Lower Fort Garry to Lake Winnipeg. In March 1969 Constable W. Townsend and Special Constable P. Benjamin, a Loucheux Indian, shown here in the lead, set out from Old Crow in the Yukon Territory on the Force's last patrol by dog team. Visiting Fort McPherson and Arctic Red River in the Northwest Territories, they returned to their starting point at Old Crow having travelled five hundred miles in sixteen days. The dogs have since been replaced by motorized toboggans and other forms of modern transport.

Members on duty at a Citizenship Court in Toronto.

To join the Force today, an applicant must be between nineteen and twenty-nine years of age and a Canadian citizen or British subject resident in Canada. In addition he must have grade eleven education or higher, pass a thorough medical examination and educational test, be of exemplary character, hold a current driver's licence and speak, read and write either the English or French language. Successful applicants are engaged for an initial period of five years. They are not permitted to marry until they have served for two years and are twenty-one years of age. Recruits are posted to "Depot" Division, Regina, where they undergo an extensive course of study and training lasting approximately six months. When posted to divisions in the field recruits are placed under the supervision of experienced members until they have gained sufficient practical knowledge to work by themselves. A recruit entering the Force today is embarking upon a lifetime career which offers advancement and service in many areas of modern police work.

Members of the R.C.M.P. at Montreal in 1960 with 240,000 cigarettes seized as the result of a custom's investigation.

Concealed in this peaceful pastoral scene near St. Valerien, Quebec, in 1963 R.C.M.P. investigators uncovered an illegal distilling operation manufacturing two-hundred gallons of alcohol daily for commercial distribution.

The Challenge of the Future

During the last quarter of a century police forces in Canada and elsewhere have become aware that the relations between themselves and the public they serve are a primary concern of modern police work. Given the temper of the times, the complexity and scope of today's law enforcement operations, the police role in society has become increasingly misunderstood. Throughout human history there have been periods when it has seemed that respect for law and order was declining, crime increasing, traditional authority breaking down and moral standards deteriorating. At such times the actions of those whose task it is to enforce the law are often sharply called into question. Disrespect for authority is frequently accompanied by a loss of confidence in the system of justice and an estrangement between the police and the citizens they represent.

To begin with, the task of the policeman has been made more difficult by the expanding power of the state and the growing number of laws which reach out to regulate society, imposing new restrictions and responsibilities on its members. A century ago the police were primarily concerned

François and Jean. In 1968 two younger members of the Montreal R.C.M.P. Drug Section were selected for undercover work. Their task was to infiltrate the criminal element dealing in illegal drugs. Readily accepted by Montreal's hippy community, they became known as François and Jean. Nine months later their efforts resulted in twenty-seven persons being charged with trafficking or possession of drugs.

Paraphernalia of the drug culture of the 1960s and '70s. The rapid increase in the use of illegal drugs in recent years has posed new problems for police forces throughout Canada.

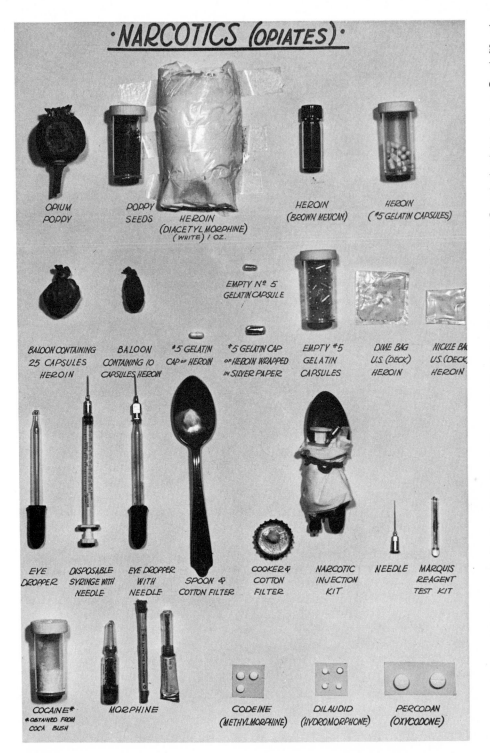

·NARCOTICS (OPIATES)·

OPIUM POPPY

POPPY SEEDS

HEROIN (DIACETYL MORPHINE) (WHITE) 1 OZ.

HEROIN (BROWN MEXICAN)

HEROIN (#5 GELATIN CAPSULES)

EMPTY Nº 5 GELATIN CAPSULE

BALOON CONTAINING 25 CAPSULES HEROIN

BALOON CONTAINING 10 CAPSULES HEROIN

#5 GELATIN CAP OF HEROIN

#5 GELATIN CAP OF HEROIN WRAPPED IN SILVER PAPER

EMPTY #5 GELATIN CAPSULES

DIME BAG U.S. (DECK) HEROIN

NICKLE BAG U.S. (DECK) HEROIN

EYE DROPPER

DISPOSABLE SYRINGE WITH NEEDLE

EYE DROPPER WITH NEEDLE

SPOON & COTTON FILTER

COOKER & COTTON FILTER

NARCOTIC INJECTION KIT

NEEDLE

MARQUIS REAGENT TEST KIT

COCAINE* *OBTAINED FROM COCA BUSH

MORPHINE

CODEINE (METHYLMORPHINE)

DILAUDID (HYDROMORPHONE)

PERCODAN (OXYCODONE)

with a small minority who transgressed a code of criminal laws that was based upon a widely accepted and understood moral code. Today almost any citizen is liable to find himself prosecuted by the police for an infraction of one of the many statutory provisions which govern the community. Usually the offence will be a minor one – illegal parking, for example. Instead of feeling guilty, however, the offender is more likely to resent the restriction of his freedom and the personal inconvenience which result. Under such circumstances the policeman is often seen as an adversary, and criticism, rather than being aimed at the law itself, is directed at a more immediate target, those who enforce it.

The growing complexity of contemporary police work, meanwhile, has also tended to change the old associations between the citizen and his local constabulary. First, modern communications, cars, radios, telephones have removed some of the personal contact. In addition, much of the work of the police goes on unnoticed by the public. Often justice is done, but it is not seen to be done. At the same time the police have developed highly specialized services to fight white-collar and organized crime. A vast array of technical aids has also been assembled to assist them – scientific skills, computers, data banks – which the citizen often feels are a threat to his already diminishing area of freedom. Minority groups are concerned

Riot control training.

front de libération du québec

communiqué numéro 9 CELLULE CHENIER – CELLULE LIBÉRATION

14 octobre 1970 , 5 heures a.m.

Après rencontre et entente entre la cellule CHENIER et la cellule LIBÉRATION, Le Front de Libération du Québec (cellule LIBÉRATION) tient à faire certaines mises au point, suite à la conférence de presse de Me. Lemieux sur les résultats des pourparlers avec les autorités en place.

1. Quant aux garanties que les autorités en place nous demandent, le Front de Libération du Québec ne peut que renouveler son **engagement** solennel devant le peuple du Québec.

   Il n'est pas question, comme le suggèrent les autorités en place, de leur livrer un membre de chaque cellule, comme garanties.

   Nous acceptons toutefois comme solution ultime, la proposition de Me. Lemieux, à savoir que le pays qui accueillera les prisonniers politiques retiennent ces derniers (ainsi que les 500,000 dollars) jusqu'à ce que nous ayons libéré sain et sauf J. Cross et P. Laporte.

2. Nous doutons sérieusement de la bonne foi des autorités concernées. Quelles " **garanties** " celles-ci peuvent-elles nous donner, quant à la cessation des fouilles, perquisitions, et arrestations de la part de leur police politique fasciste? Depuis plus de huit jours les forces policières répressives, sous les ordres du chien à Choquette, multiplient leurs perquisitions et arrestations **illégales**, malgré le

operation liberation

In October 1970 British diplomat James Cross and Quebec Labour Minister Pierre Laporte were kidnapped from their Montreal homes by members of the Front de Libération du Québec. In exchange for their safe return (Mr. Laporte was later murdered by his abductors) the terrorists' demands included the release of so-called political prisoners, the publication of a Marxist manifesto and payment of half a million dollars. The actions of the terrorist cells resulted in the proclamation of the War Measures Act and the mounting of one of the most extensive police operations in Canadian history, with the R.C.M.P. assisting the provincial and municipal police forces at the request of the Quebec authorities.

about the impartial administration of justice, while the responsibility of the police for national security tends to create suspicion. On top of this, newspapers, television and other forms of the mass media have frequently created a superficial and distorted image of the police and their duties.

No one realizes better than the police the danger in losing touch with the community they serve. Without some degree of co-operation from the citizenry, they cannot function. The need for public support and respect, therefore, has become a vital issue. In return the police must strive harder to ensure an efficient, fair and meaningful system of law enforcement. As the R.C.M.P. enters its second century, the maintenance of public confidence will be one of its foremost challenges. The development of police-community relations will be essential if the Force is to continue its part in maintaining the orderly process of law upon which our society rests.

Commissioners of the R.C.M.P.

1. Lt. Col. W. Osborne SMITH (temporary) — September 25, 1873 – October 17, 1873
2. Commissioner George Arthur FRENCH — October 18, 1873 – July 21, 1876
3. Commissioner James Farquharson MACLEOD, C.M.G. — July 22, 1876 – October 31, 1880
4. Commissioner Acheson Gosford IRVINE — November 1, 1880 – March 31, 1886
5. Commissioner Lawrence William HERCHMER — April 1, 1886 – July 31, 1900
6. Commissioner Aylesworth Bowen PERRY, C.M.G. — August 1, 1900 – March 31, 1923
7. Commissioner Cortlandt STARNES — April 1, 1923 – July 31, 1931
8. Commissioner Sir James Howden MACBRIEN, K.C.B., C.M.G., D.S.O. — August 1, 1931 – March 5, 1938
9. Commissioner Stuart Taylor WOOD, C.M.G. — March 6, 1938 – April 30, 1951
10. Commissioner Leonard Hanson NICHOLSON, M.B.E. — May 1, 1951 – March 31, 1959
11. Commissioner Charles Edward RIVETT-CARNAC — April 1, 1959 – March 31, 1960
12. Commissioner Clifford Walter HARVISON — April 1, 1960 – October 31, 1963
13. Commissioner George Brinton McCLELLAN — November 1, 1963 – August 14, 1967
14. Commissioner Malcolm Francis Aylesworth LINDSAY — August 15, 1967 – September 30, 1969
15. Commissioner William Leonard HIGGITT — October 1, 1969 –

An artist's sketch of the new R.C.M.P.
Museum in Regina which was officially
opened by Her Majesty Queen Elizabeth II
in July 1973. To its right is the R.C.M.P.
Chapel, the oldest building at "Depot"
Division.

The Honour Roll

22240   Cst. Robert Weston AMEY
Died on December 17, 1964, in hospital at Whitbourne, Nfld., from a bullet wound inflicted by Melvin Peter Young, one of four prisoners who escaped from St. John's Penitentiary.

19206   Cst. William John David ANNAND
Killed on July 13, 1963, in an R.C.M. Police aircraft which crashed and burned when attempting to land at Carmacks, Y.T.

21129   Cst. Douglas Bernard ANSON
Shot and killed on October 9, 1970, while on duty investigating a domestic dispute near MacDowall, Saskatchewan.

1065   Cst. George Pearce ARNOLD
Died on March 27, 1885, from wounds received during a skirmish at Duck Lake, N.W.T., the previous day.

19626   Cpl. Robert William ASBIL
Killed on July 13, 1963, in an R.C.M. Police aircraft which crashed and burned when attempting to land at Carmacks, Y.T.

4968   Cpl. Maxwell George BAILEY
Killed near Tofield, Alberta, on April 23, 1913, while attempting to apprehend Oscar Fonberg, a suspected lunatic.

7606   Sgt. Arthur J. BARKER
Shot and killed on March 16, 1940, in the Grand Hotel at Shaunavon, Saskatchewan, by Victor Greenlay.

13205   Cst. J. H. D. BEDLINGTON
Killed on April 30, 1943, in a motorcycle accident in England while serving with the R.C.M.P. Provost Company.

16141   Cst. R. C. BLOOMFIELD
Drowned in the Red Deer River near Swan River, Manitoba, on July 9, 1954, while on patrol.

12965   Cst. G. E. BONDURANT
Died on January 8, 1944, as a result of wounds received in action while serving with the R.C.M.P. Provost Company in Italy.

12130   Master J. W. BONNER
Killed during September 1942, when H.M.C.S. Charlottetown was sunk by enemy action.

12093   Cst. William George BOORMAN
Accidentally shot on May 26, 1937, while hunting seal in the vicinity of Elsie Island, about forty-five miles from Port Harrison, Hudson Bay, N.W.T.

979   S/Sgt. George H. L. BOSSANGE
Killed by lightning on June 21, 1919, at Spirit River, Alberta, while on patrol.

1102   S/Sgt. Arthur F. M. BROOKE
Drowned when fording the Bow River on the Blackfoot Reserve, N.W.T., September 26, 1903, while on patrol.

20824   Cst. Neil MacArthur BRUCE
Died on April 14, 1965, in hospital at Kelowna, B.C., of pneumonia resulting from a bullet wound inflicted by Russell Spears, Westbank, B.C., while investigating a complaint.

402   Cst. Patrick BURKE
Died on May 3, 1885, from wounds received during a fight at Cut Knife Hill, N.W.T., the previous day.

12856   Cst. E. A. CAMERON
Killed in action on December 28, 1943, while serving with Number One Provost Company, R.C.M.P., in Italy.

2972   Cst. Norman M. CAMPBELL
Drowned in the Stikine River, Alaska, while on patrol from northern British Columbia, on December 26, 1901.

20388   Cst. Thomas Percy CARROLL
Killed on February 11, 1966, in an aeroplane accident while in the performance of his duty at Cyril Lake, Manitoba.

S/Cst. Samuel CARTER
Died with the McPherson–Dawson patrol in February 1911.

18656   2/Cst. Henry C. A. CHANDLER
Died on June 15, 1956, from injuries received in a traffic accident at Millview, Halifax County, N.S., while on duty.

10155   Cst. Albert Joseph CHARTRAND
Died on February 13, 1942, while on duty aboard the R.C.M.P. Schooner St. Roch which was frozen in at Kent Bay, Boothia Pen., N.W.T.

12983   Cst. Wilfred J. COBBLE
Died on December 4, 1946, from injuries received when struck by a truck on the highway at Lavoy, Alberta, while on duty.

17298   Cst. J. R. COBLEY
Died on January 5, 1957, from injuries received when struck by an automobile on the highway near Salmon Arm, B.C., while on duty.

605   Sgt. Colin C. COLEBROOK
Killed by Almighty Voice, an escaped Cree Indian prisoner, near Kinistino, N.W.T., while attempting to arrest him, October 29, 1895.

S/Cst. J. E. R. CORMIER
Killed in an aeroplane accident on August 6, 1958, while in the performance of duty along the east shore of Skaha Lake, B.C.

11298   Cst. F. G. F. COUNSELL
Shot and killed on May 22, 1940, at Parkland, Alberta, by Charles Hansen, wanted for the shooting of his son.

635   Cst. David Latimer COWAN
Killed by Indians at Fort Pitt, N.W.T., on April 15, 1885, while on scouting duty.

9818   Cst. Leo Francis COX
Drowned near La Sarre, P.Q., while on duty, June 29, 1925.

13678   Cst. K. L. D'ALBENAS
Killed in action on May 15, 1944, while serving with the R.C.M.P. Provost Company in Italy.

4837   Cst. Francis Walter DAVIES
Killed by Mike Running Wolf, an Indian, near Brooks, Alberta, on June 3, 1912, while trying to arrest him.

2439   Cst. George Q. R. DE BEAUJEU
Drowned in Lake Winnipeg when the Mounted Police patrol boat capsized during a storm on September 8, 1890.

4396   Cpl. William Andrew DOAK
Murdered by Alikomiak, an Eskimo, at Tree River, N.W.T., on April 1, 1922.

3566   Sgt. Ralph M. L. DONALDSON
Drowned when police boat attacked by a walrus off Marple Island, Hudson Bay, N.W.T., on August 14, 1908.

22055   Cst. Joseph P. F. DUBOIS
Killed on January 3, 1964, in a police car accident near Fauvel, Quebec, while on escort duty.

10982   Sgt. L. R. DUBUC
Killed in action on September 27, 1941, while serving with the R.C.A.F. in Eire.

20366   Cst. R. A. EKSTROM
Killed on April 22, 1961, in a noncollision traffic accident while in the performance of duty near Lytton, B.C.

973   Cst. Frank O. ELLIOTT
Killed by Indians near Battleford, N.W.T., while on scouting duty on May 14, 1885.

19478   2/Cst. G. E. FAROUGH
Drowned in Lake Simcoe, near Georgina Island, Ontario, on June 7, 1958, while on patrol.

15802   Cst. D. E. FERGUSON
Died of carbon monoxide poisoning aboard the Hudson's Bay boat near Cape Alexander, N.W.T., on September 17, 1954, while on duty.

Insp. Francis Joseph FITZGERALD
Died from starvation, exposure and exhaustion while a member of the McPherson–Dawson patrol in February, 1911.

3617   Cst. Michael J. FITZGERALD
Drowned in White River, Y.T., on August 27, 1913.

A/Surgeon Walter Stafford FLOOD
Died from exposure while on duty near Churchill, Manitoba, on November 29, 1906.

17334   Cst. James W. FOREMAN
Died on April 24, 1963, of injuries sustained when struck by an automobile on the highway near Sangudo, Alberta, while helping a motorist in trouble.

5816   Cst. A. GAMMAN
Died on May 26, 1950, from wounds received while attempting to apprehend an armed bank robber at Montreal, Quebec.

852   Cst. George Knox GARRETT
Died on March 27, 1885, from wounds received during a skirmish at Duck Lake, N.W.T., the previous day.

1003   Cst. Thomas James GIBSON
Killed in a skirmish at Duck Lake, N.W.T., on March 26, 1885, when Métis and Indians ambushed a party of Mounted Police and Prince Albert Volunteers.

17644   Cpl. Ervin Jack GIESBRECHT
Drowned on June 20, 1964, while on patrol, when the police car went out of control and plunged into the water at the Coffer Dam at Nybord, Manitoba.

12223   3/Cst. D. E. GILLIS
Lost at sea on March 26, 1941, when H.M.C.S. Otter foundered off Halifax, N.S.

11046   Cst. Norman A. GLEADOW
Murdered at Esterhazy, Saskatchewan, on October 11, 1939, by Ernest Flook, under arrest for theft.

335   Cst. Marmaduke GRABURN
Murdered by person or persons unknown, while on duty near Fort Walsh, N.W.T., on November 17, 1879.

14740   Cst. Richard William GREEN
Killed in an aeroplane accident while in the performance of duty on August 6, 1958, along the east shore of Skaha Lake, B.C.

26402   Cst. William Joseph GREEN
Died on October 4, 1970, at Invermere, B.C., as a result of injuries received earlier in a motor vehicle accident involving the police car he was operating in response to a call.

2836   Cpl. Alexander G. HADDOCK
Drowned in the Yukon River, near Ogilvie, Y.T., while on patrol June 14, 1906.

7688   Cpl. John L. HALLIDAY
Accidentally shot on October 14, 1932, while lowering a rifle by the barrel, into a cabin sixteen miles from Simpson, N.W.T.

10946   Cst. George Campbell HARRISON
Killed on October 8, 1935, near the Eastern Gate of Banff National Park, while attempting to apprehend three young robber suspects, murderers of Const. Shaw.

17129   Cpl. Donald A. HARVEY
Killed on June 23, 1967, as a result of a bullet wound inflicted by Leonard Borg at Grande Prairie, Alberta.

3463   Cst. Spencer G. HEATHCOTE
Drowned in the Stikine River, Alaska, while on patrol from northern British Columbia, on December 26, 1901.

14890   2/Cst. J. B. HENDERSON
Drowned in the St. Lawrence River on August 7, 1948, near Gananoque, Ontario, while on duty.

913   Cst. James HERRON
Died during a blizzard, near St. Mary's River, N.W.T., while on patrol, March 2, 1891.

3106   Cpl. Charles H. S. HOCKIN
Killed at Minnichinas Hills, near Duck Lake, N.W.T., on May 28, 1897, while attempting to apprehend Almighty Voice, the Indian murderer of Sgt. Colebrook.

20307   3/Cst. John Terrence HOEY
Shot and killed at Botwood, Nfld., on November 6, 1958, while investigating a complaint.

181   Cst. Claudius S. HOOLEY
Drowned in the Belly River on July 24, 1880, while on patrol from Wood Mountain to Fort Macleod, N.W.T.

11818   Cst. George E. HORAN
Killed in an automobile accident near Belleville, Ontario, on March 10, 1937.

25165   Cst. Derek Thomas IVANY
Died on June 25, 1971, at St. Arthur, N.B., of injuries received in a police car accident the previous day.

4119   Cst. Thomas R. JACKSON
Drowned when fording a flooded stream at Battle Creek, Sask., while on patrol, June 8, 1906.

S/4218   S/Cst. H. C. JARVIS
Drowned near Lock 25, Cornwall Canal, Iroquois, Ontario, on July 15, 1941.

10063   Cst. J. C. JOHNSTONE
Lost at sea as a result of enemy action on May 1, 1941, while serving with the R.C.M.P. Provost Company.

16810   Cst. S. KASPER
Killed in an aeroplane accident in Prince Rupert Harbour, B.C., while on duty, on May 11, 1953.

19233   Cst. E. J. KECK
Shot and killed on June 18, 1962, at Kamloops, B.C. while investigating a complaint.

S/3185   S/Cst. J. H. KENT
Died on November 5, 1941, from injuries received when struck by an automobile on the Welland Ship Canal, St. Catharines, Ontario, while proceeding off duty.

3100   Cst. Oscar Alexander KERN
Drowned while attempting to ford a flooded stream near Estevan, N.W.T., while on patrol on April 26, 1896.

26042   2/Cst. James Alexander KERR
Killed in a motor vehicle accident on December 11, 1968, at St. Anne, N.B., while on duty.

3040   Cst. John Randolph KERR
Killed at Minnichinas Hills, near Duck Lake, N.W.T., on May 28, 1897, while attempting to apprehend Almighty Voice, the Indian murderer of Sergeant Colebrook.

4582   Cst. George Francis KINNEY
Died with the McPherson-Dawson patrol in February 1911.

14694   Cst. R. E. LAIRD
Killed on August 26, 1955, in a noncollision traffic accident on the Ranchville Road, near Medicine Hat, Alberta, while on duty.

5548   Cst. Alexander LAMONT
Died at Herschel Island, Y.T., on February 16, 1918, from typhoid fever contracted while nursing Vilhjalmur Stefansson, the Arctic explorer.

17368   Sgt. Kenneth Morley LAUGHLAND
Killed on July 13, 1963, in an R.C.M. Police aircraft which crashed and burned when attempting to land at Carmacks, Y.T.

19731   Cst. Collin Eric LELLIOTT
Shot and killed at Cambridge Bay, N.W.T., on January 12, 1960, while attempting to arrest an escaped Eskimo, Jimmy Ayalik.

21512   Cst. A. O. M. LEPINE
Died on July 19, 1962, from injuries received in a motor vehicle accident near Whalley, B.C., while on duty.

907   Cpl. William H. T. LOWRY
Died on May 3, 1885, from wounds received during a fight at Cut Knife Hill, N.W.T., the previous day.

9791   Cst. Ian M. MacDONALD
Drowned near the mouth of the Indian River, east of Herschel Island, Arctic Ocean, while on special duty, on August 18, 1924.

10399   Cst. Donald R. MacDONELL
Drowned on April 19, 1931, near the mouth of Fourteen River, Hudson Bay, while on patrol.

409   Sub/Cst. George MAHONEY
Drowned while crossing the South Saskatchewan River on patrol from Battleford to Fort Walsh, N.W.T., on June 19, 1877.

18570   Cst. Proctor Lawrence Anthony MALCOLM
Killed on July 13, 1963, in an R.C.M. Police aircraft which crashed and burned when attempting to land at Carmacks, Y.T.

Insp. D. J. McCOMBE
Died from exposure on December 12, 1955, while on patrol near Cutknife, Saskatchewan.

22830   Cst. Michael Robert MASON
Drowned at Courtenay, B.C., on November 26, 1971, when aeroplane he was a passenger in plunged into the Courtenay River.

19469   2/Cst. M. MELNYCHUK
Drowned on June 7, 1958, in Lake Simcoe, near Georgina Island, Ontario, while on patrol.

18050   Cst. W. L. MELSOM
Killed in a traffic accident at Port Alberni, B.C., while responding to an emergency call for police assistance on August 2, 1955.

9669   Cst. Edgar MILLEN
Killed near Rat River, N.W.T., on January 30, 1932, while attempting to apprehend Albert Johnson, a fugitive from justice.

11150   Cst. Daniel MILLER
Died on October 14, 1935, from injuries sustained in an automobile accident, when on duty with Sgt. F. Lucas near Newcastle, N.B.

12168   1st. Off. P. R. F. MILTHORP
Killed when H.M.C.S. Spikenard was sunk by enemy action in February, 1942.

487   Sgt. A. E. G. MONTGOMERY
Died on August 10, 1890, from injuries sustained when thrown from his horse, while on parade at Prince Albert on August 7, 1890.

13157   Cst. D. C. G. MOON
Died on December 28, 1943, as a result of wounds received in action while serving with the R.C.M.P. Provost Company.

6352   Cpl. M. MORIARITY
Murdered by David Knox, farmer, on April 26, 1935, at Rosebud District, Alberta, while attemtping to effect the service of a summons.

2162   Cpl. Harry Oliver MORPHY
Drowned in Lake Winnipeg when the Mounted Police patrol boat capsized during a storm on September 10, 1890.

135   Sub/Cst. John NASH
Accidentally killed while on duty near Fort Macleod, N.W.T., March 11, 1876.

12398   Cst. J. F. NELSON
Killed in action on May 22, 1944, while serving with the R.C.M.P. Provost Company in Italy.

5611   Sgt. Richard H. NICHOLSON
Killed on December 31, 1928, while conducting a search for an illicit still near Molson, Manitoba.

12572   Cst. P. S. OLIVER
Killed in action at Dieppe, France, on August 19, 1942, while serving with the R.C.M.P. Provost Company.

15190   Sgt. James Aldridge O'MALLEY
Drowned in the Kettle River near Gillam, Manitoba, on October 28, 1970, while on duty conducting a search for a drowned body, when his small boat capsized.

11003   Cst. C. F. PATTERSON
Accidentally killed on November 25, 1941, while serving with the R.C.M.P. Provost Company overseas.

23018   Cst. Gordon Donald PEARSON
Killed on November 22, 1966, as a result of a bullet wound inflicted by Charles Wilfrid Hill, when investigating a disturbance at Winterburn, Alberta.

20865   Cst. G. E. PEDERSEN
Shot and killed on June 18, 1962, at Kamloops, B.C., while investigating a complaint.

2181   Cst. A. PERRY
Drowned in the Belly River, N.W.T., while on patrol on June 8, 1889.

19879   2/Cst. D. M. PERRY
Drowned in Lake Simcoe, near Georgina Island, Ontario, on June 7, 1958, while on patrol.

Surgeon M. POWERS, B.A., M.D., C.M.
Killed on October 20, 1943, in an aeroplane accident while in the performance of duty near Red Pheasant, Saskatchewan.

6177   Cpl. Leonard Victor RALLS
Killed by escaping thieves whom he was trying to intercept near Foam Lake, Saskatchewan, on July 5, 1932.

19915   2/Cst. G. H. E. RANSOM
Drowned in Lake Simcoe, near Georgina Island, Ontario, on June 7, 1958, while on patrol.

10655   Cst. H. G. RAPEER
Killed while endeavouring to stop a runaway team at Regina, Saskatchewan, on May 23, 1940.

2086   Cst. William T. READING
Died on December 14, 1890, from injuries received at Calgary, when Supt. J. H. McIllree's horse – which he was exercising – fell on him.

15303   Cst. C. W. REAY
Drowned in the Churchill River at Island Falls, Saskatchewan, on October 6, 1955, while on duty.

12690   Cst. W. E. RHODENISER
Shot and killed on August 26, 1939, near Carlyle, Saskatchewan, while leading a posse in search of Nelson Sammy, an Indian, wanted for questioning in connection with the murder of his wife and her parents.

9951   Cst. Frederick RHODES
Died on December 6, 1926, from injuries received when the police detachment at Rae, N.W.T., burned to the ground.

20598   Cst. David Brian ROBINSON
Died in hospital at Saskatoon, Sask., on February 2, 1965, from an accidental bullet wound inflicted by another member while cleaning a service revolver preparatory to inspection.

10880   S/Sgt. S. S. ROTHWELL
Killed on August 6, 1958, in an aeroplane accident while in the performance of duty along the east shore of Skaha Lake, B.C.

4152   Cst. Joseph RUSSELL
Drowned at Cape Fullerton, Hudson Bay, on July 5, 1905.

11371   Lawrence Percival RYDER
Died on January 20, 1943, of cerebral haemorrhage at Fisher Memorial Hospital, Woodstock, N.B., possibly caused by injuries sustained while on duty.

S/Cst. Stick SAM
Drowned when fording Kaskawulsh River, Y.T., while on patrol, on July 29, 1903.

Insp. Lorne James SAMPSON
Died on May 8, 1933 as a result of injuries received in a fall from his horse while on duty endeavouring to suppress a disturbance at Saskatoon, Saskatchewan.

14819   Cst. J. K. SANDER
Drowned on July 9, 1954, in the Red Deer River, near Swan River, Manitoba, while on patrol.

15445   Sgt. Robert James SCHRADER
Shot and killed on October 9, 1970, while on duty investigating a domestic dispute near MacDowall, Saskatchewan.

4995   Sgt. Arthur George SEARLE
Drowned on May 15, 1921, near Creston, B.C., while on patrol after whisky runners, when a flooded stream washed the road away.

22976   Cst. Harold Stanley SEIGEL
Shot and killed on September 26, 1971, while attempting to dislodge a person, later declared insane, from a house at Iles-des-Chênes, Manitoba.

11582   Cst. John George SHAW
Murdered on October 4, 1935, near Benito, Manitoba, by three Doukhobor suspects while transferring them to Pelly, Saskatchewan.

20958   Cst. W. SINCLAIR
Died on September 17, 1961, of injuries received in a noncollision traffic accident on Highway No. 6, near Regina, Saskatchewan, while on duty.

565   Cpl. Ralph Bateman SLEIGH
Killed on May 2, 1885, in the fight between the Government forces and the Indians at Cut Knife Hill, N.W.T.

14588   Cpl. H. M. SMART
Drowned in Lake Simcoe, near Georgina Island, Ontario, on June 7, 1958, while on patrol.

12108   Cst. D. C. STACKHOUSE
Killed in action on May 31, 1944, while serving with the R.C.M.P. Provost Company in Italy.

18165   Cst. C. L. SUNDELL
Accidentally shot on July 14, 1958, at Herschel Island, Y.T., while on duty.

4346   Cst. Richard O. H. TAYLOR
Died in February 1911, with the McPherson–Dawson patrol.

18200   Cst. J. T. THOMPSON
Died at Selkirk, Manitoba, on December 18, 1961, of injuries received while on duty on September 26, 1957, when Police Transport was struck by wheels of landing aircraft near Lethbridge Airport, Alberta.

24014   3/Cst. Philip John Francis TIDMAN
Killed on April 20, 1966, in a police car accident near Wakaw, Sask., while on escort duty.

25214   3/Cst. Terry Eugene TOMFOHR
Accidentally killed on June 3, 1967, while in the performance of duty at Burnaby, B.C.

6096   Cpl. Ernest USHER
Killed on August 7, 1920, while attempting to arrest train bandits at Bellevue, Alberta.

25094   3/Cst. Robert William VARNEY
Killed on August 17, 1967, in a police car accident near Raymond, Alberta, while on duty.

Cst. Adam WAHL
A recruit from Eastern Canada; drowned in the Missouri River, U.S.A., while en route with other recruits to Fort Macleod, N.W.T., 1882.

11326   Sgt. Thomas Sellar WALLACE
Killed near the Eastern Gate of Banff National Park, on October 8, 1935, while attempting to apprehend three young Doukhobor robber suspects, murderers of Cst. Shaw.

13064   Cst. T. C. N. WATTS
Killed in action on December 28, 1943, while serving with the R.C.M.P. Provost Company in Italy.

20215   Cst. D. G. WEISGERBER
Shot and killed on June 18, 1962, at Kamloops, B.C., while investigating a complaint.

857   Sgt. William Brock WILDE
Killed on November 10, 1896, by Charcoal, alias Bad Young Man, a Blood Indian fugitive murderer, near Dry Forks, the Kootenai River, N.W.T., while attempting to arrest him.

23499   3/Cst. Reginald Wayne WILLIAMS
Drowned on December 19, 1964, while on patrol, when the police car skidded and plunged into the water off the slippery Government Dock at Sooke, B.C.

19508   Cpl. Terry Gerrard WILLIAMS
Drowned in a boating accident in Sheet Harbour Passage, Halifax County, N.S., while on duty, on June 8, 1969.

4584   Cst. George Ernest WILLMETT
Murdered by a burglar on April 12, 1908, in the town of Frank, Alberta, while on night patrol duty.

11645   Cst. Carl F. WILSON
Died on September 9, 1948, from injuries received when struck by an automobile, while directing traffic at the scene of a highway accident near Portapique, N.S.

14757   Cst. H. T. WOOD
Died on July 16, 1950, from injuries received in a police car accident near Glacier Park, Montana, U.S.A., while on duty.

The names of those members above who have given their lives in the performance of their duties are inscribed upon the Memorial Tablet which stands on the Barrack Square at "Depot" Division in Regina.

Index

Designed by Julian Cleva and Brant Cowie

DISCARD